1986

The Remedial Reading Handbook

Bonnie Lass
Boston College

Beth Davis
Brandeis University

Prentice-Hall, Inc., Englewood Cliffs, New Jersey 07632

Library of Congress Cataloging in Publication Data

Lass, Bonnie.
    The remedial reading handbook.

    Includes bibliographies and index.
        1. Reading—Remedial teaching—Handbooks, manuals,
etc.   2. Individualized reading instruction—Handbooks,
manuals, etc.   I. Davis, Beth.   II. Title.
LB1050.5.L33   1985   428.4'2   84-22289
ISBN 0-13-773482-4
ISBN 0-13-773474-3 (pbk.)

To Our Families

Illustrations by: Marc Mannheimer
Cover design: Wanda Lubelska Design
Manufacturing buyer: Barbara Kelly Kittle

Printed in the United States of America

10 9 8 7 6 5 4 3 2 1

ISBN 0-13-773482-4   01

ISBN 0-13-773474-3   {pbk}

Prentice-Hall International, Inc., *London*
Prentice-Hall of Australia Pty. Limited, *Sydney*
Editora Prentice-Hall do Brasil, Ltda., *Rio de Janeiro*
Prentice-Hall Canada Inc., *Toronto*
Prentice-Hall Hispanoamericana, S.A., *Mexico*
Prentice-Hall of India Private Limited, *New Delhi*
Prentice-Hall of Japan, Inc., *Tokyo*
Prentice-Hall of Southeast Asia Pte. Ltd., *Singapore*
Whitehall Books Limited, *Wellington, New Zealand*

Contents

Introduction

Individually designed instruction is essential for students with reading problems. Current research in effective reading instruction confirms this (Blair, 1976; Harris, 1979) and teachers themselves recognize its importance. In one recent study, seventy-four elementary teachers ranked individualizing reading instruction as second among ten teacher skills. Only the ability to motivate was considered more important (Jackson and Sui-Runyan, 1981).

Providing individualized remedial reading instruction, however, is a challenge. Since few specialists have the luxury of a tutorial, extra planning is necesary; sometimes separate lessons are required for each child in a group. In addition, there is insufficient time to spend with each needy student. Management and attentional difficulties also can arise when students are engaged in independent work. This further curtails a teacher's time for individual instruction.

Our reason for writing this book is to provide help for both (1) the college student who has already had a first course in teaching reading and (2) novice and experienced teachers who wish to accept the challenge of individualizing instruction for their remedial students. To set the stage, Figure 1 illustrates our view of the model "diagnostic-prescriptive teacher."

No teacher rings the bell with each strike of the mallet. Moreover, it is not our intention to explore all of the steps of diagnostic-prescriptive instruction outlined in the diagram. Much literature is already available to provide help with both reading skills identification and testing procedures for diagnosis. But assistance with test interpretation and suggestions for skill instruction based on these results are lacking. We hope this book will make a contribution in these areas.

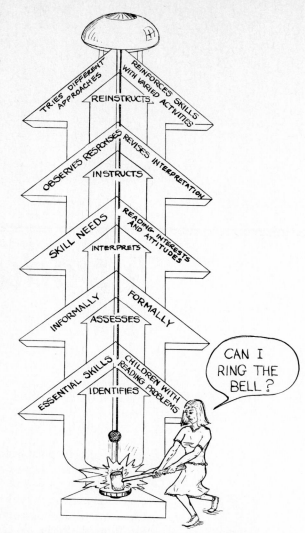

~ THE DIAGNOSTIC PRESCRIPTIVE READING TEACHER ~

HANDBOOK FEATURES

As can be observed from the table of contents, the reading skills considered in this handbook are clustered into four sections: (1) Word Identification Problems, (2) Comprehension Difficulties, (3) Underdeveloped Study Skills, and (4) Affective and Linguistic Roadblocks.

Each of the fourteen chapters follows a similar format. First, the skill considered in a chapter is defined and followed by reasons why students might be deficient in it. Selected diagnostic procedures come next and a case study protocol provides results which we interpret. We have tried to vary the diagnostic tool used in each case study for two reasons:

1. No one test can assess all of the skills we are writing about.
2. We would like to show the wide range of assessment tools available to the teacher for obtaining skill deficit information. These range from standardized instruments, to informal tests both published and teacher-made, to interviews and classroom discussion.

We are in no way advocating that a teacher use the particular test we have chosen for each case study nor are we attempting to instruct teachers in the administration of these instruments. Moreover, by using a single child and a single test in each section, we do not wish to imply that all children with that skill deficit will perform in the same way. What we wish to focus on is the technique of analyzing whatever errors are made, to show teachers how tentative hypotheses for remediation are derived. Following this, a few other tests that help assess the skill are usually listed. Interested readers may wish to refer to a text on reading diagnosis for further recommendations.

The advice for remediation comes in two forms. First, we have provided a set of briefly explained techniques or references for the remedial teacher. We have not attempted to match these techniques to the etiologies listed under Reasons for Skill Deficiencies; such matches don't always work. Students with identical problems often respond to very different solutions. We urge teachers to read the entire Techniques for Remediation section with this in mind.

Second, games and worksheets are found in the Activity Index. Teachers will find them to be timesavers. Two activities are provided for each chapter, and each one, when adapted, is appropriate for at least one other skill area. We have provided specific suggestions of alternate uses for activities, and we are sure that teachers will find still further applications.

Student-centered skills instruction based on continuing diagnosis is our approach to remediation. Although each chapter contains one test protocol, we are concerned with *patterns* of error. One error does not a skill deficiency make. We hope that any "hints" discovered in formal diagnosis will be confirmed in classroom performance before a program of remediation is adopted.

Once remediation begins, however, direct teaching in the reading and language-related skills that a student lacks seems logical and has been successful for us and for the teachers we have trained. We are equally concerned with increasing the enjoyment of students during reading instruction, perpetuating the reading habit, and increasing a failing student's self-esteem. We believe that effective remediators are, at times, counselors or librarians. In seeking to work with students wholistically, successful remedial teachers combine a student's interest and mood with skill needs.

One

Insufficient Sight Vocabulary

SKILL DESCRIPTION

Sally, attempting to read "Neanderthal man lived long ago," stumbles over the first word but the rest of the sentence she reads quickly and easily. We can assume the last four words are a part of Sally's sight vocabulary.

Sight words are those words the reader identifies instantly. The words have been memorized and one look at a word can bring an immediate verbal response. This is why a sight approach is often referred to as "look-say". Able adult readers identify almost all words by sight. Therefore, a constantly growing sight vocabulary is the ultimate goal of all word identification instruction.

An early grasp of a large number of sight words is important for achieving success in reading skills (Hood, 1977). Even if a phonics or linguistic approach constitutes a child's beginning reading instruction, there are a number of frequently occurring words which may only be learned through memorization because of their irregular spelling (*of, two*) or which need to be learned quickly, usually before the sound-symbol elements are taught in the child's program (*game, go*).

Durkin (1976) recommends that the word identification techniques that students should be helped to utilize in reading are: sight, context, structural analysis, and phonic analysis, in that order. Although this order is appropriate for proficient readers in attempting to read an unknown word, beginning readers may use a different learning sequence. We have ordered our chapters: sight words, phonic analysis, structural analysis, and context. We agree with Durkin that sight words should be considered first since (1) naturalistic studies of reading acquisition show that most children begin this way (Durkin, 1966; Lass, 1982) and (2) other word identification instruction is facilitated by a student's grasp of a number of sight words which illustrate the sound symbol or morphologic relationship in question.

What are the appropriate words to teach as sight vocabulary? One answer comes from lists of high frequency words which have appeared in the reading literature. Dolch,

Fry, Harris-Jacobsen, Johnson, and Kucera-Francis are some authors of lists of high frequency words. Included here are the Ekwall "Basic Sight Words" and Johns' list for older disabled readers.

Basic Sight Words[1]

Words

a	play	him	big	then	it
did	too	look	get	where	of
have	are	run	house	can	three
know	down	water	my	good	will
one	here	be	the	in	oh
to	little	for	what	not	you
and	put	his	but	this	your
do	two	make	go	who	
her	away	said	I	come	
like	eat	we	no	has	

Primer	about	all	an	as	blue	by
	call	could	find	from	give	green
	had	help	is	let	may	me
	mother	old	other	ran	ride	sat
	see	so	something	take	them	there
	time	up	very	was	went	when
	after	am	around	back	by	saw
	came	day	fly	funny	green	they
	he	how	jump	man	may	would
	now	on	over	red	ride	yes
	she	some	stop	that	them	
	tree	us	want	way	went	

First Reader	again	were	than	pull	name	side
	boy	ask	why	their	read	took
	fun	buy	ate	work	think	black
	long	got	cold	been	door	fast
	or	Mrs.	happy	cry	began	light
	soon	please	morning	into	laugh	night
	well	tell	pretty	must	never	sleep
	any	white	thank	rabbit	shall	under
	brown	at	with	these	thought	father
	girl	children	ball	yellow	better	walk
	Mr.	high	color	before	far	five
	out	more	if	dog	light	four
	stand	party	much	just	new	

2-1 Level	always	end	head	once	sit	while
	does	hand	near	should	warm	full
	going	many	say	until	clean	last
	live	right	together	bring	found	still
	pick	thing	both	fall	keep	wish
	sure	best	every	hot	our	gave
	another	enough	hold	only	six	left
	each	hard	next	show	which	year
	grow	men	school	wait	cut	
	made	round	told	carry	friend	
	place	those	box	first	kind	
	ten	book	eye	hurt	own	
	because	even	home	open	start	

2-2 Level	dear	done	drink	off	most	people
	seem	seven	sing	small	such	write
	today	try	turn	use	wash	present

Third Reader Level	also	eight	kind	upon
	don't	goes	leave	grand
	draw	its	myself	

[1]Ekwall, Eldon, E., "Basic Sight Words" from *Locating and Correcting Reading Difficulties, 4th edition* (Columbus, Ohio: Charles E. Merrill Publishing Co., 1985), ©1985 by Eldon E. Ekwall. Used with permission.

A Supplement to the Dolch Word Lists[1]

1. more	15. world	29. used	43. united	57. yet
2. than	16. still	30. states	44. left	58. government
3. other	17. between	31. himself	45. number	59. system
4. such	18. life	32. few	46. course	60. set
5. even	19. being	33. during	47. war	61. told
6. most	20. same	34. without	48. until	62. nothing
7. also	21. another	35. place	49. something	63. end
8. through	22. white	36. American	50. fact	64. called
9. years	23. last	37. however	51. though	65. didn't
10. should	24. might	38. Mrs.	52. less	66. eyes
11. each	25. great	39. thought	53. public	67. asked
12. people	26. year	40. part	54. almost	68. later
13. Mr.	27. since	41. general	55. enough	69. knew
14. state	28. against	42. high	56. took	

[1] Johns, Jerry L. "A Supplement to the Dolch Word Lists," *Reading Improvement*, Winter 1971–72, p. 91. Used with permission.

A study of the words in either list above will reveal two word classes: form words and function words. Form words are an open class of words consisting of nouns, verbs, adjectives and adverbs. As new words enter the English language, this class expands. Function words, however, are a closed class of about 135 words. Articles, conjunctions, prepositions and interjections comprise this category and differ from form words in that:

1. they usually have syntactical rather than lexical meaning and therefore are difficult to visualize or explain.
2. they occur over and over in written language. In the sentence, "A boy went to the store," three of the six words are function words.

For both reasons and because the sound-symbol relationship for function words is often irregular (*to, the, of, they*), it makes sense to teach function words as sight words.

A third source of sight words may come from words which children indicate a desire to know and are often gleaned from language experience stories. Words that are meaningful to a child are more easily learned than those selected by the teacher (Ashton-Warner, 1963). Moreover, researchers (Hargis and Gickling, 1978) have found that high imagery words, words like *dog* and *tree* (as opposed to *time* and *thing*) have also been shown to be words that are learned and retained more readily.

Very few children learn sight words at a single exposure. Most children need twenty repetitions (Ekwall and Shanker, 1983) before they automatically identify a word. This means that the teacher must find varied and motivating ways to provide "old-fashioned" drill. We believe as carpenters do that drills are tools. In reading, they are tools for building fluency. Isolated word drill can be a first step, but reading is not word list identification. A connected and pleasurable reading experience is our ultimate goal.

Although isolated skill practice may be valuable as a first step, the reader should be encouraged quickly to recognize these words in a single fixation when they are part of two-or three-word phrases. Phrase reading is an essential technique the fluent reader uses in connected reading and helps to discourage word-by-word reading. Recent research tends to show that learning words in isolation does not assure their recognition in context (Ceprano, 1981). Words appearing in isolation *and* in context should be utilized both for instruction and for evaluating instruction. The Dolch list of sight phrases included below will be useful to the teacher both for instruction and evaluation.

Dolch* Sight Phrases

can live	on the chair	is coming
down the hill	with mother	will go
will walk	down there	for the girl
in the barn	my father	if I must
they are	so much	as he did
if you can	his brother	when I wish
what I say	you will do	the small boy
all day	so long	it was
some bread	must be	down the street
you were	will buy	the red apple
to the farm	some cake	the little pig
her father	as I said	the little chickens
on the floor	too soon	with us
from the tree	what I want	would want
was made	I was	all night
at home	at once	her mother
the black horse	for them	is going
you will like	will think	ii is
went away	the black bird	will read
in the window	a new hat	to the school
in the box	about it	they were
for him	he is	he was
I may go	to go	in the garden
from home	we were	from the farm
the old men	the little dog	my brother
for the baby	at school	your sister
the new coat	by the tree	too little
a big horse	up here	I will come
then he came	would like	could make
by the house	went down	I will go
the old man	the yellow cat	to the barn
the small boat	up there	can fly
I am	the funny man	a big house
a pretty picture	I may get	about him
as I do	if you wish	then he said
he would try	can play	could eat
we are	has made	to the nest
a pretty home	when you know	did not fall
must go	in the grass	in the water
his sister	a new book	will look
if I may	the red cow	the yellow ball
you are	the little children	was found
did not go	to stop	your mother
has come back	when you come	can run
as he said	the new doll	to the house
the funny rabbit	when I can	the white sheep
at three	has found	
has run away	the white duck	

POSSIBLE REASONS FOR SKILL DEFICIENCY

1. Some students are presented with too many sight words in one lesson and therefore fail to learn any.

2. Some students have poor visual memory skills and need phonics skills, meaning, visualization, and/or kinesthetic or tactile reinforcement to impress words on their memories.

3. Students have not focused on the word. Sometimes students look up at a teacher to have words pronounced instead of looking at words as they are read.

*Dolch, Edward, *Dolch Sight Phrases* (Champaign, IL: Garrard Publishing Co., 1949). Used with permission.

4. Students are focusing on the beginning letter or on another recognizable part of words rather than looking at the whole.

5. Students have not learned to discriminate visually between minimally different letters and therefore do not see the difference between *map* and *nap,* for example.

6. Students confuse words that are similar in appearance and need to see the words together and to have the differences highlighted. *What* and *that* are an example.

7. Students in phonics-oriented programs sometimes overanalyze words.

8. Students have not had enough exposure to certain sight words to have committed them to memory.

9. Students who have concentrated on words in isolation may not recognize the words when they appear in connected reading. The surrounding words may confuse the reader.

10. The words are not a part of students' speaking/listening vocabularies.

SELECTED DIAGNOSTIC PROCEDURES

There are many tests available to assess sight word knowledge. Generally the tests provide a list of ten to twenty words at various reading levels. The student is given one list at a time and reads the words aloud. If the student reads 80 percent of the words correctly (sometimes 70 to 90 percent, depending on the specific test), this is usually thought to indicate instructional level. Often some sort of tachistoscopic device in which the word appears in a window for a brief viewing time is used to ensure that the students' exposure to the words is limited and that their use of decoding skills is precluded.

A number of reading tests purport to measure sight word knowledge by asking the student to choose the visual representation of a word pronounced by the teacher. Usually three or four choices are shown, with the distractors varying in difficulty.

Example: The teacher reads, "Circle the word *guess.*"

> *guest*
> *guess*
> *guessed*
> *gas*

Although this kind of test is easier to administer because it can be done with the group as a whole, it is not asking the child to demonstrate the production skills needed in reading sight words. In a real reading situation, the students must indicate that they know the pronunciation of a word by naming it rather than merely recognizing it. Success with this kind of typical workbook page does not guarantee sight word knowledge of the words used.

CASE STUDY*

The Botel Reading Inventory (1978)† has eight lists of twenty words each, progressing from the preprimer through the fourth-grade reading level. Students are asked to read each list until they fall below 70 percent on two successive levels.

Although Jason, a second-grader whose results appear below, scored 75 percent and 60 percent on lists *A* and *B,* respectively, he hesitated for a long period on enough words in both lists to justify stopping. The long hesitation enabled him to read the words eventually but indicated to the authors that he did not have sight recognition of the words.

In the lists below, the word that was asked for is given first, followed by Jason's response. Only errors are shown.

*See Introduction for function of Case Study.
†Botel, Morton, *Botel Reading Inventory,* "Word Recognition Test" (Cleveland, OH: Modern Curriculum Press, 1978). Used with permission.

	A			B	
father	from		boat	bill	
make	milk		kitten	kit	
mother	_____		now	what	
ride	read		put	pout	
want	want—rhymes with		saw	said	
	ant		thank	this	
hesitations occurred for:			three	this	
ball, house			train	time	
			hesitations: all,		
			there, like		

According to this testing, Jason's knowledge of sight words is at a primer level. One encouraging note in examining errors is that he makes use of the initial sound and sometimes the final consonant in guessing high-frequency words. He needs more practice in attending to all parts of a word and more practice with the words he missed. Although the tester responded "good" after each word was read, Jason knew when he didn't know the word and questioned each time whether his incorrect responses were right. This would indicate that, in fact, Jason is aware of his need.

Other Assessments

1. *Durrell Analysis of Reading Difficulty.* New York: The Psychological Corporation, 1980.
   Subtests: Word Recognition, and Visual Memory for Words
2. Gates, McKillop, and Horowitz, *Reading Diagnostic Tests.* New York: Columbia University, Teachers College Press, 1981.
   Subtest: Words: Timed
3. LaPray, Margaret, and Ramon Ross, "The Graded Word List: Quick Gauge of Reading Ability," *Journal of Reading,* January 1969, pp. 305–07.

TECHNIQUES FOR REMEDIATION

Find the Lucky Number

Experiment with the student to determine the number of sight words that can be learned in one sitting and remembered the next day. Do not attempt to teach more than this number in a single lesson. It's conceivable that this number will be "one" at first; however, slow but steady progress is preferable to no progress. As the student acquires a larger repertoire of sight words, his/her learning capacity may increase. Continuing evaluation is important.

Banking Words

You may wish to make a word box or word bank for each student. As words are presented to students, they write each word on a 3″×5″ card. They may illustrate the word if possible, and then they should write the word on the back of the card with a sentence using the word. The illustrated side of the card is for learning the word; the back of the card is for testing the student. Divide the box into two sections, and as words are learned they should be entered into the "learned" section (to be distinguished from the "working on" section). Students enjoy seeing the learned section grow steadily. These words can be used for all of the practice ideas listed later in the chapter.

Variation: Keep the words that the students are working on in their word boxes. As they learn the words, have the students write them on circle coin cards (25¢) (10¢) (5¢) (1¢) that they can deposit into piggy banks made of boxes without a top to which you have pasted the picture of a pig. A slit must be made in the pig's body to bank the "coins." The students can review their words by reading them and counting their money. Harder words should go on coins of greater value.

Trace and Read

1. Some children need to trace or write the word as well as say, see, and hear it. Have the student trace over the word at the board using colored chalk. A color felt-tip pen may be used if the student is tracing the word on a piece of paper. Then have the students write the word themselves, always saying the word at the finish.

2. Tracing the word in a low box filled with dry, flavored gelatin helps the student get the feel of the letters in the word. This kind of kinesthetic approach often is helpful to the slow learner who needs lots of sensory input. Licking fingers afterward is a reward, let's hope second only to the thrill of learning! Have the student write words with finger paints if you don't mind the mess.

3. Writing missing letters of the word and tracing over the others eventually leading to writing the whole word is good practice for some students. The student reads the word aloud each time.

Example: the   He is *the* boy.
          _ he
          _ _ e
          _ _ _

If these are done on laminated cards, they may be used again.

Spelling To Jog Memory

For some students, spelling out the letters of the word and then immediately pronouncing it is helpful as a beginning crutch. The spelling triggers the memory of the word. Eventually, the spelling is dropped.

Visualize the Word

Have the students look carefully at the word and then to try and see it with their eyes closed, perhaps even writing the word in the air and pronouncing and/or spelling it with eyes still closed. The students may then open their eyes, check the word again and proceed to write the word on paper with eyes open, again simultaneously pronouncing the word.

Call Attention to All Parts of the Word

Many students fixate on the beginnings of words. When they are learning colors, for example, they easily learn "blue," and then "black" or even "brown." Once all three words have been taught, however, seeing "blue" can easily evoke a response of "black" or "brown." Try to encourage students to focus on features in the middle and endings of words as well as in their beginnings. Ask "How are these words alike and how are they different?"

Feature the Features

In teaching the sight word, have the student participate in a discussion both of meaning and of distinguishing features. Ask the students to think about and tell you how they can best remember the word. In searching for these distinguishing features, their memory will be enhanced.

Example: One student explained that she could distinguish between *want* and *went* because she *wants* an ant farm and ant is in *want* but not in *went.*

Distinguish Visually Similar Words

1. Use a homemade tachistoscope to practice these words in isolation or in phrases (*bother, brother; though, through, thought*). The tachistoscope may be an animal head with the visually similar words appearing in the eyes or the phrase in the mouth.

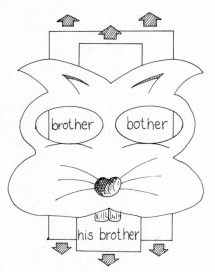

2. Help students utilize context for determining a word by providing sentences missing the sight word. Give visually similar words to choose from.

Example: The boy went _____ the door.
                      though   through

3. Have the student find the word in a word search. Use visually similar words as distractors. Have the student trace the word with a color felt-tip pen rather than circle it.

Example: B T H O U G H D F P A
                   T H G H T H R O U G H
                   O U G H T T H O U G H

Multiplying Sight Words

When you are teaching a verb—the word *jump,* for example—it is a good idea to show the student the words *jumps, jumped,* and *jumping* so that the students understand from the start that inflecting roots will enable them to read a great many more words. You might want to encourage students to cover any "ing," "s," or "ed" at the end of a word with their finger to facilitate identifying the root.

Practice Simple Function Words So That They Become Automatic

1. Have the students use one or two long articles from the front page of the newspaper and circle every *of* or *the,* pronouncing the word each time they circle it. This should be done quickly. A timer may be used. The students may count the number of times *of* appears. They can then try it with *the, in, on,* or another frequently appearing word and can compare scores.

2. Create a number of simple phrases using the function words (*at the top, in the hole, to a boy, for her mom*). Be sure the noun used is an easy, familiar one. Have the student flip through the phrases with a timer, trying to improve his or her speed.

Provide Numerous and Varied Repetitions

1. Many games that practice sight words require pairs of cards. Having the student make the second or matching set of cards for games like "Go Fish," "Concentration," or "Old Maid" provides additional motivating reinforcement.

2. Have a ring (notebook type) that can open and attach to a student's belt loop or can be pinned to a piece of clothing. Put sight word cards on the ring each day. At several points during the day, have the student read the words to you or to another student. Have the student bring the ring home each night to practice reading the words.

3. Give each student a word to read for the day. Before leaving the classroom for recess, lunch, gym, or changing classes, the students must read their words to you.

4. *Board games.* A number of different kinds of board games allow the student to read aloud the sight word, phrase, or sentence in order to move or advance toward winning the game.

Examples include:

a. Any kind of game in which words or phrases are written on the board or appear in packs of cards. The students move the appropriate number of spaces. If they can read the word on the space or the card they've picked, they stay there and continue on at their next turn. If they can't read the word, they may be penalized.

b. Football fields, baseball fields, checkerboards, spaces leading to an airplane hangar, a ladder top, or just a plain board with an interesting shape are examples of the kinds of boards that may be used.*

5. *Chance reading.*

a. Students must reach into a bag and pick a card at will. If they can read the word, phrase, or sentence, they keep it.

b. The teacher holds up cards. If a student can read the card, s/he keeps it. A variation has cards with directions. For example, "Jump up and down." If the student can do what the card says and then can read the card aloud, s/he keeps the card.

c. Students fish with a pole to which string and a magnet are attached. Word cards shaped like fish each have a paperclip on them. The magnet pulls up a card. If a student can read it, s/he keeps it.

Helpful Hint—If word packs are used, each student may pick from his/her own pack so that the word practice may be individualized.

In all instances, the object is for the student to end up with more cards than the teacher or the other players.

6. *Self-checking devices.*

a. A board can have flaps stapled at the top with colors, numbers, or picturable nouns written on each flap. As the students read each word, they check the accuracy by picking up the flap to see the circle of color, number, or picture under the flap.

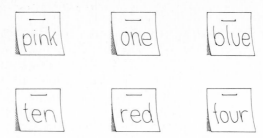

A number name or color name on each flap

b. Students may place lists of words or phrases on strips for individual tachistoscopes. After practicing the words, the students turn on a teacher-made tape recording of the list and listen to see if they were correct.

Read, Read, Read

Easy reading materials that frequently repeat words help students see sight words in context and gain automaticity. Don't be afraid of letting students read easy material. It builds sight-word knowledge as well as success.

Focus on Word Meanings

If a student's listening/speaking vocabulary does not contain the sight word being taught, it is unlikely that the word will be learned. As stated earlier, students' ability to relate to a word's meaning has been shown to influence the ease with which they learn the word. In any case, be sure the students know the meanings of the words they are learning and can use the words correctly.

In choosing sight words to introduce, you might try to cluster words around similar themes or meanings. TV words, color words, and sports words are examples. Words occurring in stories read to children offer another source.

Chapter Six offers suggestions for building meaning vocabulary. Many of these techniques for generating vocabulary provide opportunities that foster sight vocabulary building as well.

ACTIVITIES INDEX

DON'T GET BEHIND THE EIGHT BALL
GO FLY A KITE

REFERENCES

Ashton-Warner, Sylvia, *Teacher,* rev. ed. New York: Simon & Schuster, 1963.

Ceprano, Maria A., "A Review of Selected Research on Methods of Teaching Sight Words," *The Reading Teacher,* December 1981, pp. 314–322.

Durkin, Dolores, *Strategies for Identifying Words.* Boston: Allyn & Bacon, Inc., 1976.

_____, *Children Who Read Early*. New York: Columbia University, Teachers College Press: 1966.

Ekwall, Eldon E., and James Shanker, *Diagnosis and Remediation of the Disabled Reader*. Boston: Allyn and Bacon, Inc., 1983.

Hargis, Charles H., and Edward E. Gickling, "The Function of Imagery in Word Recognition Development," *The Reading Teacher*, May 1978, pp. 870–874.

Hood, Joyce, "Sight Words Are Not Going Out of Style," *The Reading Teacher*, January 1977, pp. 379–382.

Lass, Bonnie, "Portrait of My Son as an Early Reader," *The Reading Teacher*, October 1982, pp. 20–28.

Two

Problems with Phonic Analysis

SKILL DESCRIPTION

Letter–Sound Relationships

How much phonics instruction belongs in the teaching of reading? The answer to this question has ranged from "a lot" (Flesch, 1981) to "none" (Smith, 1979). The expert reader is a sight reader and relies very little if at all on phonics. Most reading educators, ourselves included, however, suggest that for the beginner a certain amount of phonics is necessary to develop independent reading (Heilman, 1981; Lamb, 1975).

Most phonics teaching, especially that taught within the context of the basal reader, begins with consonant sounds. Consonants provide the "backbone" of words. "C__n y____ r____d th__s?" is probably decodable for most readers, whereas "__a__ __ou __ea__ ____i__?" is not. To work successfully with consonant letters and sounds, a student must first be able to identify the sound of the consonant letter whether it is found in the initial, medial, or final position in a word. Consonant digraphs (*ch, gh, ph, sh, th, wh, ng*) are often most successfully taught next since they are taught and reinforced in an identical manner to individual consonants. Like individual consonants, they produce a single sound, and blending of sounds, which is a more difficult task, is not necessary. Consonant clusters are taught next. With consonant clusters, the student learns to blend together the two or three individual sounds.

Vowels are more unpredictable than consonants and are therefore best taught later to remedial students. Individual vowel letters may represent several different sounds. The letter *o*, for example, sounds different in the words *hot, ought, home, out,* and *orange.* Moreover, a vowel sound may be spelled in a number of ways. Long *e* can be spelled in any one of seven ways as seen in the words: *see, sea, Pete, receive, he, believe, key.*

Decisions about vowel sounds in relation to vowel letters are not easy. There are, however, syllable patterns which indicate that a particular vowel sound is likely (CVC, CVCe, etc.). These patterns are rarely without exceptions, so that while they are helpful it is essential that we teach students to be flexible decoders. When one vowel sound produces a nonsense word, a student should be ready to try another vowel sound.

Blending

Even though students know the sound-symbol relationships for consonants and vowels, they must be able to blend together the sounds to produce a word. This is not always an easy task. Linguistic basic readers were an attempt to deal with the problems that arise when some students are learning to blend sounds. In these readers, whole words are taught with minimal variations in pattern (*cat, hat, rat, Nat, fat*), and individual sounds are never taught apart from the whole word. Not all students, however, can perceive what sound a letter produces when it is part of a word. These students need to learn sounds in isolation and consequently need to learn blending skills as well.

POSSIBLE REASONS FOR SKILL DEFICIENCY

1. Sometimes the student is taught too many sounds too quickly and hasn't had a chance to master any. In our attempt to get through all of the reading material we feel we need to in a school day, we sometimes teach too much too fast. Moreover, a student's ability to display short-term memory skills may trick a teacher into believing that a skill has been learned permanently. As the teacher forges ahead, the student falls further and further behind.

2. Many students cannot separate one sound from another within a word.

3. Students may fixate on the letter name(s) instead of the letter sound(s).

4. Although students have progressed to the stage of recognizing sounds, they cannot yet produce sounds upon seeing the letter(s) in isolation or within words. (See the difference between recognition and identification discussed in ''Diagnostic Procedures below.'')

5. With consonant digraphs or vowel digraphs and diphthongs, a student may identify the letter combinations as individual sounds and read *ch* as ''kuh huh'' or the *oi* in *oil* as ''oh ǐ''. With consonant clusters, a student may use only one of the letters, usually the first (*black = back*).

6. Students who have been exposed primarily to a sight approach may not have been taught enough phonics to help them analyze new words. For example, a student may not know the syllable patterns and the generalizations that apply to them and cue the appropriate vowel sound (e.g. CVC pattern usually produces a short vowel sound).

7. Students who have learned vowel generalizations may be inflexible decoders. Having tried, for example, to pronounce the word *find* as *fǐnd,* they may have difficulty trying a different vowel sound, especially if the alternative doesn't conform to rules they've learned.

8. The student may have learned individual sounds in isolation. This can lead to incorrect pronunciation of the consonant with an ''uh'' sound following it, possibly resulting in blending problems. For a fuller discussion of this topic see Haddock, 1978.

9. Students have not learned to blend quickly enough. Hesitations between letters, regardless of how slight they appear, keep students from recognizing the parts as a whole familiar word.

10. Students are using phonics exclusively. They need to realize that they must use context clues to confirm attempts at phonic analysis. For example, in the sentence ''He was wearing a *bow* tie,'' *bow* may be read incorrectly to rhyme with *cow.*

11. Students may not have a sufficient listening-speaking vocabulary. When they attempt to decode or blend, they don't recognize a real word as the result of their efforts. This may be less of a problem when the word appears in context.

SELECTED DIAGNOSTIC PROCEDURES

A student's ability to use decoding skills effectively to aid word identification may either be observed in connected oral reading performance or tested directly through the use of formal or informal phonics instruments. In either type of observation, the teacher is looking for patterns of error.

Oral reading, whether it occurs as a natural part of classroom instruction or as a part of any of the diagnostic batteries (e.g., Gates-McKillop-Horowitz Reading Diagnostic Tests), offers the teacher the chance to note whether errors are caused by inadequate phonics skills. Consonants, for example, may be omitted in words in which consonant clusters are present. The medial parts of one-syllable words with a particular vowel combination (*taut, haul, pound, shout*) may be mispronounced.

Formal or informal phonics tests look at a student's ability to make sound-symbol relationships with: sounds in isolation and/or within words, words in isolation and/or in context, and real and/or nonsense words. Moreover, these tests can help a teacher to discover whether a student understands sound-symbol relationships simply at a recognition or beginning level. Students may be asked to listen to a word pronounced by the teacher and then to point to one of three or four words that begin, end, or have the same vowel sound as the word that has been read to them. This is different from real reading, which asks students to pronounce the word independently. The first task is important as an initial step but, as reading teachers, it is the second or *identification* task we are concerned with in this chapter. When you are testing phonics knowledge, be sure that you have asked students to produce sounds or words themselves before making the judgment that a particular sound-symbol relationship is known.

The BAF Test (Frank B. May and Susan B. Eliot, *To Help Children Read,* 1978)* is a quick and easy measure for determining specific needs with consonant and vowel sounds as well as with blending. This test utilizes nonsense words in isolation. For the occasional student who cannot perform with nonsense words, a different test would be advisable. Information about skill needs gleaned from the results of this test should be confirmed in a reading situation that uses real words.

With the BAF Test, the student is taught the nonsense word "baf." The student is then asked to read aloud a list of nonsense words utilizing the "af" phonogram and consonant substitutions. Vowel substitutions follow, utilizing the same "baf" syllable. Ability with consonants, vowels, and blending can be assessed.

*May, Frank B., and Susan B. Eliot, *To Help Children Read, 2nd edition,* "The BAF Test" (Columbus, OH: Charles E. Merrill Publishing Co. 1978), Copyright 1978 by Bell and Howell Co., pp. 213–214. Used with permission.

CASE STUDY*

Lily's testing results are shown below. She was tested at the beginning of third grade. Her errors are shown in parentheses. A number of additional nonsense words have been added by the authors to the vowel digraph and diphthong columns of May's original test.

Consonant Letters

baf	kaf	tab
caf	laf	vaf (wuh a f)
daf (baf)	maf	waf (wuh wa)
faf	naf	yaf (yuh a f)
gaf	paf	zaf (zee af)
haf (have)	raf (rat, ră f)	baf
jaf (juh a f)	saf	bax
		quaf[1] (kew—I don't know)

Consonant Digraphs

chaf (juh huh af)	phaf (puh huh af)	shaf (ss huh af)
thaf (taf)	fack (fa kuh kuh)	fang (fan)
whaf (waf)		fank (fan)

[1]See Introduction for function of Case Study.

Consonant Blends

blaf (baf)	braf (buh bee—I	stopped subtest
claf (kuh el af)	don't know)	

Vowel Letters, Digraphs, Blends

baf	bafe	barf (baf)	baif (ba if)	bawf (I don't
bef	befe	berf (bef)	beaf	bewf know
bof (bŭf)	bofe	borf (bor f)	boaf	bouf the
bif	bife	birf (bir brif)	beef[1]	bauf[1] rest)
buf	bufe	burf (burif)	boef[1] (bu ef)	boif
			bayf[1]	bowf[1]
			bowf[1] (b—	boyf[1]
			I don't	boof
			know)	

[1]Words added by the authors

The patterns that emerge from the results of Lily's consonant tests show that she has mastered most single consonant sounds and can use them appropriately in the initial position. *D, q, v,* and *z* sounds need further checking. Consonant digraphs and consonant clusters seem unknown. Lily has shown problems blending certain consonants. The use of the added "uh" to the consonant sound seems to get in her way. Although at times Lily's desire to make real words emerged, she was able to control this.

In the vowel tests, it appeared that Lily probably can read short vowel words. Short *o* should be checked in other situations. With long vowels, she seems to have mastered the vce syllable pattern but only the most common vowel digraphs (*ee, oa, ea*) are familiar. Vowel digraphs and vowel diphthongs need to be taught, and *r*-controlled vowels are not known.

Other Assessments

1. "El Paso Phonics Survey," in *Ekwall Reading Inventory,* Eldon E. Ekwall. Boston: Allyn and Bacon, 1979. (This test is similar to the BAF Test.)
2. *Botel Reading Inventory.* Chicago: Follett, 1978.
   Subtest: Decoding
3. *Diagnostic Reading Scales,* George D. Spache. Monterey, CA: McGraw-Hill, Inc., 1981.
   Subtests: Supplementary Tests of Word Analysis
4. *Durrell Analysis of Reading Difficulty.* New York: The Psychological Corporation, 1980.
   Subtests: Word Analysis, Identifying Sounds in Words, Sounds in Isolation, etc.
5. *Gates-McKillop-Horowitz Reading Diagnostic Tests.* New York: Columbia University, Teachers College Press, 1981.
6. *Roswell-Chall Diagnostic Reading Test.* San Diego, CA: Essay Press, 1976.

TECHNIQUES FOR REMEDIATION

The techniques described below begin with suggestions for help with individual sounds both in isolation and within words, continue with hints for blending sounds within words, and finally move to words in larger thought units—phrases, sentences, and paragraphs.

Know Where You're Going, Proceed Step-by-Step, and Don't Rush

1. Decide on your approach to phonics. Will you use whole words to demonstrate letter sounds (analytic phonics), sounds in isolation that you will then help students to blend (synthetic phonics $/b/ /a/ /t/ = /bat/$), or a combination?
2. Next, decide on the sequence of sounds you will teach.

3. Progress systematically, making certain students have success with a sound before teaching a new one.

4. Provide continued practice with old sounds when new sounds are taught.

5. Put words into context as quickly as possible and always discuss a word's meaning to assure that students recognize the word they have sounded.

6. Provide connected reading to practice sounds in context.

Help Students Learn Sound-Symbol Relationships

1. Use pictures that highlight a letter's configuration. When possible, give students pictures that begin with a letter and remind them of its written form and sound.

Example:

See *Beginning* **(Developed by Boston Educational Research Company for J. B. Lippincott Co., 1978) for ideas for letters.**

You can't always find a picture which portrays the letter's shape. But pictures can serve as key words. Display the pictures in the classroom to serve as reminders of sound and symbol. Emphasize that the letter name and letter sound usually differ.

2. Practice having students identify sounds within words.

a. Write the letter you hear at the beginning (middle, end) of each of these words: *bad, baby, bug, bottle, bitter, berry,* etc.

b. Make class or group collages for letters. Have students paste pictures that begin (end) with the sound on a large sheet of paper. The letter may be painted on afterward and the collage displayed in the room.

c. Make posters of letters with pockets into which the students can place cut out pictures that begin or end with the letter sound. Medial vowels can also be used. At various points in the day or week, the teacher can sort through the pictures with the students to reinforce the sound and correct errors.

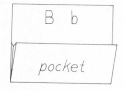

d. *Picture cards.* (1) Prepare picture cards with the beginning, ending, or vowel letter written on the back. (e.g. A picture of a cat may have a *c*, an *a*, or a *t* written on the back.) Have two students work together to test each other. (2) Give students laminated pictures with space beneath the picture to write the initial, vowel, or final letter. Have the students say aloud what the picture shows before writing the appropriate grapheme. The teacher may have the grapheme written on the back for self checking.

e. *Bat a Round.* Place a picture of a baseball bat on one side of an oaktag folder with letters written in spaces around the perimeter of the bat. The other side of the folder should have two pipe cleaners attached to it with the headings *Cards* and *Used Cards,* respectively. Picture cards representing initial, final, or vowel sounds are placed on the *Cards* pipe cleaner. Students take turns moving one space at a time and picking a picture card. If the card matches the letter in the space (for initial, final, or vowel sound—any one or any combination may be used), the child keeps the card. Otherwise, it goes on the *Used Cards* pile. When the cards are used up, the children play with the *Used Cards* pile. The child with the most cards at the end wins. One child may play alone to see if s/he can better a previous score.

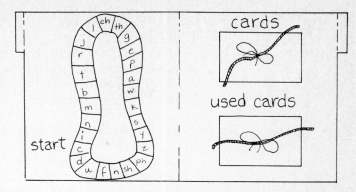

f. *Climbing Up.* A ladder is drawn diagonally on one side of the oaktag folder with pipe cleaners attached to each rung. The other side of the folder has two attached pipe cleaners headed *Letters* and *Pictures.* Cards for each are placed on the appropriate pipe cleaners. Students place a letter card at the top of the ladder. They then look for pictures which begin with the sound the letter represents (or ending sounds and/or vowel sounds may be used) and place one on each rung. Pictures may have the relevant letter written on the back for self-checking.

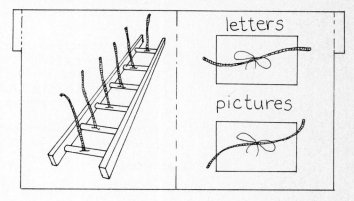

g. *Word chains.* Write and/or read a word that begins with a particular letter. Have the student volunteer another word that begins or ends the same way.

You may play the game this way. Say a word—e.g., *bat.* The student must give a word that begins with the ending sound of *bat*—e,.g., *top.* Continue in this fashion.

Teach Digraphs and Clusters in the Initial Position First

1. Show students that when consonants combine with *h* (*ch, ph, sh, th,*) a brand-new sound results, different from either letter alone. Use pictures or sound images to reinforce the sound. Ch, ch, ch, ch—choo choo train; sh, sh—quiet; th— tongue between your teeth; wh—whistle (purse your lips).

2. Have students read the words *sip* and *lip.* Then combine the *s* and *l,* making *slip.* Do this with each of the clusters so that the students see how the cluster is formed.

3. Form cluster wheels in two steps. To teach *l* or *r* clusters, have a center word such as *lack* or *rack.* Have an outer wheel with single consonants that turns to form words with the center word.

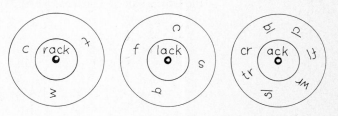

Then proceed to a center wheel with the phonogram *ack* and the clusters on the outer wheel.

4. You might wish to play "one sound or two" with students. As you flash a card with a consonant digraph (*ch*) or a consonant cluster (*cl*), students may state whether these letters generally refer to one or two sounds. You might ask for a word that demonstrates their response.

For Some Students, Learning the Vowel Generalizations Proves Useful

It is helpful to remember that these generalizations apply to syllables. Since most beginning reading words have one syllable, the generalizations are applicable right from the beginning. Always help the children to use the generalizations flexibly, recognizing that exceptions are rarely the exception. Useful rules to teach include:

1. When there is one vowel at the end of a word or syllable, it is usually long (*gō, na/tion*).
2. When there is one vowel in a word or syllable that is not the final letter and it is not followed by an *r*, it is usually short (*add, best, trip, hot, trust, gym*).
3. A vowel followed by an *r* has neither the long nor short sound (*her, car*).
4. When there are two vowels in a syllable, the first one is often long and the second one is silent (*rain, like*).
5. *Y* has the long *i* sound when it is the only vowel in a one-syllable word and is the final letter of the word (*sky*).

   In words of two or more syllables, the final *y* preceded by a consonant has the sound of long *e* (*baby, happily*). When *y* is preceded by a vowel, it is usually part of a vowel digraph or diphthong (*play, key, toy*).

The following table shows syllable patterns useful in determining vowel sounds.

Syllable Patterns*

short	long	other sound
vc	cv	vr
cvc	cvce (usually long, sometimes short)	aw, au, al
		oi, oy, ou, ow (as in *owl*)
	cvvc (usually for *ai, ay, ee, ea, oa;* sometimes for *oe, ow*)	oo (both long and short variant— *book, moon*)
	(Note: *ea* often has short sound— *ow* can have sound heard in *owl*)	*v = any vowel c = any consonant

Climbing Ladders

Have children read up and down vowel ladders to show how the vowel changes the word. The words on the ladders should conform to syllabic patterns. Explain that some of the words will be nonsense words.

bag	*ha*	*make*
beg	*he*	*meke*
big	*hi*	*mike*
bog	*ho*	*moke*
bug	*hu*	*muke*

Reinforce Vowel Sounds

1. Using one sound at a time, have children read a number of words using that sound.

Example: short vowel /ă/–*bat, bag, bad, man, map, cap, dam*

2. Contrast two sounds using minimal pairs.
   a. short vowels

      Example: *mat, met,* etc.

   b. Silent e (vce)

      Example: *cap cape, pet Pete,* etc.

   c. vowel digraphs

      Example: *ran rain, men mean, got goat,*
                 red reed, pan pawn, Hal haul, etc.

   d. *r*-controlled vowels

      Example: *cat, cart;*
                 chip, chirp, etc.

Here's How

1. When vowels are particularly problematic, it is useful to provide a method or sequence for word attack. Have the student: (1) identify the vowel sound first; (2) add the ending; and (3) blend in the initial grapheme.

Example: *cat = ă at   cat*
           bake = ā ake bake
           rest = ě est rest

This is not appropriate for students who have problems with left-right sequencing (see Chapter Five).

2. For certain students, you may wish to use word families to build words. Teach the students two or three word families (*at, en, ill, ot,* etc.) and have them try to make real or nonsense words by blending a consonant, consonant digraph, or consonant cluster to the beginning—i.e., *dat, den, dill, dot.* For ending sounds, use consonants with vowels (*bă, bě, bǐ, bǒ, bŭ, bee*) to which students add the ending consonant sound—i.e., *bat, bet, bit, bot, but.* Using homemade anagrams can be an effective way of practicing. Cut one-inch squares of oaktag and write a separate letter on each square. Have many squares for each letter, especially the vowels.

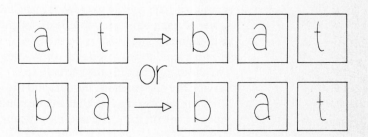

Variations: a. Using words the students already know, the teacher may try consonant substitution asking the students to quickly read the two words.

Example: *cat rat*   *or*   *cat cab*

b. Try teaching students to separate phonograms from initial sound and then blend them by clapping them together. The students say the initial sound looking at their left hand and then the phonogram looking at their right hand. They then say the word clapping the sounds and their hands together.

Some children do better by learning to blend an initial consonant plus a vowel (*ma*), then clapping on the final consonant. Have the children practice by adding the same final consonant to a number of beginning word parts with differing vowels.

Example: *mă t, mě t, mǐ t, mŏ t, mŭ t*

3. Show students how to use their knowledge of vowel sounds flexibly. When the expected pronunciation of an unknown word does not work, have students try another vowel sound. If in the sentence, *He ate the bread,* long *e* (brēd) does not work, have them try short *e* (brĕd). When neither long *e,* nor short *e* decode *break,* have them try other vowel sounds until the word is discovered.

Example: Please don't *break* that.
          brēk, brĕk, brăk, brĭk—Oh, I know—*brāk.*

Take Some Tips from Published Reading Series

Many students who know letter sounds cannot blend them to form words without instruction (Haddock, 1978). Below are some approaches that various reading series advise.

1. Begin to practice blending with vowels and consonants which are continuants like *m, n, r, s.* Write the word *am.* Point to the *a* and have the child give the short sound and hold it. Then, without taking a breath, add the *m* sound. Next have the child say the word quickly. Demonstrate if necesary. Continue with *in, on.* Proceed to words beginning with a consonant such as *man, Sam.* Have the child hold the first letter and add succesive letters without taking a breath. Then say the word quickly. (See the Lippincott *Basic Reading* Series, Book A, McCracken and Walcutt, 1975, for a complete description of this approach.)

2. Continue the one-breath procedure by having three children stand up, each holding a card to form a word such as *man.* Have the first child pronounce the *m* sound and bump up against the second who adds the *a* sound and bumps up against the third who adds the *n* sound. The word is then pronounced quickly. (See *Alpha One,* Reiss and Friedman, 1982, for a more complete description of this approach.)

3. If kids get stuck on slow decoding, use the DISTAR method of "say it fast." (*DISTAR Reading,* Englemann and Bruner, 1983.) Students slowly sound out the letters in a word (sss aaa mmm) and then blend the sounds by saying them fast (Sam).

Baseball Catch Blending

Using an oaktag folder, draw or paste a baseball glove on one side with an empty pipe cleaner attached to the palm. On the other side, attach to a pipe cleaner a number of laminated balls with a narrow oaktag slide that can be woven through two cuts in the center of each ball. On one side of the slide, write single consonants, and place consonant digraphs and clusters on the reverse side. Next to the two cuts on the ball, write a phonogram that will produce words when combined with the initial letters on the slide. The slide may be used on some balls to provide either the final consonant or the vowel by varying the placement of the cuts and the letters written on the ball. If students can read all of the words on a ball that can be made by pulling the slide, they put the ball on the pipe cleaner on the glove and have "caught" that ball.

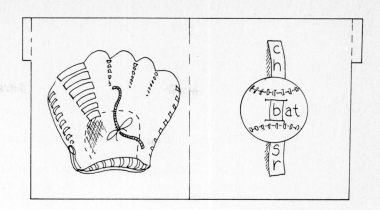

Words in Phrases and Sentences

As soon as possible, put words into phrases and sentences to practice letter sounds. Be sure students recognize that they must use context to confirm their analysis of a word. Have students respond to the sentences in various ways.

Example: Make a silly or serious face after each sentence.
      Bob bit the bug.
      Chip can chop wood for a chair.
      Green grapes grow in gravy.
      Big Tim will hit with his fist.

Write "yes" or "no" after each sentence.
      Can you cut a cord?   Yes
      Can ships shout?   No
      Are blue and black colors?   Yes
      Can you bake a game?   No

Analyze Words in Sentences

Using sentences such as "Sam has a *cap*," ask the child why the underlined word can't be *hat,* emphasizing that though the context and general size of the word fit, attention must be given to letters too.

Graduate from Sentences to Longer Passages

Move from isolated word practice to phrases and sentences to reading paragraphs practicing the elements being taught. Several publishing companies that put out small storybooks that do this are listed below:

Primary Phonics, Educators Publishing Service, Inc., Cambridge, MA.
Super Books, J. P. Lippincott Company, New York, NY.
K and Preprimary Readers, Modern Curriculum Press, Cleveland, OH.

A variation would be to write your own short story (book) using the appropriate phonic elements. Leave the hero/ine's name blank so students may fill in their own (____*had a sad cat,* etc.) We all like to read about ourselves. Laminate the pages so that the book may be used by everyone. When one student finishes the book, s/he wipes off his/her name.

ACTIVITIES INDEX

REFERENCES

Englemann, Seigfried, and Elaine Bruner, *Reading Mastery: DISTAR Reading.* Chicago: Science Research Associates, 1983.

Flesch, Rudolph, *Why Johnny Still Can't Read.* New York: Harper & Row, 1981.

Haddock, Maryann, "Teaching Blending in Beginning Reading Instruction Is Important," *The Reading Teacher,* March 1978, pp. 654–58.

Heilman, Arthur W., *Phonics in Proper Perspective.* Columbus, OH: Charles E. Merrill, 1981.

Lamb, Pose, "How Important Is Instruction in Phonics?" *The Reading Teacher,* October 1975, pp. 15–19.

McCracken, Glenn, and Charles C. Walcutt, *Basic Reading.* New York: J. B. Lippincott, 1975.

Reiss, Elayne, and Rita Friedman, *Alpha One.* New York: Arista Corporation, 1982.

Rowland, Pleasant T., *Beginning.* Boston, MA: Boston Educational Research Co., 1978.

Smith, Frank, *Reading Without Nonsense.* New York: Columbia University, Teachers College Press, 1979.

Three

Poor Structural Analysis

SKILL DESCRIPTION

It is not uncommon to meet a student who reads a selection quite competently until encountering a long, multisyllabic word. Typically the student looks up for help, without even attempting to read the word. The sheer length of the word engenders inaction. In most cases, however, the difficult word is easily decoded by dividing it into smaller, more manageable segments. Morphemic and syllabic analysis, components of structural analysis, offer the student approaches for accomplishing this.

When students encounter an unknown word that they cannot identify through the context, they should be encouraged to look within the word for a recognizable root and its accompanying prefix and / or ending(s) (Durkin, 1983). This is morphemic analysis: a concern with the meaningful parts of words—roots, prefixes, and suffixes.

A morpheme is classified as bound or free. A free morpheme is equivalent to a root word and can stand alone. Sometimes two free morphemes comprise a word as in *playground* and other compound words. A bound morpheme, such as the *s* in *boys,* which signifies that the noun *boy* is plural, only exists in connection with a free morpheme, in this case the word *boy.* All plurals, as well as derivatives, comparatives, and possessives combine bound and free morphemes. The meaning transmitted by each of the bound or free morphemes contained in the categories above aids the student in reading the resulting words. In the word *walked,* for example, the student identifies the *-ed* inflectional ending as a past tense marker. Although the *-ed* marker can be pronounced in three different ways (/ed/, /d/, or /t/), the student automatically responds with the correct pronunciation for the past tense of *walk,* since this word is in his / her listening-speaking vocabulary. How morphemic analysis helps to *build* vocabulary will be discussed in Chapter Six.

When morphemic analysis does not work in enabling the student to read the word, he or she may need to segment the word in a different way. The student is then encouraged to consider syllabic analysis, the other component of structural analysis. Syllabic analysis deals with a word's structure by dividing the word into its syllables (word segments, each containing one sounded vowel) so that the smaller segments can be more readily identified. The student then blends these segments to produce the word.

When the student divides the word into its syllables, the resulting word segments produce either open or closed syllables with their corresponding vowel sounds. An open syllable ends in a vowel (CV) and usually produces a long vowel sound. A closed syllable (VC or CVC) ends in a consonant and usually produces a short vowel sound. Students can identify the *ri* in *rifle* as a syllable requiring a long sound so that the word is pronounced correctly as *rīfle* rather than *rĭfle*. Although *canteen* may look like an unfamiliar and therefore difficult word, once the word is syllabicated, the two parts *can* and *teen* are easily read.

Unfortunately, because of accenting and resulting *schwa* sounds, open and closed syllables are most effective for decoding a stressed syllable, usually the first syllable, but this is often enough to get the students into the word and to facilitate their identifying the word as a whole. Usually simple generalizations for correct accent and an understanding of the *schwa* sound are taught along with generalizations for syllabic analysis. (See Techniques for Remediation later in this chapter.)

Syllabic analysis is a controversial topic. Ordinarily, dictionary syllabication is the accepted way of dividing words. The dictionary provides the verification for the rules which students are taught in the classroom. Lately, however, reading specialists have questioned the validity of dictionary syllabication (Groff, 1971; Seymour, 1973). Waugh and Howell (1975) insist that syllabication rules should follow speech patterns. This may mean, for example, keeping like consonants together since they produce one sound (*lett/er*) rather than adhering to the usual VC/CV generalization (*let/ter*), which in this instance distorts the pronunciation of the word.

But dividing after the double consonant has its problems as well. Following speech patterns, the consonant sound actually belongs with the second syllable rather than the first. This inaccurately leaves an open syllable which should be read with a long vowel (*lē/tter*). Moreover, it is the rare student who, if he or she pronounced a double consonant twice (*let/ter*), consequently failed to identify the word correctly. Our approach therefore is to apply the VC/CV generalization to like or unlike double consonants. (When a double letter ends a root and an affix is attached, division occurs between the root and the affix. Examples are: *hill/y, miss/ing.*)

POSSIBLE REASONS FOR SKILL DEFICIENCY

1. The length of the word frightens certain students. They will not even attempt a pronunciation.

2. In reading inflected words, the student might also need to be using context as a cue and is failing to do so. Consequently, the student reads, "He jump ed off the box," an error that s/he would not make if s/he were attending to the content.

3. Students may not recognize certain affixes as such. Therefore they cannot separate the root and the affix to facilitate pronouncing the word.

4. The student may be falsely identifying a prefix when in fact the letters do not act as a prefix in the given word (*rem*nant, *un*ite). Moreover, they may be looking for little words in big ones (*or* in *word*) rather than looking for root words with prefixes and suffixes.

5. The student may be unfamiliar with the pronunciation of certain affixes (*anti*trust, ela*tion*, rest*ive*).

6. Students may not know the generalizations for adding endings to words and may misread (C)VC words to which an ending beginning with a vowel has been added. (Example: They read *hŏping* for *hoping* or *nŏtable* for *notable*.)

7. Students may not have learned the syllable generalizations and their resulting effect on vowel sounds.

8. Improper use of accent and/or lack of familiarity with the schwa sound can prevent students from recognizing their pronunciation of the word.

SELECTED DIAGNOSTIC PROCEDURES

There isn't one test that diagnoses all of the components of structural analysis. It is often done best through listening to students' oral reading and noting whether they evidence problems in any of the areas concerned. It is important to distinguish, however, between nonstandard English errors or dialect errors that may result in omitted endings, and those errors that show problems in reading words with inflectional endings. For a fuller discussion of this topic, refer to Chapter Thirteen.

CASE STUDY*

The structural analysis section of the Green Level Stanford Diagnostic Reading Test (Karlsen, 1976)† was administered to Ted, who was finishing fifth grade. It is important to note that this is a group silent reading test. The test is shown below. Only Ted's errors are circled.

Test 4: Structural Analysis Part A

Samples

A tiptoe	t	ti	*tip*	15 almost	a	al	almo
B captain	ca	*cap*	capta	16 headline	he	head	headl
1 sometimes	so	some	somet	17 report	re	rep	repo
2 invent	i	in	(inve)	18 buying	bu	buy	buyi
3 surely	su	sur	sure	19 pirate	pi	(pir)	pira
4 tonight	to	ton	toni	20 accent	a	ac	(acce)
5 forget	fo	for	forge	21 doghouse	do	dog	dogh
6 outdoors	ou	out	outd	22 exclaim	e	ex	(exc)
7 unknown	u	un	unk	23 thoughtless	thou	though	thought
8 kindness	ki	kin	kind	24 station	sta	(stat)	stati
9 alive	a	al	(ali)	25 picnic	pi	pic	picni
10 platform	pla	plat	platfo	26 seashore	sea	seas	seash
11 flashlight	fla	flas	flash	27 pretend	pre	(pret)	prete
12 complete	co	com	compl	28 action	a	ac	acti
13 hopeful	hop	hope	hopef	29 elect	e	(el)	ele
14 future	fu	(fut)	futu	30 perhaps	pe	per	(perha)

*See Introduction for function of Case Study.
†Reproduced by permission from the Stanford Diagnostic Reading Test: 2nd Edition. Copyright © 1976 by Harcourt Brace Jovanovich, Inc. All rights reserved.

Of the ten items that Ted failed, seven were concerned with syllabication. The remaining three dealt with affixes. It seems evident that this young man could benefit by instruction in the VCV syllable rule. Work with some common prefixes may also be in order. Before conclusions are drawn, however, it would be important to see whether the student can read these words aloud. Perhaps Ted's only problem is in isolating the first syllable, the task the directions ask for. If he can pronounce the words correctly, his problem may reflect difficulty with the testing task rather than a reading deficiency.

Other Assessments

1. May, Frank B. and Susan B. Eliot, *To Help Children Read*. Columbus, OH: Charles E. Merrill, 1978.
   Subtests: Meaning of Contractions, Recognition of Roots and Affixes.
2. Pearson, P. David and Dale D. Johnson, *Teaching Reading Vocabulary*. New York: Holt, Rinehart and Winston, 1978.
   Subtests: Plurals, Possessives, Affixes.
3. Rae, Gwenneth and Thomas Potter. *Informal Reading Diagnosis*. Englewood Cliffs, NJ: Prentice-Hall, Inc., 1981.
   Subtests: Syllabication Structural Analysis Tests: Levels I, II, III.
4. *Roswell-Chall Diagnostic Reading Test*. Sacramento, CA: Essay Press, 1976. (Section V.)

TECHNIQUES FOR REMEDIATION

Get to the Root of Things

Before attempting to divide a word into syllables, teach the student to look to see if a recognizable root is present. *Unreadable* may seem impossible to decode until the student sees the root word *read* and then sees that a prefix and suffix are attached. By looking for roots, the student can avoid such errors as treating the *re* in remnant as a prefix.

Teach Affixes When a Root Word Is Learned

When students learn the verbs *like, jump,* and so on, teach them *likes, liked, liking, jumps, jumped, jumping* at the same time so that they get used to seeing the root with endings and can recognize it as such. Don't wait for a special lesson on *ed* or *ing*. Practice using words with inflectional endings in cloze sentences so that students recognize that context must be used with structural analysis.

Example: John was _____ up and down.
               jumps   jumped   jumping

Learn the Common Affixes and Their Meanings

Plan specific lessons in which you teach common affixes (*re, un, im, in, less, ful, able*). Show how they are added to a root and change its meaning.

Ekwall and Shanker (1983), in agreement with Russell Stauffer, claim that disabled readers need not be concerned with the meanings of suffixes and that only eleven prefixes (*re, un, en, ex, de, com, in [into], in [not], pre, sub, dis*) are useful to learn. However, they feel that teaching common prefixes and suffixes by sight aids word identification. We feel that it is useful for students to know the meaning of some of the more common suffixes and that awareness of meaning aids word identification as well.

Use Your Fingers

Have students cover affixes with their fingers as soon as they can spot them. Once they have decoded the root word, the affix is easy to add and the word as a whole seems less difficult.

System Analysis

In a sentence such as "She was unforgettably beautiful," the student meets a multisyllabic word composed of a root with a prefix and suffixes.

Durkin (1983) recommends that the student use the following system in attempting to read a word such as *unforgettably:*

1. remove the prefix	*forgettably*
2. remove the last suffix	*forgettable*
3. remove the next suffix	*forget*
4. decode the root and then working backward	
5. put the first suffix back	*forgettable*
6. put the next suffix back	*forgettably*
7. put the prefix back	*unforgettably*

A student enjoys the security that a reliable system offers.

Bob's Reading Bill's Books

Teach the differences between contractions, possessives, and plurals. Many students tend to confuse contractions and possessives because of the apostrophe, possessives and plurals because of the *s* ending. Help students to understand the meanings of individual contractions. Often they do not relate the printed word to what is commonplace in their oral usage.

Useful exercises for distinguishing between contractions, possessives, and plurals might include:

1. Match the underlined word in the following sentence to the correct meaning:
    a. He's coming with us.
       he is   many boys
    b. The boy's hat blew off.
       the hat of the boy   boy is
2. Choose the correct word for each sentence
    a. _____ hat blew off.
       Bill   Bill's   Bills
    b. _____ my house.
       Here   Here's   Heres

Teach Spelling Rules for Suffixes

When looking at root words and suffixes (derivational or inflectional), students often have problems reading words like *hoped* or *hoping* (see Possible Reasons for Skill Deficiency). The teacher may feel the need to show students how to add suffixes that begin with a vowel.

1. Double the final consonant for CVC single-syllable words or accented CVC last syllables.
   tap = tapped, tapping
   omit = omitted, omitting

2. Drop the final *e* for VCe words.
   faked, faking, faker

3. Change the *y* to *i.* *
   carried, carrier

*Unless: (1) a vowel precedes the *y—player;* (2) the suffix is *ing—carrying.* For plurals, the *y* (when preceded by a consonant) changes to *i* and the *es* is added—*penny, pennies.*

Although these generalizations are usually relevant for spelling purposes, students may need to learn them for decoding as well.

Syllable Generalizations

Although we recommend that students in need become familiar with these generalizations, we stress that they must be used flexibly. Clymer (1963), for example, in citing the percentage of utility for certain generalizations, found the V / CV rule (see 5. below) to be applicable only 44 percent of the time. We would suggest that the percentage would be a great deal higher if we encourage students to try VC / V when their first attempt does not produce a real word.

Any order may be taught for syllabication rules. The order we find useful is found below. It is important to remember that these generalizations offer students a means of visually segmenting words so that they may then decode only three or four letters at a time. Segmenting words that can be pronounced is foolish. If a student can already pronounce the word, it is a waste of time to divide it into syllables.

1. *Every syllable has a sounded vowel.* A syllable may have three vowel letters but since two of the vowels are silent, it is still a single syllable (*geese*).

2. *Compound words*—Divide between the two words.

   Example: *play/ground*

3. *VCCV*—When two consonants appear between two sounded vowels, divide between the two consonants. This normally will leave a CVC first syllable which is easy to decode and gives the student a good start on the word. *Remember that a consonant digraph and some consonant clusters act as a single letter and relate to the VCV generalization below.*

   Examples: *win/dow* **but:** *le/thal   a/pron*
   VC/CV   V/CV

4. *Cle*—In words that end in *le,* keep the consonant that precedes the *le* with the *le* syllable. This leaves either an open or closed first syllable with its corresponding long or short vowel sound. This is a good time to illustrate how syllabication aids understanding of which vowel sound to use.

   Example: *rifle = rī fle* not *rĭf le*

   When the *tle* follows an *s,* the *t* is silent—*castle, rustle.*
   ck remains with the first syllable (*nick / le*).

5. *VCV*—When one consonant appears between two sounded vowels, first try dividing after the first vowel (*pa / per*). If a recognizable word is not found, try dividing after the consonant (*rob / in*). The concept of open and closed syllables is reinforced here. *Consonant digraphs and certain consonant clusters act as one consonant (le / thal, a / pron).*

6. *Root words*—If a word has an affix (prefix and / or suffix or inflectional ending), divide between the root and the affix.

   Examples: *re/write   un/like/ly*

7. *Inflectional endings*—As a past tense ending, *ed* forms a separate syllable only when it is added to a root word that ends in a *d* or a *t* (*plant/ed   need/ed*).
When *ion* is added to a word ending in *t, tion* becomes a syllable.

Example: *elect   elec/tion*

8. *Double vowels*—Sometimes double vowels do not form digraphs or diphthongs but are read separately, forming two syllables.

Examples: *d<u>i</u>/<u>e</u>t, d<u>u</u>/<u>e</u>t, nu/cle/<u>u</u>s, ra/d<u>i</u>/<u>o</u>, cre/<u>a</u>te, <u>o</u>/<u>a</u>/sis.*

Concentrate on the First Syllable

Help the students to see that the first syllable of a root word is usually a CVC or CV configuration and is easily decoded. If the students can read the first syllable, this is often enough to give them the confidence to proceed with the word. The context provides additional help.

The teacher may wish to compose cloze sentences using the first syllable of a difficult word for the deleted word to illustrate the usefulness of the initial syllable plus context.

Example: Tom needed to <u>prac____</u> his math.
                                     (practice)

Decode One Syllable at a Time

Sometimes it helps students to overcome their fear of long words by isolating the first syllable and then covering the rest of the word with their finger. Four letters at a time is "do-able" when the whole word is formidable.

Use Most Common Accent Generalizations

Help the student to understand stress or accent. Show the student that:

1. Most two syllable words have the stress on the first syllable unless the second syllable has a long vowel sound.

   Example: *car' pet   com plain'*

2. Root words are usually accented rather than their affixes.

   Example: *un hap' py   care' ful*

3. The syllable before certain suffixes is often an open syllable with a long sound and is accented.

   Example: before *tion: re la' tion   sol u' tion   com mo' tion*

Schwa

Teach students about the *schwa* sound (this usually sounds quite like the short *u* sound /*uh*/—*a gree,* but sometimes may sound like short *e* or *i*—*de cide*—depending on an individual's dialect). It is especially confusing with syllables like *age* (*usage*), *ite* (*composite*), *ive* (*explosive*) where the silent *e* leads the student to expect that the preceding vowel will be long. Because the syllable is unaccented, the vowel produces the schwa rather than the long sound. The schwa sound appears in most unaccented syllables.

Provide Lots of Practice

Examples of practice techniques may include card games.

1. *Concentration*—Pairs could include contraction and meaning (*we've   we have*), root and derivative (*do   undo*), two syllables that comprise a word (*sta   tion*), etc.
2. *Calling All Cards*—Using fifty-two cards, thirteen packs of four cards each are put together. Each pack uses a different verb, thirteen in total. The four cards of each pack all include the verb and three endings—i.e., *jump, jumps, jumped, jumping*. On each of the four cards, a different word is underlined. It is useful to choose the verb and have the student write it and each of the three inflections for each card.

<table>
<tr><td><u>jump</u></td><td>jump</td><td>jump</td><td>jump</td></tr>
<tr><td>jumps</td><td><u>jumps</u></td><td>jumps</td><td>jumps</td></tr>
<tr><td>jumped</td><td>jumped</td><td><u>jumped</u></td><td>jumped</td></tr>
<tr><td>jumping</td><td>jumping</td><td>jumping</td><td><u>jumping</u></td></tr>
</table>

Procedure: Three or more may play. Each player is dealt four cards and the remainder of the pack is placed face down. The first player looks at one of his cards and asks for a word on the card which is not underlined on that card or any of his cards. If he gets it, he may ask again. Otherwise, he draws from the remaining deck. When four cards of a book have been completed, the book is placed on the table. The player with the most books wins.

ACTIVITIES INDEX

CAN YOU STRIKE 100?
REROUTED

REFERENCES

Clymer, Theodore, "The Utility of Phonic Generalizations in the Primary Grades," *The Reading Teacher,* January 1963, pp. 252–258.

Durkin, Dolores, *Teaching Them to Read.* Boston: Allyn and Bacon, Inc., 1983.

Ekwall, Eldon E., and James Shanker, *Diagnosis and Remediation of the Disabled Reader.* Boston: Allyn and Bacon, Inc. 1983.

Groff, Patrick, "Dictionary Syllabication: How Useful?" *Elementary School Journal,* (1971), pp. 107–117.

Seymour, Dorothy Z., "Word Division for Decoding," *The Reading Teacher,* December 1973, pp. 275–283.

Waugh, Ronald P. and Kenneth W. Howell, "Teaching Modern Syllabication," *The Reading Teacher,* October 1975, pp. 20–25.

Four

Inability to Use Context Clues

SKILL DESCRIPTION

Contextual analysis requires the reader to attend to the whole sentence or text in order to identify an unknown word within it. In a context, the reader is given numbers of cues. These cues are usually semantic (meaning), syntactic (grammatical), and/or pictorial (nonverbal).

For the able reader, contextual analysis is a skill in constant use. The capable reader predicts and then accepts or rejects word identification on the basis of whether or not the word fits the sense of the sentence. Selecting from the available cues, readers use their experiences with and understandings about language to make predictions. An interaction takes place between contextual and graphophonic cues so that the importance given to any one cue is always a relational one and dependent on the particular sentence. For example, in the sentence "She read the _____," the appropriate word is limited syntactically to a noun and semantically to something that can be read (book, note, paper, newspaper, etc.). The beginning and ending letters *p* and *r* narrow the choices still further. The word *paper* is the logical choice given these cues and, if looked at still more closely, it becomes the only choice. Psycholinguists (Goodman and Burke, 1980; Smith, 1978) stress this interaction between word identification and meaning. Moreover, empirical studies (e.g., Kleiman, 1977) have confirmed that previous context lessens decision time in identifying expected words.

Although children may need to be taught to use the clues the context provides to help them identify unknown words in reading, they are continually processing context cues in spoken language. Use of context is not, therefore, a totally unfamiliar skill and should be used as an aid to identifying words in reading from the start.

In addition to assisting unknown word identification, contextual analysis aids in determining correct pronunciation or stress for certain words (*rēad, rĕad, objéct, óbject*). It also plays an active role in vocabulary building, often providing meanings for new words or alternate meanings for known words. For further discussion of this last aspect of contextual analysis, see Chapter Six.

1. Students have concentrated on either sight-word identification or phonic analysis with words in isolation. Accustomed to seeing the word as an individual unit, they fail to consider the word as part of the larger sentence and do not understand that the rest of the sentence helps them to predict what a word will be. They do not use context as an aid. What occurs naturally in oral language is not recognized as applicable to written language or reading.

2. If an unfamiliar word appears at the beginning or middle of a sentence, the student often "stops dead" rather than continuing right on to see if the rest of the sentence will aid in identifying the unknown word. Once an interruption has occurred, the student may not be able to sustain the sense of the sentence.

3. Students use only one kind of context clue, ignoring the others.

Examples: Given the sentence "The walls were painted red," the student reads:

"The walls were bright red."   (semantic cue only)
"The walls were pond red."   (graphophonic only)
"The walls were climbed red."   (syntactic only)

4. The graphophonic cues do not conform to the student's contextual expectation for the word. Nonflexible readers become stymied and, unable to consider another possibility that might better fit all available cues, omit the unknown word.

Example: Students may want to read (for the sentence in 3 above) "The walls were *colored* red." Because the graphophonic cues don't fit, they may not supply a word at all.

5. Students' experiences are not wide enough to allow them to use context as a clue to word identification. When reading about something familiar, students are able to predict what the information and the vocabulary will be. When content doesn't match students' experiences, use of context is less productive.

SELECTED DIAGNOSTIC PROCEDURES

A student's ability to utilize context effectively can be measured in two ways. The first occurs whenever a child reads orally during instruction. This reading offers the teacher an informal opportunity to analyze miscues to determine whether the student is using the semantic and syntactic cues as aids for word identification.

According to psycholinguists Goodman and Burke (1972), the seriousness of a miscue is judged by how far the miscue deviates from what is acceptable in semantic and syntactic terms. What matters is whether or not the student is comprehending the passage. Sometimes students substitute words because their expectations are so strong that the graphophonic cues are quickly translated to conform to the stronger semantic and syntactic cues. For example, "The child rode a small horse at the fair" might be read as "The child rode a pony at the fair." A far more serious miscue would have the student read "The child rode a small house at the fair."

Cloze passages are another way of determining a student's use of contextual analysis. By deleting words either randomly (every nth word) or purposely (choosing a particular part of speech or meaningful unit), the teacher can note how the student responds to the deletions and whether the accompanying context is taken into account.

In studying how children best utilized context when a word had been deleted from a sentence, Emans and Fisher (1967) came up with a hierarchy that they claim progresses from easiest to most difficult. They say that the more information that is given or noted, the easier it is for students to determine the word, so that beginning and ending letters given—for example, "He read the b __ __ k,"—is easier than just context alone—"He read the _____." It is possible that this hierarchy will differ among children. Some children, for example, may find that word length—"He read the _ _ _ _"—is a more difficult cue than beginning letter—"He read the b_____"—although Emans and Fisher do not agree. Durkin (1983) utilizes a teaching sequence that asks for:

1. No cues other than context
2. Beginning letter given
3. Beginning and ending letter given

She suggests that providing letters also provides constraints and limits choices.

Cloze exercises can be developed utilizing different kinds of cues to determine which ones a particular child finds most troublesome. Below is an example of such a cloze test that we have devised, using a selection from the basal reader *People Need People* (Evertts and Weiss, 1980).* Context alone, beginning letter given, beginning and ending letter given, and word length were each used for five successive deletions to determine if any of these kinds of deletions enabled the student to use surrounding context most effectively. At the same time, the tester should analyze the words chosen as fill-ins to determine whether they reflect problems that are either semantic or syntactic in nature.

CASE STUDY†

Matthew's results are found below. He was assessed in the middle of third grade. We have written in his answers above each line.

Long, long ago, there *were* no people in the world. But *there* were animals. One of these *animal(X)* was the dinosaur. Some dinosaurs were *the* biggest animals that ever walked in the *world*. One was t *(X)* than a house of three floors. But s *ome* were as small a *(X)* cats.

Some dinosaurs a *are(X)* meat. These were fighters and k *(X)* other dinosaurs. Other dinosaurs ate p *lant* s. These were not fighters and d *(X)* d not eat o *(X)* r dinosaurs.

Tyrannosaurus was o *n* e of the dinosaurs that ate meat. It was a f *ighte* r. Tyrannosaurus was about 50 feet long and 20 *feet* tall. It *(X)* on two big legs. The arms of Tyrannosaurus were *(X)*. But it could hold and kill other *fighter* *(X)* with *big* *(okay—should be its)* arms.

More than one factor must be considered when looking at Matthew's performance. First of all, it seems quite clear that for this child, context alone was the easiest cue. His only error (*animal* instead of *animals*) is a syntactical one that doesn't disrupt meaning. Word length alone or just first letter given were categories that both seemed to provide distracting cues. Although one might make an argument for the possibility that Matthew tired as he proceeded, it then becomes difficult to assess why he succeeded quite well with the third category, first and last letters given.

Perhaps what this performance says to the teacher is that s/he might try to have Matthew cover an unknown word with his finger, read the sentence without the troublesome word, and then attempt to find an appropriate word, possibly checking first and last letters if he is still having difficulty. Only after coming up with a word should he check to see if all the graphic cues (letters and length) conform.

†See Introduction for function of Case Study.
*Evertts and Weiss, *People Need People* (New York: Holt, Rinehart and Winston, Publishers 1980), pp. 125, 126. Used with permission.

1. Rae, Gwenneth, and Thomas C. Potter, *Informal Reading Diagnosis.* Englewood Cliffs, NJ: Prentice-Hall, Inc., 1981.
   Subtests: Cloze Reading

2. Pearson, P. David, and Dale D. Johnson, *Teaching Reading Vocabulary.* New York: Holt, Rinehart, and Winston, 1978.
   Subtests: Cloze, Intruded Word, Nonsense Word

3. May, Frank B., and Susan B. Eliot, *To Help Children Read.* Columbus, OH: Charles E. Merrill, 1978.
   Subtests: Contextual Analysis

4. Miller, Wilma, *Reading Diagnosis Kit.* New York: The Center for Applied Research in Education, Inc., 1974.

5. Goodman, Yetta, and Carolyn Burke, *Reading Miscue Inventory.* New York: Macmillan Publishing Co., Inc., 1972.

6. Heilman, Arthur, et al., *Principles and Practices of Teaching Reading.* Columbus, OH: Charles E. Merrill, 1981.
   Subtests: Use of Context Clues in Sentences, Use of Context Clues in Sustained Reading

TECHNIQUES FOR REMEDIATION

Spoken Language Demonstrates the Use of Context

Show student(s) how context helps one to anticipate what an unknown word might be. Omit words in several sentences spoken orally and ask the student(s) to supply the missing word.

Examples of appropriate sentences might be:

Please pass the salt and _____.

The boy at bat hit a home _____.

The child likes to _____ rope.

We _____ in a house.

Move from Use of Spoken Language to Written Language

1. Explain that exactly the same process used above is at work in determining what an unknown word is in a reading selection. With spoken language, the word was omitted; with written language, the word is unknown. It's as if it were omitted.

   a. Write a sentence on the board with an easy word omitted.
   b. Write the sentence with the first letter of the word written or the first and last letters written.
   c. Write the sentence with the whole word.
   d. Repeat the procedure, this time using a difficult, unknown word.

2. Demonstrate this process in a book by covering words that are easily predicted. Show the children that they can guess what the word will be. Remove the covering slowly from the left, revealing a letter at a time to confirm the guesses.

Don't Stop

Difficult words appearing at the end of a sentence are the easiest to identify when using context. For unknown words that appear at the beginning or in the middle of a sentence, be sure to have the child read the entire sentence before attempting the word.

Example: The *raft* was made of wood so it would float.

Sometimes the sentences before and after must also be read.

Example: The boy watched the *parade*. First came the bands, then the floats, and then the clowns.

1. Have students substitute a silly word for every unknown word. The child might read, "In the kazoom (*parade*), there were bands, floats, clowns, and marchers." By substituting a word, students may continue with the sentence without losing continuity of thought. They may then go back and fill in the appropriate word if the context has enabled them to think of a word that both fits the sense of the sentence and the letters shown.

2. To determine appropriate pronunciation or stress, students should read the whole sentence.

Some words can only be identified in context—words like "live," "refuse." Always teach the two pronunciations from the start and illustrate how only context can help the child to know which word is being used.

Examples of other ambiguous words:

1. Vowel change—*read, lead, bow, sow, wind, wound, tear.*
2. Stress change—*object, present, rebel, conduct, permit, record, digest, escort, annex, combat.*

Here's How

Omit words in written sentences (The cat _____ the milk quickly. I read a good _____ today.) Ask the children to supply possibilities for the missing word in each sentence. Discuss with the children how they came up with these choices. What helped them? By verbalizing what they are doing, they will become more aware of how context is used and what factors (syntax, meaning, letters) must be satisfied. Nonsense words can be used effectively instead of blanks.

Examples: We ate at our new seppin and chairs.
We should walk and not lub in the halls.
The car stopped at the blag light.

Covering Up

It often helps to have the child cover the difficult word with his finger and try to think of an appropriate word before seeing whether the graphophonic and word length cues fit. Too much information to deal with at one time may be overwhelming for some children.

What Do You Know?

When assigning reading, be sure that you do not skip the prereading discussion. With all age groups, familiarize students with the words and concepts they'll be meeting before they begin the reading. By doing this, you will help to establish appropriate expectations and maximize potential use of context clues.

Encourage Rereading and Self-Correcting

When students try an unknown word in oral reading and substitute a nonmeaningful pronunciation for that context, urge them to start the sentence again, or repeat the preceding one to two sentences to get into the "swing" of meaning and thus utilize available context clues. When a self-correction occurs from this process, liberal praise for the student is suggested.

ACTIVITIES INDEX

FILLING IN
CONCENTRATE

REFERENCES

Durkin, Dolores, *Teaching Them to Read.* Boston: Allyn and Bacon, Inc., 1983.

Emans, R., and G. M. Fisher, "Teaching the Use of Context Clues," *Elementary English,* March 1967, pp. 243–246.

Goodman, Yetta, and Carolyn Burke, *Reading Strategies: Focus on Comprehension.* New York: Holt, Rinehart and Winston, 1980.

Kleiman, Glenn M., *The Effect of Previous Context on Reading Individual Words.* Technical Report #20. Urbana, IL: Center for the Study of Reading, February 1977.

Smith, Frank, *Understanding Reading.* New York: Harper and Row, 1978.

Five

Limited Background in the Language of Reading

SKILL DESCRIPTION

The suggestions in this book are directed toward children who have already begun reading instruction and usually have many of the prereading skills such as letter knowledge and a small, functional sight vocabulary. Nevertheless, our experiences have shown a number of crucial prerequisite skills imperfectly learned, or absent among disabled readers. Deficiency in these skills is manifest, for example, when students display consistent difficulty during story discussions, cannot find the first word in an array or the last picture or sentence on a workbook page, and/or cannot identify the individual sounds in a slowly pronounced three-letter word. These students often lose their place and exhibit an unusual number of reversed elements (letters or words) while reading, suggesting underdeveloped left-right orientation to print.

The prereading skills lacking in students with the above reading behaviors can be clustered together and labeled metalinguistic—that is, they often deal with knowledge about the conventions of written language (its form) rather than with language meaning. Poor readers may not know that (1) a stream of oral language can be broken into discrete units called words, (2) words can be divided into syllables and sounds, and (3) words and lines of print are scanned consistently from left to right.

Additional skills, those normally acquired in a gradual fashion during beginning reading lessons, more directly concern the vocabulary of reading instruction. Teachers' directions and the written directions in workbooks often include terms like "beginning letter," "matching sound," and "next to." For many disabled readers, these terms reflect imperfectly learned concepts and cause problems in formal reading instruction.

Finally, readers need to have an awareness of story structure or predictable narrative patterns in order to comprehend stories. Understanding narratives involves more than understanding the individual sentences. Readers need to know that a story has a beginning, middle, and end. More specifically, in terms of cognitive theorists, narratives have (1) scene and character background, (2) a precipitating event or problem, (3) attempts to resolve the problem, (4) a climax, and (5) a conclusion. Two familiar stories can be analyzed this way—*Caps for Sale* (Slobodkin, 1947) and *Bread and Jam for Frances* (Hoban, 1964):

Caps for Sale	Bread and Jam for Frances
(1) A cap salesman has a bad day and goes for a walk in the country. He falls asleep under a tree. (2) While he sleeps, monkeys snatch his caps. (3) The salesman, now awake, shakes first one fist, then both, one leg, then both, while shouting at the monkeys to return his caps. The monkeys shake their limbs in response, but don't return the caps. (4) In exasperation, the salesman throws his cap to the ground. (5) The monkeys, in imitation, throw the snatched caps to the ground. The salesman retrieves them and saunters back to town.	(1) Frances, a badger child, is a picky eater. She's repelled by anything but bread and jam. (2) Mom decides to use reverse psychology and offer only bread and jam at every meal. (3) At first, Frances is happy about this turn of events. But her interest in food variety is piqued by a gourmet friend and a food-adventurous baby sister. (4) Finally, Frances breaks into tears at a family dinner when she is served a jam sandwich. (5) Mom serves her the family's meatballs and spaghetti, and Frances finds she likes it.

Characters in simple stories can function categorically too. Foxes are sly, wolves are villainous, and pigs are clever. After several encounters with these animals in traditional stories like Little Red Riding Hood, The Three Little Pigs, and The Fox and the Crow, children presumably know what to expect when they meet such animals again in contemporary stories like *The Amazing Bone* (Steig, 1976) or *Mr. and Mrs. Pig's Evening Out* (Rayner, 1976).

POSSIBLE REASONS FOR SKILL DEFICIENCY

1. Children may have had insufficient preschool exposure to printed language. Because they have not been frequently read to or exposed to written words in meaningful contexts, they may lack metalinguistic concepts related to print. Specifically, left-to-right orientation, story sense, and word awareness may be deficient.

2. Even with adequate exposure, some children, out of disinterest, have not attended to the relevant experiences. During early childhood, other cognitive and social demands may claim exclusive attention for certain youngsters. Oral language and physical development, emerging social skills, as well as the quest for a measure of independence—all major achievements—may leave little room for some youngsters to attend to printed stimuli and stories.

3. Immaturity may prevent some students from benefiting from preschool exposure. Piagetian scholars (Westby, 1981; Ehri, 1979) have claimed that certain of the skills mentioned above, particularly story sense and phoneme segmentation, cannot be realized until a child learns to conserve, an achievement normally attained at age seven. Westby found that mature narratives emerge from youngsters only in the last stage of story-telling development, at about seven years of age. Ehri noted that word and sound sense was absent in many six- and seven-year-olds. It should be noted that seven years and the end of first grade coincide for many children. Therefore, it is difficult to tell if the onset of mature word and story sense is purely developmental or the result of a full year of formal reading instruction.

4. Even after a full year or more of reading instruction, some children continue to have difficulty with these prerequisites. One reason is that these skills are not frequently singled out for direct instruction but are, instead, taught along with skills such as word identification and comprehension. Instructional language like "cross out," "find the one that doesn't belong" may go along with the directions for a workbook page, but

direct instruction in these concepts is rare. Remedial students often need direct instruction in one thing at a time and cannot learn a subordinate skill such as instructional language while focusing on a lesson's primary goal—phonics, for example.

SELECTED DIAGNOSTIC PROCEDURES

Readiness tests are not particularly useful for assessing difficulty with the metalinguistic prereading skills, primarily because they are group tests and an individual child's strategies for approaching print cannot be ascertained. Moreover, such tests do not directly assess ability in these skills.

More useful are individually administered diagnostic reading tests since the examiner can monitor the child's reading and certain sections of these tests assess metalinguistic readiness skills directly. In our opinion, most helpful is an informal assessment of the instruction in which a child is currently engaged. Comments made during reading lessons can be quite revealing of student need. As Durkin (1980) has pointed out, a child who sees the word *red* and identifies it as "red fire truck" must have an inadequate concept of what constitutes a written word.

CASE STUDY*

What follows is an author-made informal inventory that directly assesses ability with certain prereading skills. The administration of this inventory might follow a series of naturalistic observations made during instruction to confirm suspicion of inadequately developed prereading skills. It was administered to a seven-year-old who is reading at primer level. Carl's teacher noticed an unusual number of word reversals (e.g., "top box" for *box top*) in his oral reading and difficulty with workbook page directions and phonics instruction. Moreover, Carl rarely participated during story discussions, although he happily took part in the grouped oral reading.

1. **Teacher Directions**

Point to the word on the top of the box. Find the word to the left of the box. Now find the one to the right of the box. Which one is under the box?

What child sees

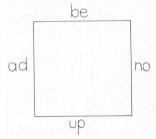

Results

Carl indicated *no* was the left-hand word and *ad* the right-hand one.

2. **Teacher Directions**

Show me the first letter of the top word. Now the last letter. And the middle letter? (If failure with the top word, have student attempt the second one.)

*See Introduction for function of Case Study.

What child sees

cheat
eat

Results

Successful identification of letters in the longer word.

3. Teacher Directions

a. Point to the middle word in this sentence. The first one now. And the last word? How many words are in the sentence? (If a student succeeds with this task, request a word count for sentences b and c.)

What child sees

a. Ted can jump.
b. Ted can jump high.
c. Ted and Sue can jump high.

Results

Carl was successful with all sentences.

4. Teacher Directions

Listen to this sentence. What is the first word? Last word? How many words do you hear? If the child cannot count "in his head," have him tap out the words. Too, if difficulty occurs with the six word sentence, try the shorter sentences in descending order.

What child hears

I see the red car go.
I see the car go.
I see the car.
See the car?
I see.

Results

Carl usually identified the last word spoken as the "first word" and next to last word spoken as "last word." Using a pencil to tap out words was successful with only the three- and two-word sentences.

5. Teacher Directions

Listen to these sentences and tell me the first word I say. Now I will read the sentences again. This time, tell me the last word.

What child hears

I eat spaghetti.
Pet my sheepdog.
Cover the dish.
Anybody can jump over.

Results

He identified the last word spoken as the "first word" in each case. *Spaghetti, pet, cover,* and *over* were chosen as last words.

6. Teacher Directions

What is the first sound you hear in these words? (Read list). The ending sound? (Reread list).

What child hears

soup
home
lane
star
show

Results

At first Carl was confused by the task. But when the words "What sound do you hear at the beginning?" were substituted for the first sentence in the examiner's directions, the child was successful with the first three words. For the last two, responses were "r" + /s/, respectively. When asked for an ending sound, the child gave a rhyme word in every case—i.e., "so" for *show*.

7. Teacher Directions

Each word I will say has two parts. Say the beginning part after I finish the word. (Do not exaggerate syllabic division.)

What child hears

raffle	*shipment*
toaster	*jacket*

Results

Nonsense rhymes were given for each stimulus word—i.e., "caffle."

8. Teacher Directions

How many word parts do you hear? (If a child cannot hear syllables, have him tap them out. Do not exaggerate syllabic division.)

What child hears

lick
teapot
supermarket
umbrella

Results

Carl responded correctly to first two and then misidentified the number of syllables in *supermarket* as three and in *umbrella* as four.

9. Teacher Directions

Find the word that is the same as this one (point to the first *ham*). Now find the word that is different from this one (point to the first *eggs*).

What child sees

ham   ahm   mah   Ham

eggs   eggs   segg   EGGS

Results

Correct identification made.

10. **Teacher Directions**

Tell me a story about a boy who gets lost at the supermarket. (If the supermarket theme doesn't inspire, try "in the park," "on the beach.")

Results

"A boy went to the supermarket and he got lost. He didn't know where he was going. And then he went to the bakery. But he was lost. And then he went to the comic-book store. But he was lost. And then he went home. And then he went back to the supermarket. And then he went home."

11. **Teacher Directions**

Show what happened first, next, and last with these pictures.

What child sees

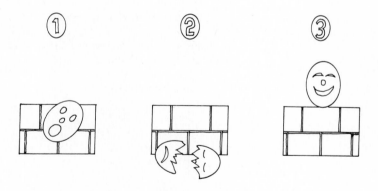

Results

Child was able to put pictures in order and recited Humpty Dumpty rhyme.

12. **Teacher Directions**

If a lion got loose in a zoo and climbed out of his cage, what would happen?

Results

"A doctor would come."

13. **Teacher Directions**

A witch put a magic spell on a frog. Tell what happened.

Results

"He turned into a tiger. He turned the lion into a mouse."

Other than left-right labeling confusion, the visual skills displayed by this seven-year-old are stronger than his auditory skills. When given a visual stimulus, Carl could count words and identify beginnings, middles, and ends. Carl had no problem with first and last elements when applied to written words and sentences.

Auditory segmentation caused problems, however, along with the terms *first* and *last* when applied to the sounds of a word.

Carl's narrative showed immaturity as well. Really a listing of events, they lacked precipitating events, solutions, and logic.

Carl may need help with auditory segmentation, both syllables and phonemes, developing story sense, and instruction in several reading terms, including left-right, first-last, rhyme, last sound, and word part.

Other Assessments

1. *Durrell Analysis of Reading Difficulty.* New York: The Psychological Corporation, 1980.
   Subtests: Prereading phonic abilities inventories—Syntax Matching, Identifying Letter Names in Spoken Words, and Identifying Phonemes in Spoken Words.
2. *Gates-McKillop-Horowitz Reading Diagnostic Tests.* New York: Teachers College Press, 1981.
   Subtest: Auditory Blending
3. *Brigance Inventory of Early Development.* Woburn, MA: Curriculum Associates, 1978.
   Subtests: Responses to and Experience with Books, Directional/Positional Concepts
4. *Concepts about Print Test* (Marie Clay). Exeter, NH: Heinemann Educational Books, 1972.

TECHNIQUES FOR REMEDIATION

Orientation to Print

Green Means "Go"

Modify texts in any or all of the following ways so that students will begin at the left side of the page and/or the left side of a word and progress to the right: (1) color the first letter of each word green, (2) use a green vertical line at the beginning of each line of text, (3) number the words in the order in which they are to be read, (4) number the letters of a word in the order in which they are to be decoded, (5) use left-to-right arrows underneath a line of print. It is important to fade gradually whichever cues are used so that students don't use the cues as crutches.

Left, Right

When reading words from the board or from text that a student can also see, the teacher can sweep his or her hand or finger underneath words and phrases as they are pronounced. Write so that students can see each word or line revealed from left to right. Controlled readers, machines that highlight chunks of text at varied rates, can be used at their slowest speed to encourage left-to-right text analysis. It makes sense for students then to imitate these models by using their fingers or a marker.

Start at the Beginning

For children with orientation problems, certain methods of word analysis can compound their reading difficulties. For example, urging such students to decode a word from the vowel to the final consonant and then to attach the initial consonant (*a-t, c-a-t, cat*), or via identification of graphemic base first (*-at, cat*) may disrupt their shaky hold of left-right. Likewise, a search for a word's root or pronounceable syllable may cause students to start reading in the middle of a word.

Better word analysis techniques for these students would be left-to-right phonic or structural analysis, kinesthetic techniques where students trace the letters of each word as it is decoded, and the use of tachistoscopes, devices that frame a word or phrase and reveal a little of it at a time in a left-to-right progression.

Word and Letter Consciousness

Marking a Text

The teacher and student can mark a xeroxed text by circling, underlining, or X'ing each word, marking and counting letters and/or words, putting boxes between or around words, and the like.

Carefully Prepared Materials

If letter and word boundaries are not clearly delineated in teacher-made materials, remedial students may have difficulty. Care needs to be taken to space letters so none touch (e.g., *c* and *l* together look like *d*) and to leave evenly sized spaces between words.

Word Searches

These puzzles are found everywhere, from airline magazines to the daily newspaper. Some of these, though, embed words vertically, diagonally, and backwards. For beginners, teacher-made versions that embed words only horizontally from left to right are appropriate. The task in a word search is to separate a group of letters that yield a word from arrays of random letters. A variation is word (or letter) tracking, which requires that a child find and mark a specific word in a field of distractor words. Distractors may be similar graphically and/or semantically.

Example: Find *cookie:*

> *shook crook cookie cook*
> *cake cookie cracker jam pie cookie*
> *cookie ice cream tart cookie pudding*

Find the Letters, Find the Words

To help children distinguish between letters and words, have them circle the letters and underline the words. Explain how *I* and *a* fit in both categories or omit them from your exercise.

Example: (b)   *be*   *only*   *on*   (a)

In later exercises, real words can be contrasted with letter clusters and then with nonsense words.

Labeling

Affixing labels to a selected number of objects in a room, on bulletin boards, and on job charts helps students learn that one word equals one thing or concept. To be effective, overlabeling should be avoided. Moreover, the words should be used in other language arts activities, and seen frequently in other meaningful contexts like on signs and in stories.

Cut and Match

Have students cut apart familiar words or sentences and put them back together.

Voice Pointing

This refers to the technique of pointing to each word in a known or memorized story as it is read aloud. This allows students to learn what the words they are saying from memory look like. It also aids awareness of spaces between words.

Language Experience Approach

Showing children that what they say can be written is recommended to increase their written word and left-to-right concepts. Durkin's (1980) guidelines for using the approach to teach the meaning of *word* are excellent:

1. Say each word as you print it.
2. Read the entire story in a natural speaking fashion, pointing to each word as it is read.
3. Suggest to the children that they might like to read it too (as the children read, read along with them, all the while moving your hand across each line of text from left to right).
4. Point to and identify words that appear more than once. If children seem interested, let them read these words.
5. Make a comment like, "there are so many words up here!" Then count them, pointing to each one. Show how a space separates one word from another. Now let the children count the words. Point to each one as it is counted.
6. Reread the entire account. Encourage the children to read along with you (p. 104).

Instructional Language

Listen Carefully

Depending on the age of students, a number of oral language activities could be employed for practice in reading terminology. For very young children, the records of Hap Palmer or Ella Jenkins provide songs that require physical response based on oral directions. For somewhat older children, the familiar songs and games The Hokey-Pokey and Simple Simon may be helpful. Hot and Cold, a game in which children search for a hidden object with hints from the teacher like "more to your left," "you were closer before," "look below the table," is a tried and true favorite.

Circle, Underline, Cross Out, Etc.

Lessons in instructional vocabulary are advised. For example, a lesson in *same* and *different* could focus on how words are the same when their letters are the same and in the same order—even when written in different typefaces and in different places. GUM, gum, *gum*, *gum*, are the same while *gym* and *mug* are different from *gum*.
  Some of the key terms for beginning reading found in instructional materials are:

circle	before	letter	end
underline	after	sound	then
cross out	word	first	alike
above	below	over	under
next to	beside		

DISTAR (Englemann and Bruner, 1983)

This approach to beginning reading was initially prepared for culturally different children who may come to school without facility with school language. Children are actively involved with clapping and reciting in response to teacher direction and teacher-modeled language. Some of the lesson content of DISTAR Kits and much of the technique are appropriate for children with problems in instructional language.

Sound and Syllable Sense

The object of these recommendations is to raise a child's consciousness about how words can be auditorially separated into parts. (Matching sounds or syllables to their visual counterparts is the content of Chapter Two.) Because researchers have found syllable sense to precede the ability to separate phonemes (Lieberman and Shankweiler, 1979), we recommend starting auditory (but not necessarily visual) instruction with syllable exercises.

Get the Beat

Start with easily separable or syncopated rhythms so that students can tap out the beat with percussion instruments or with a pencil on the desk. This will be the only time in school that this activity is teacher-sanctioned! Move on to rhythmic poetry and then to activities in which words are said slowly and syllables or sounds are identified or counted.

Antidisestablishmentarianism

Students' interest in the sounds or parts of words can be piqued by unusual language—rhymes, alliterations, the "gulps," "pows," and "tee-hees" of comic book language, and by long unknown or nonsense words (*supercalifragilisticexpealidotious*). Such words are found, for example, in literature in the books of Dr. Seuss, William Steig, and in the *Ten-Word Texts* by Patty Wolcott.

Guess the Word

Riddles with both meaning cues and the initial syllable or sound prod children to think about and use word parts.

Examples: I'm thinking of a word that rhymes with glove and means "push."

Which word starts with /p/ and means "water on the sidewalk after it rains"?

Guess this word—it means "short coat" and starts with "jac."

Divide and Conquer

Provide experiences with auditory analysis and synthesis. Take words apart and put them together in a variety of ways: syllable by syllable (*splin-ter*), cluster by graphemic base (*spl-inter*), or cluster by cluster (*spl-in-ter* or *spl-int-er*). The Glass Analysis (1978) provides a cluster-by-cluster model for visual/auditory analysis that could easily be adapted for auditory practice alone.

Reading to Students

Naturally the best way to increase story sense is exposure to many stories, particularly classically structured ones. Fairy and folk tales, fables and contemporary children's literature will provide experiences with plot, character, theme, setting, and style. It makes sense to have a daily story time in remedial sessions for children who haven't developed a story sense. Questions to assess comprehension should be omitted at these sessions, which should be as informal as possible in imitation of early home story experiences. However, *reactions* to the books should be encouraged. Also, comments can be made which focus attention on story parts (beginning, middle, end).

Student-authored Stories

Ask students to make up a story. If this task is too challenging, ask the student to retell a familiar story. The teacher can copy, in outline form, the essential story elements. When a story is missing aspects of plot that are needed to make it a satisfying narrative, teacher questions can help elicit these facts or details. For example, when a child tells a story that is essentially a listing of events ("The frog wanted to eat from the princess' plate. He wanted to sleep in her bed. Then he got turned back into a prince"), teacher questions could focus on sequence, cause and effect, and details (Did he want to eat or sleep first? Why did he insist on eating from her plate, sleeping in her bed? Which part did you like best? Please tell me more about that part.).

Comparing Student-authored to Published Stories

Sometimes student narratives are not stories but retellings of personal experience. To show the connection between "books and life" or the personal and other-authored narrative, find books that parallel student experiences. A child's story about his trip to a zoo can be followed by an authored story on the same topic. Comparisons of the two stories can be made.

Children's Literature

Some children's books are particularly useful for teaching narrative structure in a more indirect way than previously mentioned techniques. In *Albert's Story* (Long, 1978), an older sister prods her brother so that he will elaborate on a story that he first presents simply with one sentence. In *The Tyrannosaurus Game* (Kroll, 1976), a class of children make up a group oral narrative, each child adding a part to the story. Wordless picture books are wonderful sources for eliciting narratives from children. The ones by Fernando Krahn and Mercer Mayer are particularly good for story sequence and development.

What Comes First?

Putting the events of a wordless picture story together is useful for reinforcing beginning, middle, and end. Four to five pictures can be given to a child in an envelope with the direction to put them in story order from left to right. Source material for this activity includes comic strips and Developmental Learning Materials' *Open Sequence Cards* (Niles, IL, 1974).

ACTIVITIES INDEX

A DAY AT SCHOOL
STORY SHAPES

REFERENCES

Durkin, Dolores, *Teaching Young Children to Read.* Boston: Allyn & Bacon, 1980.

Ehri, Linnea, "Linguistic Insight: Threshold of Reading Acquisition," in *Reading Research: Advances in Theory and Practice,* eds. Waller, T., and Mackinnon, G. E. New York: Academic Press, 1979.

Englemann, Siegfried and Elaine Bruner, *Reading Mastery: DISTAR Reading.* Chicago: Science Research Associates, 1983.

Glass, Gerald, *The Glass Analysis for Decoding Only.* Garden City, NJ: Easier-to-Learn, 1978.

Hoban, Russell, *Bread and Jam for Frances.* New York: Harper & Row, 1964.

Kroll, Steven, *The Tyrannosaurus Game.* New York: Holiday House, 1976.

Lieberman, Isabel and Donald Shankweiler, "Speech, the Alphabet, and Teaching to Read," in *Theory and Practice of Early Reading,* eds. Resnick, L., and Weaver, P. Hillsdale, NJ: Lawrence Erlbaum, 1979.

Long, Claudia, *Albert's Story.* New York: Delacorte Press, 1978.

Slobodkin, Esphr. *Caps for Sale.* New York: Scott, 1947.

Steig, William, *The Amazing Bone.* New York: Farrar, Straus, Giroux, 1976.

Rayner, Mary, *Mr. and Mrs. Pig's Evening Out.* New York: Atheneum, 1976.

Westby, Carol, "Children's Narrative Development—Cognitive and Linguistic Aspects," in *Language, Learning and Reading Disabilities: A New Decade.* New York: Queens College, 1980.

Wolcott, Patty, *The Ten-Word Texts* (i.e., *Double-Decker, Double-Decker, Double-Decker Bus*). Reading, MA: Addison Wesley, Various publication dates.

Six

Poor Meaning Vocabulary

SKILL DESCRIPTION

The definition of "a good reader" is one who is successful *both* in word identification and in comprehension. Central to each is a well-developed meaning vocabulary. When students' attempts at pronunciation do not produce a word that they have heard before, their ability to identify words may be affected adversely. Similarly, understanding an author's message is difficult when the vocabulary used conveys little or no meaning to the student. In reading "Margaret offered fulsome praise for the project," it is easy to assume that Margaret loved the project and was full of true praise for it, unless the meaning of *fulsome* (excessive or insincere) is known.

Knowledge of word meaning is a prerequisite to understanding sentences or passages. Davis (1944), in measuring the various subskills of reading comprehension, determined that memory for word meaning is one of the two most important factors in reading comprehension, reasoning being the other. Klare (1974, 1975) found that varying the vocabulary within a sentence is more likely to contribute to comprehension difficulty than varying the structure of the sentence.

Often the meaning of a passage is distorted or not fully appreciated when a student knows only one usage for a word and another meaning is indicated. Unfortunately, it is usually the more common words that have the most meanings (examples: *run, point, light*). Moreover, knowing that a word has multiple meanings is not always enough. Can the reader discern from the text which meaning is intended? For example, in the sentence "The singer had a long *run* at the theater," the student recognizing that *run* has several meanings may choose to relate this "long run" to a ripped stocking.

Knowledge of multiple meanings also involves a consideration of connotation and denotation. A word *denotes* a specific meaning or a number of specific meanings which may be found in a dictionary. Words also *connote* meanings, however, which may vary from person to person. Connotations reflect emotions and experiences. Whereas the word *fire* connotes warmth and happiness to one who pictures a homey scene in front of a fireplace on a cold wintry night, the same word can connote fear and anger to someone who has experienced the ravaging aspects of fire. Readers therefore need exposure to varieties of experiences to comprehend both a word's denotation and its connotation.

Complicating the issue further are the slight variations of meaning that context helps the reader to identify. Words rarely have precise meanings. Their definitions and synonyms reflect their context. Therefore the definition of a word in isolation is altered somewhat when the word is put into a sentence or paragraph. For "The boy was faced with a *dilemma*," the decision of whether this is a simple problem or a complex predicament can only be clarified by the surrounding context.

Students possess four different vocabularies: listening, speaking, reading, and writing, which normally develop in that order. Although at first a student's listening vocabulary exceeds all others, good readers find that their reading vocabulary eventually outdistances the other three. Listening and reading are receptive skills. These vocabularies tend to be easier to measure and are more representative of word knowledge than the vocabulary evidenced by speaking or writing, the expressive modes. Many of us recognize the meanings of hundreds of words in print that we have never attempted to use. When a student uses vocabulary, however, either through speaking or writing, competence in the receptive skills is assumed and reinforced. Use of the expressive modes, therefore, is to be encouraged.

Meaning vocabulary expands throughout one's lifetime. Dale (1965) determined that at the end of first grade, children have an average meaning vocabulary of about 3000 words, and that during their school years they add 1000 words a year. This number appears to be far greater for more gifted children since intelligence is closely related to the size of a child's meaning vocabulary. In addition, vocabulary development is affected by health, socioeconomic status, background, geography, and instructional opportunities.

Finally, vocabulary builds most rapidly when words are met often and in varying circumstances. A papier-maché figure is strengthened by pasting layer upon layer of paper stripping. A single layer of stripping is far too fragile and will not last. Each time students encounter a word, they add another layer to the word's meaning foundation.

POSSIBLE REASONS FOR SKILL DEFICIENCY

1. Students' experiences may be limited, thereby curtailing their exposure to the concepts that prompt language. A wonderful example is the child who, riding in the country for the first time, looks out of the car window at a barn and says "Oh, there's the pancake house." Perhaps this child knew about farms and barns from books, but his primary experience was with a pancake restaurant that was shaped like a barn.

2. Problems occur when students know only one meaning for a word and the context calls for a different meaning.

Example: "He saw the bird *light* on the tree and then fly away."

If a student defines *light* as a type of lamp, the sentence will not make sense. Even when students are aware of a number of meanings, they frequently are unable to select the appropriate meaning for the context or, even more commonly, tend to focus on the meaning they know best.

3. The ability to recognize when a word is part of a figurative expression may be difficult for students who react literally to language. "Get off my back," the second grade boy shouted. "But I wasn't on his back," his tormenter whined. "What's he talking about?"

4. Homothones (words that sound alike but have different spelling and meaning— *blue, blew*) and homographs (words that look alike but are pronounced differently and have different meanings—wound (oo), wound (ow)) are word categories that can prove confusing to readers.

5. Instruction in using morphemes (roots and affixes) is often limited to word identification. Students consequently do not use affixes and common roots to help unlock meaning.

Example: Because his work was *substandard, the teacher asked that he do it over.*

Using the prefix *sub,* which means "under," the meaning of the unfamiliar word is more easily uncovered.

6. New vocabulary that is not practiced or used is usually not retained after the initial introduction (Pany and Jenkins, 1977). Repetition cements memory. Sometimes the circumstances in which a student learns or hears a word are so vivid or important that the word becomes deeply etched in the student's memory after only one meeting. Usually, however, a student needs to experience the word in a variety of ways—reading, speaking, and/or writing the word frequently and in differing contexts—before it is truly learned. One of us met the word *shibboleth* once every year or so and for a number of years faithfully looked it up and promptly forgot it by the next encounter. Finally, after recognizing that this was happening and consequently making a conscious effort to use the word, she "learned" it. By the way, a *shibboleth* is an identifying catchword or slogan of a particular group.

7. Students may not use context to assist in comprehending meaning even when a sentence is contextually rich. Sometimes they are able to use certain contextual cues but not others. For example, a student reading "John was loquacious, talkative" might understand the meaning of loquacious. Meeting that word in the sentence "Although John was loquacious, his brother hardly said a word," the student might not take note of the signal word *although,* which indicates contrast.

8. Conversely, some students often become accustomed to using context to reveal meaning and do not take the time to analyze the meaning of an unfamiliar word. When the material is not contextually rich, the students may not have substitute strategies for obtaining meaning.

SELECTED DIAGNOSTIC PROCEDURES

Johnson and Pearson (1978) have commented on the difficulty of measuring a student's meaning vocabulary. Their research shows that to a large extent the testing format influences whether or not the student can show that s/he knows a word's meaning.

Common ways of testing word meaning are:

1. *Matching words and pictures*—This is a valid way of testing; however, the tester must be on guard for pictures that are ambiguous. If a student fails an item, it might be advisable to have the student orally identify the pictures in question as a means of ruling out this pitfall. Testers using this format must recognize as well that many words are difficult or impossible to picture (*democracy; if*).

2. *Matching synonyms or antonyms*—Again, this is a valid measure, but requires that the student know the meaning of two words, not just one. When multiple choice is given (Synonym Example: *confused*—(a) *baffled,* (b) *certain,* (c) *positive,* (d) *careful*), the process of elimination might be used to identify unknown words. Although *baffled* might not be known, the student recognizes that none of the other choices fit. Therefore, *baffled* must be the correct answer. This is a pitfall with picture matching as well.

Synonyms and antonyms may also be used in a context format.

Example: Find the synonym for the underlined word.
            The music was strident. *harsh   soft   loud   melodious*

3. *Context.*

    a. Words may be used in context that requires a true-false or yes-no response from the student (*Birds fly* or *Do birds fly?*). As with synonyms and antonyms, the student must relate two words, this time a noun and a verb. Unfortunately, the guessing factor becomes significant with this format.

    b. Another context format for assessing vocabulary is the cloze procedure.

        Example: She dressed in a new skirt and _____.
                  blouse   *trouser*   *swatch*

    Here the student's knowledge of word meaning is extended beyond one or two words. In the example sentence, *skirt, she,* and *dressed* all contribute to the correct answer. Knowledge of syntax is also needed. Depending on the words tested, this approach may be useful for getting shades of meaning difficult to test in single-word formats.

    4. *Supplying definitions*—This may be done orally or in writing. Although this may be the purest test of vocabulary, often students know a word's meaning but have difficulty finding the appropriate words to express themselves. Were they to encounter the word in a reading situation, however, they would have no trouble comprehending its meaning. It may not be valid therefore, to use an expressive mode to measure receptive vocabulary.

    All of the formats suggested may be done as listening or as reading tests. If words are a part of students' listening vocabularies, the students then have the means to comprehend these words in a reading experience—assuming, of course, that they can also decode them.

    The reasons for testing a student's vocabulary are varied. Students with wide and varied meaning vocabularies may be capable of reading more challenging material than that currently offered them in the classroom. Students with comprehension difficulties may be having problems because they lack the appropriate concepts to understand grade level material. If the problem is not a lack of an adequate meaning vocabulary, the teachers will have learned that they must look elsewhere for the cause of their students' comprehension problems.

CASE STUDY*

The Durrell Analysis of Reading Difficulty (3rd ed., 1980)† provides a subtest for diagnosing listening vocabulary. Word-picture matching is the technique utilized. Three pictures are shown for each column of words. The student is read the word and must point to the picture for which the word is appropriate.

    The results below are those of a boy at the end of third grade, reading below grade level. His problems in comprehension may be in part the result of a meaning vocabulary low (high second-grade level) for his grade level. Although test instructions ask that each list be stopped after three errors, the tester felt that the boy would not be unduly frustrated by continuing and she was eager to see what the child might know.

*See Introduction for function of Case Study.
†From the Durrell Analysis of Reading Difficulty: 3rd edition. Copyright ©1980, 1955, 1937 by Harcourt Brace Jovanovich, Inc. All rights reserved. Reproduced by permission.

List 1		List 2	
+	1. red (3)	+	1. tree (1)
+	2. large (2)	+	2. glad (2)
+	3. huge (2)	+	3. leaf (1)
+	4. year (1)	+	4. dime (3)
+	5. enormous (2)	+	5. pleased (2)
+	6. gigantic (2)	+	6. delight (2)
+	7. century (1)	+	7. coin (3)
−	8. eternity (1)	+	8. foliage (1)
−	9. scarlet (3)	+	9. elated (2)
+	10. tremendous (2)	+	10. finance (3)
−	11. colossal (2)	−	11. ecstatic (2)
+	12. decade (1)	−	12. currency (3)
−	13. azure (3)	−	13. herbaceous (1)
−	14. magenta (3)	−	14. rapture (2)
−	15. millennium (1)	−	15. deciduous (1)

List 3		List 4	
+	1. horse (3)	+	1. rain (1)
+	2. scare (2)	+	2. words (1)
+	3. fear (2)	+	3. march (2)
+	4. glow (1)	+	4. hike (2)
+	5. flash (1)	+	5. sprinkle (1)
−	6. timid (2)	+	6. discuss (3)
+	7. mammal (3)	−	7. stride (2)
+	8. panic (2)	+	8. declare (3)
+	9. rodent (3)	+	9. humidity (1)
+	10. canine (3)	−	10. saunter (2)
+	11. intimidate (2)	−	11. articulate (3)
−	12. apprehensive (2)	−	12. precipitation (1)
−	13. luminous (1)	−	13. irrigate (1)
−	14. translucent (1)	−	14. loquacious (3)
+	15. marsupial (3)	−	15. inundate (1)

List 5	
+	1. dress (3)
+	2. lunch (2)
+	3. music (1)
+	4. whistle (1)
+	5. feast (2)
+	6. costume (3)
+	7. discord (1)
+	8. apparel (3)
+	9. devour (2)
−	10. reverberate (1)
+	11. carnivorous (2)
−	12. resonant (1)
−	13. raiment (3)
−	14. clamorous (1)
−	15. accouterment (3)

LISTENING VOCABULARY

	Score	Grade
List 1	9	
List 2	10	
List 3	11	
List 4	8	
List 5	10	
Total	48	H2

A real interest in animals was reflected in the child's word knowledge (*canine, marsupial, carnivorous*.) When looking at the words Rob did not know, it is surprising to see that he knew these three words. This suggests that perhaps an appropriate way to develop vocabulary might be through an area that is of interest to him. Because some of the words he missed were words one would expect a third grader to have in his receptive vocabulary (for example *scarlet* and *colossal* from the first column), it is probable that his difficulty with literal comprehension would improve with added vocabulary knowledge.

Other Assessments

1. Vocabulary sections appear on all major achievement tests.
2. *Gates-McGinite Reading Tests.* Boston, MA: Houghton Mifflin, 1978.
   Subtest: Vocabulary
3. *Stanford Diagnostic Reading Test.* New York: Harcourt Brace Jovanovich, 1976.
   Subtests: Red, Green, and Brown Levels, "Auditory Vocabulary" Blue Level, "Word Meaning"
4. Warnecke, Edna W., and Dorothy A. Shipman, *Group Assessment in Reading.* Englewood Cliffs, NJ: Prentice-Hall, Inc., 1984, pp. 114–21.

TECHNIQUES FOR REMEDIATION

Techniques for building reading vocabulary generally:

1. Expand students' listening-speaking vocabularies
2. Improve their use of context to discern meaning.

Regardless of how the words are introduced or encountered, an effective means of promoting retention would have the student:

1. Discuss the word with its various meanings
2. Use the word orally
3. Write the word, following it either with a picture, a definition, a synonym, or a sentence which utilizes it
4. Practice using the word:
   a. In a worksheet format, examples of which might be a crossword puzzle or word search, a matching word to definition exercise, or an exercise which has the student filling the word into an appropriate sentence. An example of the last might be:

   The boy couldn't play and was forced to be a _____ at the game.
   spectator   player   participant

   b. In a game format that might range from Concentration, which matches word and definition (or synonym or cloze sentence), to bingo games in which synonyms for words read are covered, to dice games in which words might appear on each die. When a die is spun, the student must use the word in a sentence or be eliminated (or receive points, etc.).
   c. In expressive activities such as drama, conversation, and composition.

SUGGESTIONS FOR EXPANDING LISTENING-SPEAKING VOCABULARIES

Reading to Students

Reading aloud to students cannot be stressed enough as an essential means of introducing students to words. Not only are words used in differing contexts, but often subtleties of meaning are conveyed naturally.

Reading aloud to poor readers is especially important. Poor readers, lacking the tools needed to take advantage of the same opportunities for exposure to language and concepts that are accessible to good readers, find themselves in a bind. Because reading is difficult for these students, they are unlikely to elect it as a leisure activity. Even should they choose to read, the complexity and amount of vocabulary they meet is necessarily limited by the level of the books they are capable of reading. They are therefore prevented from learning new concepts through reading. Moreover, oral language exposure cannot be a substitute, because the sophisticated sentence structure and language usage found in written language rarely occurs in speech.

By reading aloud to students daily, the teacher can help to provide poor readers with the vocabulary they are not attaining on their own. The discussion that follows an oral reading should incorporate some of the new concepts or vocabulary. By varying the material chosen (novels, poetry, biographies, essays, news articles, scientific findings, etc.), exposure is increased.

Go and Do

We all learn best by doing. Therefore, first-hand experiences are invaluable vocabulary builders. Children who watch a cow chewing on grass and then get to participate in the milking process, understand *cud* and *udder* far better when these words are used or explained than if they had simply heard the teacher define the words. One of the authors recalls how rereading Hal Borland's *When the Legends Die* brought far greater understanding and appreciation after having been to the West, where she saw the lodge pole pines so vividly described in the book.

Take kids on field trips, bring experiences to the classroom, and talk. First-hand experience is not always possible in a remedial setting, but pictures, models, or films act as appropriate backup. As noted in the chapter on sight vocabulary, use of more than one sense enhances memory. A corollary to all of the above would urge teachers not to spend their whole day on reading instruction and math, thereby eliminating social studies, science, art, and music from the curriculum. A great deal of concept building takes place during these subjects, which can only enhance reading abilities.

What Do You Like?

Utilize areas of interest as a focus for developing vocabulary. An interest in biking, for example, might generate words such as *gears, axle, accelerate, decelerate, spoke,* and *incline.* Multiple meanings could be a part of any discussion utilizing certain of the above words. Charts indicating words developed around a theme might result and be displayed with words regularly added.

Preview Vocabulary

Most teacher's manuals that accompany basal and other reading material recommend that vocabulary be previewed before reading a selection. We agree. Preteaching is done to facilitate both understanding of word meaning and word identification. Use this opportunity to expand on the words by discussing (1) synonyms and antonyms; (2) multiple meanings; and (3) other words utilizing the same root.

A little of this goes a long way, however, as students are usually eager to get started with the story. To reduce distraction, be sure the books are not yet opened during the preview.

Zero In on Meaning

There are numbers of ways to help students recognize the multiple denotative and connotative aspects to every word. Below are a few suggestions:

Semantic Mapping

Smith and Johnson (1980) describe a technique in which a stimulus word is chosen. Students then brainstorm, trying to uncover every word they can think of that is related to the stimulus word. As words are provided, they are grouped into an appropriate category. Discussion, of course, reveals the reasoning and the shades of meaning that define the categories.

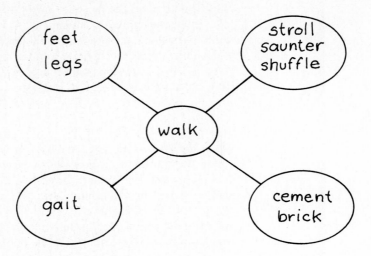

Teamwork

The group is divided in half. The teacher calls out a word. The first team must supply either a synonym, an antonym, complete an analogy, or supply a word for a category. The teacher may choose to work on one or all of these. If successful, the team gets a point and the next team has a turn.

He said and she said and I said and they said

Try to demonstrate to students that the English language offers wonderful alternatives to overworked words. In fact, the use of more precise language helps the reader visualize or comprehend more clearly. Encourage the use of a thesaurus and a dictionary.

Have students act out a sentence such as "I like that book," *said* John, using replacements for *said*.

Examples: *stated, exclaimed, spoke, shouted, whispered, cried, asserted, uttered, expressed, voiced, affirmed, declared, proclaimed, articulated, mumbled, muttered, informed, announced, ranted.*

Games

Practice games and exercises that require the student to think about a word in a variety of ways are useful. The following are examples:

1. A deck of cards is used. A number of words with multiple meanings are selected (examples: *box, point*). One word is written on each card. The first student picks a card and uses the word in a sentence. Each member of the group then uses the word in a sentence using the word differently each time. This continues until a student cannot think of a sentence and therefore receives a point. A new word card is then chosen. The student with the least points at the end is the winner.

Examples: run   I can run fast.
                  I saw the water run off the counter.
                  My stocking has a run in it.
                  The movie had a long run.
                  He hit a home run.
                  There was a run on chicken soup at the market.
                  Is there a dog run in the back yard?

2. A series of definitions can be written for a word or dictionary definitions can be used. Sentences using the word in a variety of ways can be matched by the student to the appropriate definition. This may also be used in card-game form (Concentration) where the appropriate definition is matched to a sentence with an underlined word.

3. An exercise with fifteen to twenty cloze sentences might have only three or four word choices for the deletions. Because each word would have to be used for several sentences, the sentences would require the use of each word in different ways.

4. *Puns intended*—A young boy dressed in red pajamas was refusing to go to bed on time. "You're really making me see red," chuckled his mother.

Punning is lots of fun. Use puns deliberately, corny as they may be. When kids discover that playing with language can be fun, they are more receptive to vocabulary building.

Hear What We Have Here

Students frequently assign a word its homothone's meaning. When discussing a word's meaning, it is often useful to introduce the homothone (if there is one) at the same time so that students may compare and contrast.

Example: He was asked to pay the *fare*.
               The test was *fair*.

Rooting Out Meaning

By learning the meaning of prefixes, roots, and suffixes, the meanings of words are often revealed. Knowing that the prefix *dis-* means "the opposite of," the meanings of such words as *disappear, disprove,* and *dissatisfied* are easier to figure out. Students must watch out for words like *distinct,* however, where *dis* is not a prefix.

Introducing students to Latin and Greek roots will uncover still more words. The Latin word *porto* (carry) helps students with words such as:

Example: *transport*—to carry across
               import—to carry in
               export—to carry out
               portable—able to be carried

particularly when common prefixes and suffixes are known.

Dictionaries indicate whether a Greek or Latin root is present in a word. Students, when discovering a root, might attempt to find other words using the root. Have students participate in root searches. Or, assign one or two words at a time to see what students can compile to share with others in terms of roots, prefixes, and suffixes and related words. This is a good activity for remedial students to be able to share with their higher achieving classmates.

From Louis Pasteur—"Pasteurize"

Knowing how a word has entered the language offers a student a larger framework within which to fit a new concept, and thereby increases the likelihood that the word will be remembered. Moreover, word histories often add interest and provide motivation for learning words. Appropriate source books are:

Epstein, Sam and Beryl, *The First Book of Words.* New York: Franklin Watts, 1954.
Kohn, Bernice, *What a Funny Thing to Say.* New York: The Dial Press, 1974.
Longman, Harold, *What's Behind the Word.* New York: Coward-McCann, Inc., 1966.
Nevins, Ann and Dan, *From the Horse's Mouth.* Englewood Cliffs, NJ: Prentice-Hall, Inc., 1977
Nurnberg, Maxwell, *Wonders in Words.* Englewood Cliffs, NJ: Prentice-Hall, Inc., 1965.

A Word a Day

Let each student select a word to be learned each day. Each student must use his or her word five times during the course of the day. Students should keep a booklet with a week's words on each page using sentences and / or pictures to illustrate the words. Frequently during a creative writing exercise, ask students to include the week's words in their story or literary creation.

A Word a Week

Ask students to find an unfamiliar word in their reading each Monday. It may be in any subject or from any book. Have them recount the subsequent number of times they encounter the word during the week whether at home or school, orally, from television or in reading. Chances are, students will be surprised at how often the word suddenly appears when previously it had never crossed their paths.

SUGGESTIONS FOR IMPROVING THE USE OF CONTEXT

Categorically Speaking

Many researchers (Artley, 1943; Pearson and Johnson, 1978; and others) have categorized the various kinds of contextual aids that reading material often provides to illustrate word meaning. An understanding of kinds of contextual clues helps students notice unknown words and to note how the context has enabled them to achieve meaning. The most common categories include:

Definition or Synonym

The definition or synonym of the unknown word appears in the makeup of the sentence itself (To *divulge* the news is to reveal it), in the following sentence (The news was *divulged* slowly. Bit by bit it was revealed), in apposition or parentheses (The news was *divulged,* revealed, slowly), or in an example that follows (The news was *divulged* slowly as one piece at a time was revealed.).

Antonym

Frequently antonyms or word opposites are contrasted with the unknown word. The antonym, often a familiar word, may be signaled by the use of words such as: *but, however,* etc.

Example: Jill was *reticent* but her sister was quite talkative.

Summary of Preceding Statements or Mood

Many paragraphs develop an idea that is expressed by a single culminating word. Although the word may not be a part of the student's receptive vocabulary, the preceeding sentences cumulatively have revealed its meaning.

Examples: (1) Students were asked to sit a seat apart from each other. Everyone received three sheets of paper and two sharp pencils. No talking was allowed during the two hours of the *examination.* (2) The children dressed up for the event. Everyone came to help celebrate. It was a *festive* time.

Groupings of Words

When related words appear successively, a reader may be unfamiliar with one of the words. Although its specific meaning is not apparent, the grouping enables the student to place the word in a category that conveys the information needed to comprehend the text.

Example: Saws, hammers, and *awls* are essential to carpenters.

Similes

Similes often reveal the meaning of an unknown term through comparison. The words *as* or *like* are used to communicate the comparison.

Example: Her skin was as white and transparent as *alabaster.*
Her white transparent skin was like *alabaster.*

Inference

When the unfamiliar word is not defined in the text, the reader is frequently able to infer its meaning from the illustration(s) provided.

Example: Watching how much food she ate, I was not surprised by her *corpulence.*

Certain contextual aids are simpler for students to recognize and use than others. Carnine, Kameenui, and Coyle (1984) found that middle-grade students used contextual information when it appeared in synonym form more easily than when it was present in inference form. Teachers might be wise to use synonyms to demonstrate the use of contextual information to reveal an unknown word's meaning. Once students are able to use context in this way, the other kinds of cues should be taught.

We Look but We Don't See

Try to get students into the habit of underlining unfamiliar words in their reading even though the general meaning is understood from context. They should then go back to check on specific meaning. This provides an opportunity for students to check their contextual guesses against dictionary definitions. Although not easy to enforce, the act of underlining proves valuable as students find that they meet the same words again and again, words that they might previously have seen but not noted.

No Nonsense

By substituting nonsense words in sentences, teachers can highlight the effectiveness of the context.

Example: The details of the news story were *pubosted* slowly. Each day brought new *pubostations.* What do *pubost* and *pubostations* mean?

I've Got a Secret

When asked to divulge how they have uncovered a word's meaning, students often articulate strategy in a way that both they and others remember more easily than a teacher's explanation. Assistance in utilizing context appropriately can be given very naturally for if one student has overlooked a relevant context clue, a peer may have the meaning key.

Supervised Practice Makes Perfect

Students need instruction and practice utilizing context to reveal meaning. Carnine, Kameenui, and Coyle (1984) have shown that practice is effective in a teacher-directed setting where immediate corrective feedback accompanies student attempts to use context clues. Independent seatwork that lacks prior instruction and immediate follow-up does not produce the same skill gain.

ACTIVITIES INDEX

DOMINATE
THE _____ HAVE IT (YEAS OR NAYS)

REFERENCES

Artley, A. Sterl, "Teaching Word Meaning through Context," *Elementary English Review,* February 1943, pp. 65–74.

Borland, Hal, *When the Legends Die.* New York: Bantam, 1964.

Carnine, Douglas; Edward J. Kameenui and Gayle Coyle, "Utilization of Contextual Information in Determining the Meaning of Unknown Words," *Reading Research Quarterly,* 1984, pp. 188–204.

Dale, Edgar, "Vocabulary Measurement: Techniques and Major Findings," *Elementary English,* December 1965, pp. 895–901, 948.

Davis, Frederick B., "Fundamental Factors of Comprehension in Reading," *Psychometrika,* September 1944, pp. 185–97.

Klare, George R., "Assessing Readability," *Reading Research Quarterly,* 1974–75, pp. 62–102.

Pany, Darlene, and Joseph R. Jenkins, "Learning Word Meanings: A Comparison of Instructional Procedures and Effects on Measures of Reading Comprehension with Learning Disabled Students," Technical Report #25. Urbana, IL: Center for the Study of Reading, March 1977.

Pearson, David P., and Dale D. Johnson, *Teaching Reading Vocabulary,* New York: Holt, Rinehart and Winston, 1978.

Smith, Richard, and Dale Johnson. *Teaching Children to Read.* Reading, MA: Addison-Wesley, 1980.

Seven

Difficulties with Literal Comprehension

SKILL DESCRIPTION

True reading does not take place without understanding. That is, pronouncing words without understanding them cannot be called reading. Most explanations of reading instruction, whether developmental or remedial, treat word identification and comprehension separately merely to facilitate discussion. We have continued that tradition in our book.

Also, most discussions distinguish literal from inferential comprehension even though they usually are needed by the reader simultaneously. We separate these skills here for convenience and because some children have considerably more difficulty with one than the other.

Literal and inferential comprehension, the latter to be covered in the next chapter, differ in one important respect. For literal comprehending to occur, one needs to understand what is actually on the page while inferential understanding requires the reader to go beyond the print to her / his own experiences. But as Anderson et al. (1978) point out, both kinds of comprehension require "bridges" between text and reader. Little if any understanding will take place if the vocabulary, syntax, and linguistic concepts in the text are not familiar to the reader. Pearson and Johnson (1978) classify factors which influence comprehension as "inside the head" and "outside the head," the former describing what the reader brings to a text encounter and the latter defining what is in the text and in the reading instruction that may accompany it. Reading demands the integration of the two categories but literal understanding needs less of what the reader brings to text than does inferential.

As important as the distinction between literal and inferential is that between recognition and recall of literal information. A reader may be able to locate data without being able to remember it, or vice versa. Because of this, memory for content and ability to locate it demand different teaching and assessment techniques.

Separating teaching from testing procedures for literal comprehension is another important consideration. The first, in the form of comprehension questions in oral or written form, is what often occurs in classrooms under the guise of comprehension instruction (Durkin, 1978–79). Although questions can be teaching as well as testing tools, they must be selected or created with care, positioned at key points during the lesson, and used diagnostically as part of the instructional dialogue.

When literal comprehension takes place, readers are able to identify the major components of a selection—the "who," "what," "when," "where," and "why" of sentences or larger units. These are called the details of a selection. They are able to understand the order in which things happen in a story, often via the use of signal words like *first, afterwards,* and *finally.* They can find or remember main ideas or themes when explicitly stated in titles, topic, or summarizing sentences. Anaphora, language devices such as pronouns and helping verbs which reduce repetition in speaking and writing, are understood by the successful literal comprehender. So too are the meanings of individual words in a selection but this chapter deals only with problems with and techniques for understanding connected discourse. Word knowledge was discussed in Chapter Six.

POSSIBLE REASONS FOR SKILL DEFICIENCY

1. Inadequate listening-speaking vocabularies are most frequently the reason given for poor comprehension. Jeanne Chall (1982) cited lack of vocabulary as the key cause in the drop of fourth-grade achievement scores. Because concepts in intermediate materials go beyond personal experience, (see reason 2, below) so does the vocabulary.

2. Students often do not have the background of experiences necessary to comprehend concepts introduced or extended in the text. This seems particularly true for materials written for intermediate and advanced readers in the content areas. These require readers to go into the abstract, not easily referenced worlds of history, math, and science. This is difficult for all students at the third-fourth grade juncture, but most seriously hurt are those students with limited linguistic and "hands-on" experience.

3. Immature word identification slows or eliminates comprehension for several reasons. First, in its beginning stages, reading may be a primarily decoding process. That is, young readers tend to overanalyze words, even those they know by sight. In their zest to practice decoding, comprehension is neglected (Chall, 1979). Second, this time in more mature readers, frequent attempts to decode unknown words can slow reading to a word-by-word rate, impeding the processing of written language in meaningful chunks. Finally, even when word-by-word reading is not a problem but certain word patterns (long vowel, multisyllabic, for example) cause difficulties, a sufficient number of words may be ignored or mispronounced rendering comprehension inaccurate.

4. Because so few teachers actually teach comprehension (Durkin, 1978–79), many children may have difficulty with it because of a lack of learning opportunities. At least two theorists (Fries, 1962; Flesch, 1981) have conjectured that comprehension instruction is unnecessary since children understand spoken language and apply this knowledge to print. But reading comprehension has its own conventions which often need to be taught directly to children.

5. Remedial students often have difficulty remembering anything of a selection other than the last thing read or a detail that "rang true" to their lives or interests. Often this is the result of not knowing what is important to remember of the great number of incidents or facts in some selections.

6. Inability to recognize information is another problem. Students with this difficulty do not know how to find information in a selection through scanning, skimming, use of synonymous terms, textual aids like topic sentences, or signal words. This last cueing system can be particularly helpful. Such words can indicate temporal sequences (*after, then*), a set of examples, (*first, finally*), main ideas (*in summary, overall*), cause and effect (*why. . . because*), or contrast (*but, whereas*).

7. Some students do quite well comprehending brief selections one or two sentences or a paragraph in length, but have difficulty with longer selections like stories or articles in which more information is presented. As Guszek (1967) posited, children in the upper grades answer recall questions with less accuracy than do children in lower grades because of the greater memory task created by larger quantity of text.

8. A book with which students have difficulty may be poorly written, beyond their conceptual grasp, or alien to their interests.

SELECTED DIAGNOSTIC PROCEDURES

Literal comprehension is assessed on every standardized reading test, whether it be an achievement test, or an individual or group diagnostic measure. With most of these tests, it is a challenge to the teacher to weed out literal from nonliteral questions to see which comprehension skill, if any, is most problematic. The Stanford Diagnostic Reading Test takes the guesswork from that effort by evenly dividing and designating the comprehension questions asked after each passage as literal or inferential. Scores for each category, as well as a composite score for overall comprehension, allow for skill contrast.

CASE STUDY*

Joe, a fifth grader with reading comprehension problems, was given the Stanford Diagnostic Reading Test, Green Level, Form A.† Of the thirty literal comprehension questions given, twenty-four were answered correctly giving Joe a grade equivalent score of 2.9. Joe's inferential score was slightly better—3.2. It is interesting to look at the passage and set of questions that gave him the most difficulty:

One summer, Ricky went camping with the Boy Scouts. He and his friends went swimming every day. They slept in tents and cooked their own food. But they enjoyed scaring the younger Cub Scouts in the next camp most. At night, they would creep through the woods to the Cub Scouts' camp, and make noises like wolves. The young boys would wake up and wonder what was outside their tents. One night, while sneaking through the woods, Ricky fell into a patch of poison ivy. The counselors had to send him home. Ricky had to spend the rest of the summer in the hot city.

Literal questions only

X (11)   What did Ricky like best about camp?

- o Walking through the woods
- • Swimming
- o Cooking his own food
- o Scaring the younger boys

X (13)   Where did Ricky go when he left camp?

- • To a Cub Scout camp
- o To another Boy Scout camp
- o To the city
- o To the hospital

*See Introduction for function of Case Study.
†Reproduced by permission from the Stanford Diagnostic Reading Test: 2nd Edition. Copyright © 1976 by Harcourt Brace Jovanovich, Inc. All rights reserved.

X (14) Ricky and his friends made believe they were—

- o animals
- • camp counselors
- o robbers
- o policemen

⌐ (15) What did the Cub Scouts sleep in?

- o cabins
- o trailers
- • tents
- o tree houses

There are several reasons that can account for Joe's failure with this selection. One is lack of experience with camping and/or scouting. Another has to do with the difficulty of the words or reading level of the selection. Perhaps Joe had decoding or meaning difficulty with key words in the selection—*wolves, counselors, scaring, noises*—that are essential for correct responses to the literal questions. A final explanation for Joe's difficulty may lie in the nature of the literal questions and their possible answers. In three of four literal errors, item language was a paraphrase of the text. Synonyms for key words in the selection were used in the correct answer choice. For example, in question (11) Joe chose swimming as Ricky's favorite camp activity, a sensible response since the passage states that Ricky and friends swam daily. Moreover, the words describing their greatest enjoyment—*scaring younger scouts*—was labeled "most" in the passage but "best" in the correct answer choice. If Joe scanned using the word "best," he would have been unsuccessful in finding the answer sentence in the selection. A second example is (14), where *animals,* the right answer, appears as *wolves* in the story.

Help with synonymous terms, difficulty with which is one explanation for Joe's poor performance on this selection, might be an appropriate remedial route. But before such a decision is made, informal diagnosis, perhaps contrasting performance on word-for-word literal questions with ones which use synonymous terms for those in the selection, is recommended.

Other Assessments

Reading comprehension sections on all achievement and diagnostic tests include literal questions.

TECHNIQUES FOR REMEDIATION

Select Reading Material Carefully

If possible, make sure that the text chosen for remedial students matches their interests, reading ability, and the length of discourse unit with which they feel comfortable. Also, take care to choose well-written selections that highlight the textual characteristic you are teaching in that lesson. For example, a lesson on literal main idea should involve material that has stated main ideas via topic sentences or titles, rather than inferred ones like themes or morals.

When students need to read a difficult text, often it is best to find another book on the same topic. You may also modify or rewrite poorly written materials and you can provide a great deal of text assistance in the form of selection readiness, passage analysis, and intermittent questions.

As much as remedial teachers wish to give their students positive experiences with wonderful books, success with assigned schoolwork is often more important. When helping remedial students deal with a difficult text or assignment via intensive preparation, the remedial teacher becomes a coach.

What's the Point?

Main ideas of sentences can usually be located by identifying the subject and predicate. With longer units like paragraphs or chapters, sources for main ideas are (1) topic or summarizing sentences, (2) bold-face headings and (3) subheadings, as well as (4) clearly stated author-purposes. Students need to be shown examples of these and how to find them on their own. The following selections illustrate several ways that the literal main idea can be found in a paragraph.

Use of Topic Sentence

> Columbus made a mistake when he called the people he met on San Salvador Indians. He named them that because he believed he had found the Indies. Instead, he landed on the continent we call America. He should have called the people living there Americans!

Use of Summarizing Sentence

> Columbus set sail from Spain for the Indies. He didn't realize that there was a continent in between Spain and the Indies. It was America, and Columbus landed on the island of San Salvador which is part of Central America. Believing he had landed in the Indies instead of in America, Columbus called the people he met there Indians instead of Americans.

Use of Boldface Heading

> **Columbus Calls the Americans "Indians"**
>
> Columbus set sail from Spain to look for the Indies. He thought he had found it when he landed on San Salvador which was on the American continent. So he called the people he found there Indians instead of Americans and the name stuck.

Remembering Details

To help children retain what they read:

1. Tell them what to look for in advance. This is often called asking purpose questions. Be selective about what you ask. No more than three items should be requested, and if possible the details should be related—all names of characters or all traits of a character, for example. Small numbers of facts and their interrelatedness maximize the opportunity for success with this task.

2. Teach note-taking skills. Sometimes just the act of placing a tiny pencil mark beside the information to be remembered will help to recall it later. Allowing students to jot down the answers to purpose questions when they come upon them in their reading and to refer to their notes during assessment instead of going back to the text helps bridge the gap for a student who can locate but not remember information.

3. Begin instruction with smaller chunks of text (phrase, sentence) to limit the number of details. Gradually increase the amount of text and number of details to be processed.

4. Help students retell narratives by providing cues like illustrations or key words in the same sequence as the story. Instead of discarding old basal texts or storybooks, separate text and illustrations. Have students read or listen to the story and then retell it using the pictures as a guide. Gradually, fewer illustrations and / or key words can be used to prompt these narratives.

5. Help children create mental images of settings and characters when such information is available. This can be done with the aid of illustrations at first, and then without.

1. Show students how to turn a question into a partial statement and scan for the answer. For example, if a selection deals with a wrasse, a fish which changes gender during the course of its maturation, change the question "How long does it take a female to become a male?" to the cloze statement "It takes _____ _____ for the female to become a male," and have students scan the selection for key words having to do with a quantity (*many, few, seven*) and with time (*hours, days, months*).

2. At the beginning stages of helping students recognize details, give them the location of answers to detail questions. Tell them the page, paragraph, sentence, or line from which information can be obtained (e.g., p. 56, ¶2, line 8). Over the course of several lessons, gradually withdraw the amount of information until only the page number remains.

3. Because much information is often presented in some sentences, it becomes important to be able to reduce that information to essential noun-predicate statements and to also be able to isolate kernel ideas from embellished or embedded ones. This latter skill is illustrated below. Students may need to break down sentences into many kernels at first but need fewer kernel sentences later.

a. Ellen's story about a tall dark man with pointy teeth whose mind was crawling with snakes and demons made my hair stand on end.

Example: Ellen told a story.
It was about a man.
He was tall and dark.
He had pointy teeth.
His mind was crawling with snakes and demons.
The story made my hair stand on end.

b. Despite his friend's warning, Will backed into the wet paint, ruining his new suit.

Example: Will's friend warned him.
The warning was about wet paint.
Will backed into the paint anyway.
His new suit was ruined.

c. Mr. Larkin, the captain of the men's volleyball team, believes it's not how you play the game, but whether you win or lose that counts.

Example: Mr. Larkin is the captain of the mens' volleyball team.
He believes that it's not how you play the game but whether you win or lose that counts.

4. Teaching the 5 W's helps students locate the *who, what, when, where,* and *why* of a sentence, paragraph, or story. A chart format such as that presented below can be particularly helpful. Of course, not every sentence will contain all of these elements.

WHO	WHAT	WHEN	WHERE	WHY
Marcia	bought a magazine	Saturday	at the pharmacy	because it had pictures of her favorite rock group.
He	missed the boat but wasn't disturbed.			
Aunt Ruth	telephoned and invited us for dinner	on Sunday	at her house	when she won a turkey in a raffle.

The horse on the outside	made its move, catching the favorite	suddenly	at the wire

Give Help in Distinguishing Main Idea from Details

Two kinds of diagrams help students conceptualize the difference between main idea and details. One visual display is a "top hat," with the main idea at the brim and the supporting details built above (Ekwall, 1982). This is especially good for paragraphs in which the main idea is found in the concluding sentence. Invert the hat as it is shown below for paragraphs with topic sentences.

> The functions of the hemispheres of the brain are quite different.
> One hemisphere is verbal, analytic.
> The other is artistic, intuitive and mute.
> This nonspeaking side is usually on the right.
> It is currently the focus of much research.
> The two brain sides are linked by nerves.
> Damaged nerves? The sides can't communicate!

Another is a semantic web, with the main idea at the center and the supporting details radiating out as strands. The web below illustrates an episode from the book *Delilah* (Hart, 1972).

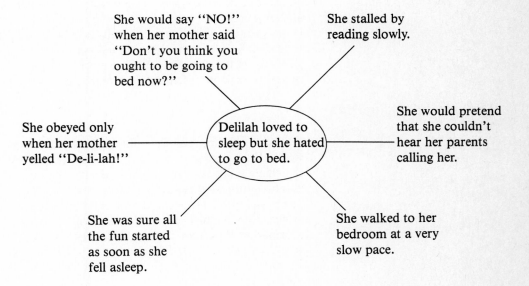

She would say "NO!" when her mother said "Don't you think you ought to be going to bed now?"

She stalled by reading slowly.

She obeyed only when her mother yelled "De-li-lah!"

Delilah loved to sleep but she hated to go to bed.

She would pretend that she couldn't hear her parents calling her.

She was sure all the fun started as soon as she fell asleep.

She walked to her bedroom at a very slow pace.

Order Counts

Sequencing is important for establishing the logical order of events in a story, chronological events in historical text, and the steps of a recipe or construction directions. Two suggestions for help with sequence are:

1. To teach the meaning and use of signal words such as: first, second, next, after, before, then, finally, following, even earlier, etc. These words are excellent cues to prompt a story retelling.

2. To provide visual displays such as outlines, timelines or flow charts to help conceptualize the events in a sequence. Time-honored techniques also include the use of cut-up comic strips or paragraphs from a story which students put in order using logic or signal words.

Cause-and-effect relationships are another kind of sequence. They differ from chronologic or story order because one event does not simply follow or accompany another but is clearly precipitated by it. The meaning and import of signal words such as "if...then" and "why...because" as well as question catch words like "happened before" "caused by," and "the effect of" should be taught.

Improving Teacher Questions

Most of the questions teachers ask in comprehension assessments are literal ones. To expand the usefulness of questions as instructional aids, they should be carefully crafted, given before the selection (particularly if recognition is the goal) and used diagnostically throughout a lesson. Moreover, teacher responses to student answers are important for redirecting and extending comprehension. For questions to be truly instructional, discussions should ensue from student answers, whether or not accurate. Requiring students to show where they found their answers and to give more than a "yes" or "no" when asked if they enjoyed a book or liked a main character may take time, but better comprehension will result.

In addition, it is important to realize that even with literal questions that seemingly have "one right answer," what is expected may not be given and yet the response may be correct. For example, a student is asked "Why did Goldilocks enter the bears' home?" after it was stated in the story that she went in because no one was home. If he answers "Because she was nosy," the teacher should realize that the child is responding to a textually explicit* question with a scriptically implicit* answer (Pearson and Johnson, 1978). That is, although the text explains that Goldilocks entered because no one was home, the student's "script," or previous experiences, will provide the label "nosy" for the nerve and curiosity that impelled Goldilocks. Under these circumstances, asking a student for a rationale for his answer is essential. Divergent answers to convergent questions should be rewarded when possible. This discussion should reveal that the line between literal and inferential comprehending can't always be sharply drawn.

What Am I Looking For?

It is also a good idea to help children decide what a question asks for and whether they can find the answer in the text. Raphael (1982) discovered that children in the intermediate grades can be taught to distinguish question-answer relationships that are literal from those that require inferencing. She labels the literal relationships "Right There"—those questions and answers that have matching key words. Questions and answers that can be found in the selection but with a bit more effort, e.g. integrating information from two or more sentences, she calls "Think and Search."

Let Me Ask You

Guiding students to ask questions of text is another important skill. This may help them improve memory for content, become independent of teacher guidance, and develop good study habits. Manzo's ReQuest (1967) is one self-questioning training procedure, a process he calls reciprocal questioning:

1. Reading selection is available to students and teacher.
2. Everyone reads the first sentence silently. Students ask the teacher as many questions about it as they can.
3. Teacher answers the questions, and requires rephrasing if the questions are illogical or poorly constructed.

*You may wish to see Chapter Eight for a fuller discussion of these terms.

4. Now the second sentence is read, but this time the teacher questions the students, and so on.

5. Teacher or student may comment on whether the question has an answer which is directly stated in the passage.

Model teacher questions and full replies are goals of the technique, so make sure your queries and answers are exemplary!

Distinguishing between Literal and Figurative Meanings

Students need to be able to separate literal from figurative expressions. While it might be adorable to see a toddler dip his eye into a glass of milk at his mother's warning to "keep your eye on the milk!" readers need to differentiate between phrases like "Wait sixty seconds" (time it, please) and "Wait a minute" (don't actually watch the clock, but I shouldn't be long). The best activities to develop this skill have students matching literal and figurative equivalent expressions or providing the figurative one for a given literal phrase or sentence, or vice versa.

Examples: Joey left but didn't know where he was going.
Joey set out for the hinterlands.
or
Joey lit out for points unknown.

It's hard to get Paco talking.
Paco keeps his mouth shut.
or
Paco is quiet as a clam.

Paraphrasing

1. Underline certain words in passages—have students generate synonymous terms (similar but not identical in meaning) for them.

Francine is a <u>nice</u> girl.
pleasant or well-mannered

Will you <u>have</u> another piece?
take or eat

2. Have students rewrite sentences, inverting the word order.

Louis and Shirley were playing softball when there was a strange noise from space.

A strange noise from space occurred when Louis and Shirley were playing softball.

3. Have students make up questions for a selection. Tell them that good questions are those which use different words from those used in the passage.

4. Do a sentence-by-sentence reading of a selection. After each one, have students tell what they read, in their own words. Teacher copies student-generated sentences and these and the text are compared for synonymous terms.

He, She, It

Sometimes authors use substitute terms, pronouns and auxiliary verbs called anaphora, to reduce redundancy in text and to provide variety. Unless readers can identify the referent for a substitute term, they may have difficulty understanding a sentence and in some cases, an entire selection. Exercises which require such identification are recommended at first as diagnosis. If a difficulty is present, continue with such exercises and add the matching of equivalent sentences, one with the anaphoric term and the other with the redundancy so students can see how "silly" the second one sounds.

I enjoyed that movie more than Marlon did.
I enjoyed that movie more than Marlon enjoyed that movie.

My sheets feel awfully cold when I crawl into them.
My sheets feel awfully cold when I crawl into my sheets.

Franklin and Suzanne ate dinner after they watched Electric Company.
Franklin and Suzanne ate dinner after Franklin and Suzanne watched Electric Company.

ACTIVITIES INDEX

REFERENCES

Anderson, Richard, et al, "Schemata as Scaffolding for the Representation of Information in Connected Discourse." *American Educational Research Journal,* 1978, pp. 433–440.

Chall, Jeanne, Address at Massachusetts Reading Association Convention. Sturbridge, Massachusetts, April 1983.

Chall, Jeanne, "The Great Debate: 10 Years Later with a Modest Proposal for Reading Stages," in *Theory and Practice of Early Reading.* Resnick, Lauren, and Phyllis Weaver (eds). Hillsdale, NJ: Lawrence Erlbaum, 1979.

Durkin, Dolores, "What Classroom Observations Reveal About Reading Comprehension Instruction," *Reading Research Quarterly,* 1978–79, pp. 481–533.

Flesch, Rudolph, *Why Johnny Still Can't Read.* New York: Harper and Row, 1981.

Fries, Charles, *Linguistics and Reading.* New York: Holt, Rinehart and Winston, 1962.

Guszak, Frank J., "Teacher Questioning and Reading," *The Reading Teacher,* December 1967, pp. 227–234.

Hart, Carole, *Delilah.* New York: Harper and Row, 1972.

Manzo, Anthony, "The ReQuest Procedure," *Journal of Reading,* November 1969, pp. 123–126.

Pearson, P. David, and Dale D. Johnson, *Teaching Reading Comprehension.* New York: Holt, Rinehart and Winston, 1978.

Raphael, Taffy, "Question-Answering Strategies for Children," *The Reading Teacher,* November 1982, pp. 186–90.

Eight

Inability to Inference

SKILL DESCRIPTION

When students have difficulty with reading comprehension, inferential comprehension is frequently the problem—i.e. using reading material to make predictions or develop ideas when main idea, sequence, character, mood, and/or outcomes are not directly stated in the text. Inferential comprehension is commonly defined as the ability to read between the lines.

All of us make frequent inferences. Picture a man attempting to open a locked door and searching his pockets, apparently in vain. It is not difficult to realize that he has failed to find a key. So too it is with written material. "The sky was looking dark, even though it was the middle of the afternoon. Suddenly the clouds let loose. Jane ran back into the house to get her _____." If a student is able to decode the words in the above passage, it is likely that appropriate words such as *raincoat, umbrella,* and *rainhat* will quickly come to mind. Yet, nowhere was it stated directly that it was raining.

There are other tasks requiring inferencing that are not as easy. Relating a number of thoughts which together yield the main idea of a paragraph or selection, for example, can be difficult for numbers of students.

In all instances, one's ability to comprehend material at an inferential level is highly dependent upon how much the reader brings to the text in background knowledge of both vocabulary and schemata (units or structures of knowledge concerning things, ideas, and events). It is the reader's ability to relate written material to these personal schemata that permits inferential comprehension to occur. Readers must have some mental concepts stored which help them to see relationships between ideas.

If a student eats mushrooms regularly at home, but has never heard that there are poisonous varieties that grow wild, s/he will not comprehend the reference in a story that says "Sally ate the mushrooms that she picked in the woods and soon was in real trouble." Perhaps the only schema the student can relate this sentence to is one about the legality or illegality of picking plants that are not on your own property. It is trouble with the law that the student will expect, rather than illness. Inferencing has occurred, the student has translated the word *trouble* which is not defined in the text into what appears to be a plausible explanation, but the inference is wrong because the student lacked appropriate background.

Comprehension, as we have stated in Chapter Seven, is often described as a literal process when the reader depends heavily on the information in the text and as an inferential process when there is a greater use of the reader's prior knowledge. Pearson and Johnson (1978) believe that the inferential process occurs at two levels. Conclusions drawn from one's reading may be *textually* implicit (two or more ideas are directly stated in the text but the relationship is inferred by the reader) or *scriptally* implicit (the reader must refer to his or her own prior knowledge or mental script to reach a conclusion). Literal comprehension, as might be expected, is described as textually *explicit*.

In H. A. Rey's *Curious George Gets a Medal,* the text reads "George did not know what a museum was. He was curious. While the guard was busy reading his paper, George slipped inside." (p. 30). A student using textually implicit comprehension concludes that George went into the museum because he was curious about what a museum holds. The connection between George's curiosity and his entering the museum is certainly implied in the writing, although it is not stated directly. A student might also determine that George went into the museum because it presented a challenge. After seeing the guard outside reading the paper, George wanted to see if he could enter without the guard noticing him. The student here is using scriptally implicit comprehension, injecting what might be his or her own personal reaction to the given circumstances.

Related skills influence inferencing ability. The student who recognizes and understands implied connectives, connotative meaning and / or figurative language, has a sense of story structure, and has a mind set for ambiguity is apt to be the most successful at discerning the inferences in an author's message.

POSSIBLE REASONS FOR SKILL DEFICIENCY

Because inferencing involves an interaction between what the reader brings to the page and what appears on the page, difficulties in making inferences or in seeing inferential relationships in reading can reflect problems that either refer to the reader (concerning experience or instruction) or are inherent in the written material that the student is asked to read.

Reader Problems

1. Students may need to be taught to apply to reading tasks the inferencing abilities they exhibit in their daily activities (Hansen, 1981). Some students who are literal readers do not realize without instruction that reading involves relating story facts and ideas to their lives and previous knowledge and experiences. This is frequently the result of too much literal comprehension instruction or a complete lack of comprehension instruction in the early grades. Since a large majority of the questions asked of students about their reading are literal-level questions (Guzak, 1967), and since very little comprehension instruction of any kind is occurring in the classroom (Durkin, 1978–79), students may not understand that inferencing is a necessary part of reading with meaning.

2. As shown in the introduction to this chapter, inferencing may occur in certain cases but because of inadequate background knowledge, the inferences made are inaccurate or inappropriate. See the example about mushrooms in the Skill Description section.

3. When students do not have language experiences that allow for understanding multiple meanings, figurative language, and other connotative aspects of words, they often miss the allusion, intentional pun, or implied humor or irony in a passage.

Example: Jane always tried to take credit for things. Although she had very pale skin and blonde hair, she could not be called *fair.*

She was on *pins and needles* waiting for the mail to arrive.

4. When interpreting reading material, students frequently rely too heavily on personal scripts, ignoring textual material. In the earlier example from *Curious George,* a student responding solely to the challenge presented by the guard has disregarded important textual information—i.e., that George was curious. Although the conclusion drawn is not incorrect, the student's reasoning is incomplete. Testing situations usually demand that a student use the textual information supplied. Class discussions may lean more heavily on scriptally implicit information where students have the opportunity to explain how they have arrived at a divergent opinion. The task, the question, and the material all determine the appropriate balance a student needs to achieve between use of text and script.

5. Sometimes students become overinvolved in relating words or ideas to their experiences so that expectations evolve, which although they have been triggered by a word in the text, bear no relation to the text as a whole. As new material that contradicts these expectations is met, students' predictions must be revised, but the students may be reluctant to relinquish their first thoughts and therefore ignore what follows. The result is that the selection is not understood. Whereas the student's reasoning given in example 4 is incomplete, in this instance it is wrong.

Tierney and Pearson (1981) use an example that illustrates this well.

Window Text

He plunked down $5.00 at the window. She tried to give him $2.50, but he refused to take it. So when they got inside, she bought him a large bag of popcorn. (p. 5)

Based on the first sentence of this example, students may be expecting a bank window or the betting window at a racetrack and fail to attend to the latter two sentences, which demand that they revise their interpretation.

Problems with Text

1. In an attempt to reduce sentence complexity to achieve an easier readability level, connectives frequently are eliminated (Irwin, 1980) and the student's inferential burden is increased.

Example: "Because I'd finished my homework, I read a pleasure book," becomes "I'd finished my homework. I read a pleasure book." The stated cause-and-effect relationship in the first sentence is implied in the second example and is sometimes missed by the elementary reader.

Conditional and sequential relationships may also be implied.

Example: "If you are having trouble, then I can help you" reads differently from "You are having trouble. I can help you."

"When it's 12:00, go to the lunchroom" is not necessarily the same as "It's 12:00. Go to the lunchroom."

2. Much of what is written can be ambiguous or subject to differing interpretations. "Because I finished my homework, I was able to read that book" may be interpreted as a cause-and-effect sequential relationship—"Once my homework was done, I had time to read that book for pleasure"—or as a simple cause-and-effect relation-

ship—"What I learned by doing my homework enabled me to read that book for pleasure."

Often, although not always, the remainder of the paragraph will clarify which meaning was intended, but students may be confused by ambiguity and lose their concentration for the remaining writing.

3. Often students make assumptions that cannot be substantiated by the amount of information appearing in the selection.

Example: The sky was looking dark even though it was the middle of the afternoon.

Although it might be correct to assume that it is December when the days grow very short, this conclusion would be difficult to justify without further information. Ambiguity should encourage students to raise questions rather than draw conclusions.

SELECTED DIAGNOSTIC PROCEDURES

CASE STUDY*

Alice is a fourth-grade student with reading comprehension problems. On the Stanford Diagnostic Reading Test,† Green Level, used for grades 3–5, she missed almost one-third of the inferential questions. This placed her at the thirty-third percentile (Stanine 4). Her literal comprehension score was above the mean at the fifty-eighth percentile but revealed that she was not remembering or locating all the facts.

Three of the paragraphs Alice was asked to read are included here.

1. Pat noticed it at the last possible moment. It was good that she had, because she had almost stepped on it. It was the most beautiful shade of blue she had ever seen. Pat decided that it must have fallen out of one of the nests in the tree above. She bent down to look at it and saw that it had not broken. "Oh, good," she thought. "Maybe if I leave it alone, it will still hatch."

2. The teacher asked Bill and Bob to roll the book cart to the front of the room. The cart was very heavy. The two boys went to it and took hold of the sides. Bill stood on one side, Bob on the other. They pushed the cart as hard as they could, but it didn't move.

3. Did you know that bananas don't grow on trees? Even though the banana plant looks like a tree, it has no trunk or limbs. Bananas are grown in South and Central America and in India where the climate is hot and damp. They grow from flowers on the plant and are cut down before they get ripe. The banana plant dies down after just one crop. Since the banana does not have seeds like an apple or pear, new plants are grown from the roots of the old plants.

Alice's incorrect responses showed two distinct patterns:

a. At times Alice was not using inferences at all but rather was latching onto literal details, disregarding the larger concepts surrounding them. With a question asking where a book cart was located, Alice marked "in the front of the classroom." Alice seized the words "front of the classroom" without analyzing the sentence as a whole. With the question "What did Pat find?" which required the answer "a bird's egg," Alice marked *nest*. Alice seemed here, too, to have responded to the sight of a word (*nest*) rather than to either what was said about it or to the paragraph as a whole.

*See Introduction for function of Case Study.
†Reproduced by permission from the Stanford Diagnostic Reading Test: 2nd edition. Copyright © 1976 by Harcourt Brace Jovanovich, Inc. All rights reserved.

b. Other errors indicated that Alice had used inferencing skills but had ignored cues from the reading, choosing instead an answer that made sense to her in general. Whereas the questions were asking Alice to use textually implicit reasoning (see introduction to this chapter), she often gave what appear to be scriptally implicit answers. As an example, when asked "After the bananas are picked, what happens to the plant?", Alice picked the response, "It grows more bananas," instead of the correct answer, "It dies down." The question demanded a textually implicit answer. Instead, Alice seemed to use her mental script that many plants continually replenish their blooms in a season, and disregarded the textual information that contradicted this general knowledge.

Remediation would have Alice first attending to the facts of the text in order to interpret or react. The teacher should ask her to justify her responses, indicating which information from her reading helped her with the answer.

In instances where inferences should or can be made, the teacher can help Alice to recognize that implied meaning is intended or is possible and should ask appropriate questions to elicit these responses.

In situations in which she calls on her own background knowledge, she must be shown that information in the text sometimes forces readers to revise their thinking by including the new facts. When Alice was asked to explain the answers she marked on the test, her reasoning indicated a tendency to overuse personal scripts. Sometimes she could provide a valid, although unusual, explanation. Alice should be instructed that in a test-taking situation, it is important to use the information that the reading provides. Standardized tests do not allow the student to explain how s/he arrived at a possibly acceptable but divergent answer.

Other Assessments

1. *Individualized Directions in Reading—Criterion-Referenced Comprehension Inventories.* Steck Vaughn Co., 1974.
2. *Prescriptive Reading Inventory.* Monterey, CA: CTB, McGraw Hill, 1977.
3. Otto, Wayne, et al., *Wisconsin Design for Reading Skill Development.* National Computer Systems, Inc., 1972.
   Subtest: Interpretive Reading
4. Rubin, Dorothy, *Diagnosis and Correction in Reading Instruction.* New York: Holt, Rinehart and Winston, 1982, pp. 232–237.
5. Warneke, Edna Wagstaff, and Dorothy K. Shipman, *Group Assessment in Reading.* Englewood Cliffs, NJ: Prentice-Hall Inc., 1984, pp. 133–140.

TECHNIQUES FOR REMEDIATION

Activating Schemata—What Do You know?

Be sure to help students review what they know about the subject matter before reading a selection. By looking at the title and the first sentence or paragraph, show them that what they already know helps them to anticipate what the selection might reveal. It is important for students to recognize that comprehending involves relating information on the page to prior understanding. Comprehension demands active readers who respond to material by accepting or rejecting the information on the page, and in the process, expanding or confirming their prior knowledge.

Direct Teaching

1. Show students directly with examples that much of what they understand after reading a sentence (paragraph, selection) has not been stated openly by the author.

Example: Jane couldn't wait to get to school.

   Do you think she walked to school quickly or slowly?

Do you think Jane expected that something exciting was happening at school?
Did Jane expect this to be a good day or a bad day?
Do you think she ate a good breakfast?

Help students to see that by putting themselves in Jane's shoes and thinking about how it feels to not be able to wait to do something, they can understand a lot more about Jane than the author has actually told them.

2. Continue by having students supply reasonable inferences for a sentence.

Example: Tom crossed the street quickly when he saw the dog.
Examples of reasonable inferences:
Tom was afraid of dogs.
Tom was afraid of that dog.
The dog was big and mean looking.

Demonstrate how sometimes tentative inferences are made and then discarded as more information is added.

Example: Tom crossed the street quickly when he saw the dog. Taffy was his favorite puppy and he was eager to play with her.

The new facts must be noted and students must be flexible enough to revise their thinking as they read.

How Would You Describe Him or Her?

Help students to recognize that much of what we learn about people and events in reading is not stated directly but rather is suggested by the examples given. This requires that students infer the "missing" meaning.

For example, in Erickson's *A Toad for Tuesday,* when Wharton risks his life to bring beetle brittle to his aunt because he thought she'd enjoy some, we can think of him as thoughtful, without the author having to use this word specifically to describe him. Moreover, if we read elsewhere that Tom was generous and friendly but his brother was just the opposite, we do not have to see the word *stingy* to apply it to Tom's brother.

Give students similar examples from their reading.

Classifying Questions

Have students attempt to ask questions about selections they read. Using the text, have them divide their questions into those which can be answered directly by the words in the text and those which require using their prior knowledge (Raphael, 1982).

Example: In Russell Erickson's *A Toad for Tuesday,* one sentence reads, "After he had gone quite a way and when the sun was directly overhead he decided to have some lunch" (p. 15). A literal question would ask where the sun was when Wharton decided to have lunch. An inferential question requiring prior knowledge would ask "What time was it when Wharton decided to have lunch?" Writing questions and having to recognize the kind of thinking called for will help students to utilize these thinking skills while reading.

Correcting Strategies

Help students to be conscious of whether they have comprehended while reading so that they can attempt different strategies to clarify misunderstandings or a lack of comprehension. If students are aware that something is amiss, they can

1. Reread the problem area and try to make sense of it.

2. Continue reading to see if the following textual material explains the confusing part.
3. Reread the material which preceded the troublesome sentence or paragraph to note details they may have missed.
4. Look for specific vocabulary which may be causing or contributing to the confusion. The student may need to look up this (these) word(s) for unfamiliar multiple meanings.

Because comprehension problems occur most frequently with inferencing, during each of these steps students should be watching for: (1) unstated connectives (cause-effect, comparison, conditional, sequential—see reasons for Skill Deficiency), and (2) ways to relate the material to what they already know about the subject.

Figurative Language

Help students to recognize comparisons made through similes, metaphors, personification. Show how each of these devices is used for emphasis.

Example: His remark was very embarrassing.
      a. Her cheeks turned as red as her ruby ring.
      b. Her cheeks turned into fiery rubies.

Both the simile and the metaphor above compare the color of her blushing cheeks to rubies, deep red stones. By providing the student with a mental picture, these figures of speech emphasize the point.

Have students write similes using *like* and *as* and then write the comparisons as metaphors. The familiarity that writing brings will transfer awareness to reading.

Use the same rationale for teaching personification.

Example: "The sun touched his shoulders, leaving them pink and burning." Does a sun have fingers that can touch? Why does the author treat the sun as a person? Help students to see that the mental picture the sentence leaves emphasizes the point in a way that is more effective than saying "His shoulders were sunburned."

Humor

Use cartoons and comics to emphasize double-entendres. Show that it is the use of double meanings that makes them humorous. The newspaper is an excellent source for material.

Riddles and puns also use double meanings to achieve humor. Use these with students, having them make up riddles or puns themselves so that they become accustomed to this use.

Example: What has an eye but can't see? A needle.

Know the Facts

In order to interpret or react to information, the student must note and recall what has actually been stated. Ask students to find the facts that allow them to make inferences. For example, in the sentence given earlier, "Jane couldn't wait to get to school," how do you know that Jane was a student? Is there enough information given? Could Jane be a teacher? Why do you assume that Jane was probably a student or a teacher?

What Happens Next?

Ask students to read part of a story and to predict what might occur next. Help students to identify the information that has already taken place which they must use to make predictions. By integrating what appears on the page with the students' prior knowledge or understandings about what has happened, a number of reasonable scenarios can be devised. These can be compared to the actual continuation of the story.

For example, in H. A. Rey's *Curious George Gets a Medal,* George lifts the gate latch to catch the large pig standing near the gate. Students can anticipate the trouble George will have because everything he has attempted to that point has backfired, leaving him more deeply involved.

An alternative activity might be to remove the last frame of a comic strip from the newspaper and ask students to try to write an appropriate frame. This can be compared to the frame that has been removed. Students often improve upon the humor.

Story Grammar

Understanding story structure helps students with predictions, because they can anticipate what should occur next. See Chapter Five for an explanation of story grammar.

It's All Right To Disagree

Stress to students that the opinions they form about character, mood, or events are opinions suggested by what has been stated but are open to differing interpretations by individual students. Using the example above from Erickson's *A Toad for Tuesday,* one student may find Wharton brave and thoughtful to want to risk danger in bringing his aunt some beetle brittle, while another may find him foolish, selfish, and insensitive to risk his life and desert his brother over such a minor deed. Even if the author tends to lead the student to react kindly toward Wharton and reinforces this by later selfless acts of Wharton's, it is not unreasonable to react differently if what *is* stated can substantiate that contradictory point of view as well.

Signal Words and Connectives

Teach students what connectives to expect in prose and give them examples of sentences in which connectives have been omitted. Let students see the relationships themselves.

Example: Sequence—"Jane walked to the store and then went for lunch, not coming home until 3:00" might read "Jane walked to the store. She went for lunch. She did not come home until 3:00." It is not clear in the second version that Jane went for lunch after going to the store. It could as easily be read that Jane went to the store for lunch.

For other examples, see Reasons for Skill Deficiencies (Problems with Text, #1).

Main Idea

Understanding the main idea when it is not stated directly involves recognizing how what has been stated relates to a category.

1. Playing categories with students and asking them to supply the categories for the examples you give (Examples: *velvet, wool, silk, cotton = fabric*) helps to clarify what you are looking for.

2. Recognizing a sentence in a paragraph which does not belong aids students in seeing that paragraphs or selections are developed around a particular idea.

Example: Jane and Jill like to play jacks together. Playing board games was another interest they shared. Jane's grandmother lived with her family. Jane and Jill even enjoyed reading to each other.

3. Finally matching (from a choice of three titles, choosing one for a paragraph) and then supplying a title ("Sharing the Fun" might be appropriate for the example given) shows students how to relate ideas.

Modeling

Model appropriate ways of reacting to reading by reading a sentence aloud and then saying "Oh, this tells me that Tom's brother is stingy" or "If the sun was overhead, that means it's noon" or "I think the author is trying to show that Jane and Jill are good friends" or "Oh yes, I thought that Wharton was kind and caring when he wanted to bring beetle brittle to his aunt and now I see that I was right because he's saving the owl's life."

ACTIVITIES INDEX

JUMPING TO CONCLUSIONS
TIC TACKY TOE

REFERENCES

Durkin, Dolores, "What Classroom Observations Reveal about Reading Comprehension Instruction," *Reading Research Quarterly,* 1978–79, pp. 481–533.

Erickson, Russell E., *A Toad for Tuesday.* New York: Dell Publishing Co., 1974.

Guzak, Frank J., "Teacher Questioning and Reading," *The Reading Teacher,* December 1967, pp. 227–234.

Hansen, Jane, "The Effects of Inference Training and Practice on Young Children's Reading Comprehension," *Reading Research Quarterly,* 1981, pp. 391–417.

Irwin, Judith Westphal, "Implicit Connectives and Comprehension," *The Reading Teacher,* February 1980, pp. 527–529.

Pearson, P. David, and Dale D. Johnson, *Teaching Reading Comprehension.* New York: Holt, Rinehart, and Winston, 1978.

Raphael, Taffy E., "Question-answering Strategies for Children," *The Reading Teacher,* November, 1982, pp. 186–190.

Rey, H. A., *Curious George Gets a Medal.* New York: Scholastic Book Services, 1957.

Tierney, Robert, and David Pearson, "Learning to Learn from Text: A Framework for Improving Classroom Practice," Reading Education Report #30. Urbana, IL: Center for the Study of Reading, 1981.

Nine

Inadequate Critical Skills

SKILL DESCRIPTION

A statement that appears in print may be true, blatantly false, or perhaps a distorted version of the truth. The fact that material is published is no guarantee of its validity. And yet many people will fervently defend a belief by claiming, "But that's what the book said" or "I read it in a book."

Comprehension is an active process requiring that the reader not passively accept all new information. Rather, s/he must integrate it into existing cognitive structures, accepting or rejecting the material read. Critical reading, evaluating what is read in the context of a reader's experiences and/or external standards, is an essential part of comprehending.

Critical reading requires that a judgment be made, taking into account author's intent, point of view, background, and use of language, usually concerning such topics as reality or fantasy, fact or opinion, relevance, bias or propaganda, and accuracy. DeBoer (1946) noted three levels of critical reading, the first relating to the relevance of the material, the second to an evaluation of the accuracy of fact or reliability of source, and the third to an appraisal of the validity of the conclusions and recognition of whether all needed facts are present. Whereas literal comprehension deals primarily with facts, and inferential comprehension with interpretation, critical comprehension is concerned with opinion, albeit substantiated opinion, and necessitates the use of both literal and inferential comprehension skills.

Clearly, critical reading demands analytical skills. Students must challenge the text with questions such as "Why?" or "Why not?" or "Do I agree?" or "So what?" To read critically means that the reader must be a skeptic. The student must be able to suspend judgment until the reading is completed and all of the material has been weighed and considered.

It is important that direct teaching of critical reading skills occurs. Relying on students to "absorb" these skills through the use of workbook pages is not enough (Patching et al., 1983)

POSSIBLE REASONS FOR SKILL DEFICIENCY

1. Many students believe that information appearing in print is infallible. They may not have been taught to question and look for verification of written material. Although they may naturally react critically to verbal interchange, written material presents an aura of authority (Baldwin et al., 1979) that they do not think to challenge. Furthermore, these students may be unaware of the kinds of questions they should ask about reading material or do not know where to go to find material to verify what they are reading. For example, checking copyright dates and knowing something about an author's background often reveals obsolete information or bias.

2. Students may lack the adequate background knowledge they need to make a judgment about the material they are reading. If they have no cognitive structure against which to verify or negate new material, it is usually accepted at face value. A student reading that mononucleosis is a bacterial disease would have no way of reacting to this statement other than to accept it if s/he (a) had never heard of mononucleosis and/or (b) did not know what was meant by bacterial disease.

3. Students may not have an awareness that authors have purposes for writing and therefore fail to make judgments as to whether these purposes have been met satisfactorily.

4. Students may need instruction in recognizing language that distinguishes fact from opinion (*think, seem, know, is,* etc.). They may also not be aware that authors use emotional words to influence the reader. A reader reacts differently to the two sentences below:

> The baby cried for a long time.
> The baby's wracking sobs lasted for an eternity.

5. Students may not recognize and consequently may be taken in by typical propaganda techniques such as the misuse of statistics and faulty use of cause and effect or logic (syllogisms). A far-fetched example might be the following:

> Ten percent of the American population drove foreign cars in 1980.
> Ten percent of the American population contracted serious illness in 1980.
> Therefore, driving foreign cars causes serious illness.

SELECTED DIAGNOSTIC PROCEDURES

There is a need for instruments which test critical reading skills (Worden, 1981). Although some of the comprehension questions in published tests may ask, for example, whether a conclusion is logical or whether a character or situation is realistically portrayed, findings about a student's ability to read critically are usually revealed informally through workbook pages, teacher-made instruments, and, most often, class or reading group questions and answers.

CASE STUDY*

Below we have included classroom dialogue that occurred between Alex, a fourth-grader, and his teacher. Alex had just finished reading the chapters on snakes in *Reptiles Do the Strangest Things* (L. and A. Hornblow, 1970, pp. 14–27) and commented that this part of the book was great.

* See Introduction for function of Case Study.

T: Alex, I can see that you're enjoying reading about snakes. You read *Crictor* (Tomi Ungerer, 1958) last week and now this. Both authors chose to write about snakes. What do you think the Hornblows' purpose was in writing *Reptiles?* Why did they write this kind of book?

A: They wanted people to read their book.

T: Yes, that's true and I'm sure that's true about Tomi Ungerer who wrote *Crictor* as well, but even though both books were about snakes, they were very different books. Do you think the authors of both books were trying to teach you about snakes?

A: Yes, but in *Crictor* you learn about one snake. In this book you learn about lots of snakes.

T: Which book had more facts about snakes?

A: This one did because you learned about rattlers and pythons and cobras, anacondas, and I forget—oh yeah, the hog nose—and *Crictor* is just about a boa constrictor but that's a python, you know.

T: Which book helped you to learn more about pythons?

A: Crictor, because the whole book was about a python, not just one chapter.

T: What did you learn about pythons in *Crictor?*

A: They wrap around things and they're long. They can form letters and numbers with their bodies.

T: Do you think pythons do that in real life?

A: Probably not the letters. But they wrap around things.

T: Why was Crictor making letters in this book?

A: Because it was a story.

T: A true story?

A: No, a made-up one.

T: All right, now let's look at *Reptiles.* What do you learn about pythons there?

A: Oh yeah, about squeezing and eating and crawling.

T: If you need to get more information about pythons, which book will help you more?

A: This one.

T: Why, Alex?

A: Because it tells more real things.

T: Even in two pages?

A: Yes.

T: Why don't you learn as much in *Crictor* even though it's the whole book?

A: Cause it's not a true story.

T: Yes. The Hornblows' purpose in writing this book was to teach or tell the reader lots of true facts about reptiles, including snakes. What do you think Tomi Ungerer's purpose was in writing *Crictor?* To teach you a lot of facts about snakes?

A: No.

T: What was the purpose do you think?

A: I guess to tell a story.

T: Yes, I think you're right. So that even if authors write about the same subject, they might write for different reasons.

Although the teacher did not in this brief interchange touch on all aspects of critical reading with Alex, it is likely that he will need direction in this area. It appears, for example, that the idea of author purpose is a new one for Alex, one that he has not thought about before. He is not yet consciously distinguishing the characteristics of fact and fiction. Interest in the subject matter seems to be his sole motivation for reading. Moreover, he seems to equate the length of selection with how much he can learn from it.

He needs to recognize what he might learn from varieties of reading material and to understand the significance of author and reader purpose. He will need practice with different kinds of writing. (See Techniques for Remediation.)

1. *Prescriptive Reading Inventory.* Monterey, CA: CTB, McGraw-Hill, 1977.
2. Warnecke, Edna W., and Dorothy A. Shipman. *Group Assessment in Reading.* Englewood Cliffs, NJ: Prentice-Hall, Inc., 1984, pp. 141–143.

TECHNIQUES FOR REMEDIATION

He Who Hesitates Is Lost

We teach critical reading skills right from the start when we ask young children "Could this really have happened? Why or why not?" "Did you like _____?" (the main character in the story) "Did you like what s/he did?" "Was this a good ending to the story?" This same way of responding to stories, relating them to personal experience and standards should continue when students begin to read for themselves but because students at first are caught up with decoding and simple comprehension concerns, the habit of reacting critically can be lost. It is important for teachers not to hestitate to teach critical reading skills, at all levels of ability, to ask the above questions even with simple stories.

Valid or Not?

Help students to be aware of features that question the authenticity or validity of a piece of writing—anachronisms, gross exaggerations, illogical conclusions. Certain cue words signal that a conclusion has been reached: *therefore, and so, from this we can see, in conclusion,* etc. Students should question whether the statement that follows has been adequately explained or prepared for. In his book *Frogs and Toads,* Charles A. Schoenknecht states on page 27, "Fish, turtles, herons, and other enemies eat many of the tadpoles. So only a small number of them live to be grown-ups." Perhaps the reader will want to explore just how many eggs are laid and what "a small number" means.

George Washington Lies

One means of bursting the "anything that appears in print must be true" bubble is to have students read conflicting accounts of the same topic or incident. Often biographies are useful for this purpose. Try to determine reasons for discrepancies—author background, copyright date, etc.

One's background necessarily influences how one perceives an incident or event and consequently affects the way one writes about it. Have two students write individual stories or reports on the same topic (about a teacher, or school event, etc.) and note how each has chosen to focus on different aspects. It is possible that one report might even contain invalid statements.

With respect to copyright date, information in a book written prior to the first moon landing, for example, might state that human beings have never set foot on the moon. Since this contradicts what students have experienced to be true, they must question the information and try to discover why the inaccuracy exists, in this case because of when the material was written. The main point is that written material is not always accurate. This always comes as a surprise to some students.

Quotations

Heilman, Rupley, and Blair (1981) suggest using quotes with which students agree or disagree, and having them provide reasons for their opinions. In this way, students may be shown the analytical skills that are a part of critical reading. Aphorisms are a handy source material.

Examples: The early bird catches the worm.
                 A stitch in time saves nine.

Do the Facts Support the Thesis?

Use content or factual material with students to see whether authors provide enough or relevant information to defend the topic sentence or concluding statements.

In *Reptiles Do the Strangest Things* (L. and A. Hornblow, 1970), the authors write that alligators sold as pets usually die and many crocodilians are killed for their skins, leaving the swamps depleted of these animals. They conclude by saying, "It is sad to think that the thundering 'song of the croc' may someday only be heard at the zoo" (p. 13), but they do not give reasons about why it is important to have crocodilians living in their natural habitat. Perhaps they are dangerous enough to man and do not provide enough value to the environment to justify the reader's feeling sad that they might soon only be found in zoos. These are questions that students should at least ask when reading this book.

Communication

When authors put pen to paper, they are speaking to a reader. Not only do they have something to say and a reason for expressing it, but their message is intended for a specific audience. Like the falling tree in the forest, their words need an ear. Authors write to inform, to entertain, to persuade, to teach or direct, and to express an idea or an emotion. Likewise, students read material for a variety of reasons—to learn, to be entertained, to find a new point of view, etc. Furthermore, both the author's and the reader's background will influence the resulting communciation.

To illustrate the importance of both author and reader interaction, ask students to read several examples of different kinds of writing—a piece of fiction, an encyclopedia entry, an advertisement, a feature article in a newspaper, a poem, etc.

Have students answer from the following questions those which seem appropriate for each piece of writing suggested above:

What is the author's purpose?
What might be a reader's purpose?
What is my purpose? (What is *this* reader's purpose?)
Does the author's background make his/her message valuable?
To what audience is the book directed?
Does a reader need additional background knowledge to fully comprehend the message?
Do I have the right background knowledge?
Is the message effectively and objectively presented?
Does this writing answer my question(s)?
Does this writing fit my mood?
Am I being influenced unfairly?

To Tell the Truth

In the early years of school, students read a great deal of fantasy. Animals in many stories dress and communicate like humans and often perform impossible feats. Although most students readily recognize that what they are reading is not real—i.e., monkeys don't talk in real life even if Curious George does—there are finer distinctions of reality that students should be encouraged to note. Much of the message and many of the characters' actions and thoughts in fictional stories (fantasy as well as realistic fiction) are real. Students might analyze stories to discover what is real and what is fantasy.

To illustrate how elements of reality are usually a part of fiction, demonstrate at the board a familiar story such as *The Three Pigs,* charting incidents of character and plot.

Reality	Fantasy
a mother leaving her children alone and telling them not to let anyone in	pigs speaking English
brothers disagreeing and each doing his own thing	pigs building homes with front doors and chimneys
brick is stronger than mud or straw	a wolf blowing a house down
one brother can be more sensible than the other two	a wolf knowing to enter a house by the chimney
boiling water can injure badly	pigs putting a pot of boiling water in the fireplace
brains can overcome physical strength and size	pigs outwitting wolves in the manner related
it often doesn't pay to take the easy way out	

Fact and fiction intermingle in other ways as well. Although the plot and characters are fictitious, sometimes the historical and geographical information is fact. Robert Lawson's *Ben and ME* (1939) relates real events from Benjamin Franklin's life as seen by a mouse. *Make Way for Ducklings* (Robert McCloskey) describes factual territory familiar to anyone living in the Boston area and yet ducks talk and act in ways that we normally attribute only to humans.

Finally, we can designate works as primarily fact or fiction. Comparing two books on the same topic, one factual and one fiction such as Charles P. Graves' *Benjamin Franklin, Man of Ideas* and Lawson's *Ben and ME,* can help students to recognize the differences and to appreciate the advantages of each.

I Believe That Is a Fact

1. To illustrate differences between factual statements (those that can be verified—proven true or false) and opinions (statements based on feelings or attitudes), look around the classroom and have students supply facts and opinions, discussing their identifying characteristics.

Examples: We can write on the blackboard.
We think the blackboard is large.

Although a good hint about whether or not a statement is fact or opinion is to have students check for words that usually signify opinion (*appear, believe, could, think, seem, perhaps, probably, possibly, in all likelihood*), sometimes these words are included in factual statements.

Example: The kindergarten children at Franklin School believe that the world is flat.

Pearson and Johnson (1978) note that statements containing adjectives related to quality (beauty, etc.) rather than quantity (a number), general statements, and those containing emotion-laden words are apt to be opinions. But often remarks can be considered as either fact or opinion.

Examples: Our high school is the best in the state.
Cancer researchers have made great strides in the last ten years.

2. Students should recognize that author-stated opinions do not necessarily equal bad writing. Some opinions are based on fact and are worthy of note; others are totally unsubstantiated. Students need to make judgments about the merit of opinions after recognizing that a statement is indeed an opinion.

3. Writing up an incident both as a news story and as an editorial to make a point (a high-school student driving while drunk is killed) helps students to understand the differences between fact and opinion, and highlights examples of their use.

Word Power

The author's purpose in writing determines the kind of language used. When the object is to entertain or amuse the reader, the writer may play with words or make use of puns as in Amelia Bedelia stories (Parish). When the purpose of the writing is to persuade, language with good and bad connotations is used. (See Namecalling below, also see Chapter Six for a discussion of denotative and connotative meanings).

1. Have students write alternative ways of saying things to show the power of language in influencing feelings.

Example: The child left.
The pouting, whining brat left.
The adorable angel of a girl left.
The nice young lady left.

Discuss the reactions of a reader to the various versions supplied. Show how certain words evoke predictable emotions or feelings and that authors use these words intentionally. In *Reptiles Do the Strangest Things,* the authors Leonora and Arthur Hornblow comment, "Only one kind of reptile carries his house on his back. That is the wonderful turtle" (p. 28). The use of the word *wonderful* immediately identifies the writers' bias and certainly can be an influence on how readers of this chapter henceforth regard turtles.

2. Ask students to bring in menus from a number of restaurants. Show how the language used in the descriptions of the same dish can affect one's perception and consequently, desire, to order a particular offering.

You Can Fool Some of the People...

Acquaint students with well-known propaganda techniques. Those usually cited are:

1. *Namecalling:* Using a label without substantiating facts for a person or a product, the author hopes the connotation of the label will transfer. "Glad names" (S/he's a beautiful person) or "bad names" (S/he's a gossip) may be used.
2. *Testimonials:* Using celebrities to endorse ideas, people, or products, the author hopes the appeal of the celebrity rather than his or her expertise will sell the product. Well-known sports figures are used for numerous food and automobile advertisements.
3. *Transfer:* Similar to testimonials, a respected object or symbol (the American flag, for example) is used with a product in the hope that feelings for the object will transfer to the product.
4. *Bandwagon effect:* When readers are told everybody's doing it, they feel they too must join the crowd. This is a technique espoused by most teenagers when dealing with their parents.
5. *Plainfolks:* The writer is appealing to the common man. Political candidates often speak of themselves as "a man of the people."
6. *Card stacking:* Statistics are presented in a manner that favors a desired conclusion. "Four out of five doctors whose patients chew gum prefer Chew-Rite." The general impression is one of four-fifths of all doctors, whereas perhaps only one in ten of all doctors or four out of the five doctors they have selected are represented.

7. *Glittering generalities:* No hard facts support the thesis. "This car is spectacular. You'll feel wonderful driving the new Cosmos. Buy it!" "What is spectacular about it?" we hope students will ask.

Having students identify television or newspaper and magazine ads that use these techniques helps students to recognize them more deftly in the future. Writing ads for imaginary products demands that students understand the emotions and attitudes to which they are appealing.

As with opinions, not all propaganda is bad but students should be aware of when it is used so that they may intelligently decide to accept or reject what is advocated. Nardelli (1957) showed that teaching sixth-grade students about the seven propaganda techniques explained above did in fact result in increased ability to recognize these techniques in a testing situation. He cautions, however, that this does not necessarily mean that students are therefore less resistant to propaganda. It is our hope that increased awareness will lead to stronger defenses as well.

ACTIVITIES INDEX

PROPAGANDA POINTS
IS THAT A FACT?

REFERENCES

Baldwin, R. Scott, and John E. Readence, "Critical Reading and Perceived Authority," *Journal of Reading,* April 1979, pp. 617–22.

DeBoer, John J., "Teaching Critical Reading," *The Elementary English Review,* October 1946, pp. 251–54.

Galdone, Paul, *The Three Pigs.* Boston: Houghton Mifflin Co., 1970.

Graves, Robert, *Benjamin Franklin, Man of Ideas.* New York: Garrard Press, 1960.

Heilman, Arthur; Timothy Blair, and William Rupley, *Principles and Practices of Teaching Reading.* New York: Holt, Rinehart, and Winston, 1981.

Hornblow, Leonora and Arthur, *Reptiles Do the Strangest Things.* New York: Random House, 1970.

Lawson, Robert, *Ben and ME.* Boston: Little, Brown, and Co., 1939.

McCloskey, Robert, *Make Way for Ducklings.* New York: Viking Press, 1941.

Nardelli, Robert R., "Some Aspects of Creative Reading." *Journal of Educational Research,* March 1957, pp. 495–508.

Parish, Peggy, *Amelia Bedelia.* New York: Harper and Row, various publication dates.

Patching, William, et al., "Direct Instruction in Critical Reading Skills," *Reading Research Quarterly,* Summer 1982, pp. 406–18.

Pearson, P. David and Dale D. Johnson, *Teaching Reading Comprehension.* New York: Holt, Rinehart, and Winston, 1978.

Schoenknecht, Charles A., *Frogs and Toads.* Chicago: Follett Publishing Co., 1960.

Ungerer, Tomi, *Crictor.* New York: Scholastic Book Services, 1958.

Worden, Thomas W., "Can Critical Reading Skills Be Measured?" *Reading Improvement,* Winter 1981, pp. 278–286.

Ten

Problems with Obtaining and Remembering Information from Text

SKILL DESCRIPTION

In order to do well in school, a student must demonstrate that s / he has learned the concepts and facts of a subject and also can apply this knowledge. Special strategies are required for gathering information from printed sources and, for those of us without photographic memories, additional strategies help us remember the information. These strategies are called study skills.

The study skills we use vary according to specific tasks. In textbook reading, for instance, to distinguish the main idea from supporting details requires perusal of headings and topic sentences for the literal main idea. On the other hand, the creation of a category which encompasses the details of a selection is necessary in the case of an inferred topic. To store the main idea for later use, a reader may make use of a written summary paragraph. However, to retrieve the details during a test, acronyms (e.g., FACE identifies the notes in the spaces of printed music while the phrase "*Every good boy does fine*" helps us remember the notes on the lines) can help.

Other abilities, those that help students make use of reference materials, are included among the study skills. Dictionaries, encyclopedias, atlases, and almanacs, while not strictly classroom materials, demand special reading techniques.

We have limited the strategies in this chapter to those associated with learning from text. Omitted are those necessary for taking lecture notes, budgeting time, or writing a term paper. Surely, these are important skills but less directly related to reading. Those we do discuss are divided into three categories when describing techniques for remediation: (1) information-gathering processes such as outlining, (2) storage techniques such as summarizing, and (3) retrieval strategies, one of which is category structuring.

POSSIBLE REASONS FOR SKILL DEFICIENCY

1. Students may not have had study skill instruction. Like comprehension, study strategies often are not taught directly. Teachers may say "read Chapter Ten and be ready for a quiz," not realizing that students haven't a notion of how textbook reading differs from processing stories or how to organize the material for later study and recall. Even when some study skills have been taught, others may have been neglected.

2. Students may have had limited exposure to expository writing. In the primary grades, most reading is fiction which ill prepares intermediate students for the demands of textbook reading and reporting. The content in texts is more objective, and students often lack the background of experiences which ease comprehension. Vocabulary and concept load is usually denser than that found in fiction, and readers are well-advised to "think like a scientist" when reading science texts, for example.

Moreover, with nonfiction, students must work harder at organizing information. Whereas most fictional stories follow a temporal sequence, history texts, for example, may follow a cause-and-effect sequence.

3. Directed reading, the primary instructional mode used in the elementary grades, involves oral discussion which allows students to respond selectively to those questions they know or are interested in, leaving unknown answers to other students. Written questions and chapter tests that accompany text learning in the middle grades place new demands on readers.

4. Students with reading or writing deficits of any kind often have problems with learning from text. Study skills assume competence in the written language for tasks such as summarizing and note-taking. When students have difficulty with either reading or writing, you can be sure merging them will be difficult.

5. The ability to use study skills may be developmental in nature. Such skills require awareness of one's own mental processes and the ability to regulate them. Sometimes termed *metacognition,* this means knowing whether you have understood and/or remembered text material and what to do if you haven't. Researchers studying metacognition believe it develops with age (Brown, 1980). Students who haven't acquired study skills even with good teaching may not yet have reached this stage.

6. It is often less difficult to "sell" a student on the merits of a story than it is to motivate the reading of a textbook chapter. The abstractness of content, the greater vocabulary load, and the responsibility for reporting on or being assessed about what has been read demand greater efforts from readers. Remedial students with a record of some failure with easier, less demanding reading tasks will need to make even greater efforts than average students. Therefore, a remedial teacher's motivation techniques must be commensurately larger.

SELECTED DIAGNOSTIC PROCEDURES

CASE STUDY*

Study skills are often assessed by the use of informal teacher-made or published inventories. The test below samples a student's ability to use a table of contents, a key skill in being able to read a textbook. It was administered to Garrett, a fourth-grade student who has poor achievement in most subjects.

*See Introduction for Function of Case Study.

Information Location Test Level 1†
Sample Table of Contents

Part A—Write the page number for the chapter that probably tells you about the following things.

1.	Indian medicine	56
2.	A famous battle	no response ✗
3.	The earliest Indians	8
4.	Pictures by Indians	23 ✗
5.	Agreements signed with Indians	8 ✗
6.	How Indians live now	112
7.	Games Indians played	8 ✗
8.	Jobs of an Indian woman	50
9.	Ways Indians wrote things down	23
10.	How a brave caught meat	42

According to these test results, Garrett's major problem with approaching a table of contents is that he uses it as he would an index. That is, he seems to expect a match, or one-to-one correspondence between the way the topic to be researched and the book chapter titles are phrased. When a key word in the topic was found in the chapter title, Garrett matched them regardless of underlying ideas. For example, for "4. Pictures by Indians," Garrett chose page 23 (Chapter 3) probably because the word "picture" appears in the chapter title.

Garrett needs instruction in distinguishing the tasks associated with index and table of contents usage. For example, "games" would be listed in an index, even if the chapter title for that idea were *Indian Sports* since the detail "games" would be found in that chapter. Indexes are comprised of both details and main ideas while tables of contents list only the latter.

Other Assessments

1. *Stanford Reading Diagnostic Tests,* Karlsen, Bjorn et al. New York: Psychological Corporation, 1976.
   Subtests: Brown and Blue levels, Skimming and Scanning

2. *BRIGANCE Diagnostic Inventory of Basic Skills.* Woburn, MA: Curriculum Associates, 1977.
   Subtests: Reference Skills (criterion referenced)

3. Warncke, Edna Wagstaff, and Dorothy A. Shipman, *Group Assessment in Reading.* Englewood Cliffs, NJ: Prentice-Hall, Inc., 1984. (Chapter 4.)

†Gwenneth Rae and Thomas C. Potter, INFORMAL READING DIAGNOSIS: A Practical Guide for the Classroom Teacher 2nd Ed., © 1981, pp. 119–121. Reprinted by permission of Prentice-Hall, Inc., Englewood Cliffs, N.J.

Laying Foundations

Before students can outline, it is necessary that they be able to distinguish between the main idea and details of a selection. This is a literal skill when authors include headings or topic sentences in textbook writing. But such explicit information is often absent from expository writing and main ideas often need to be inferred, usually by giving a category name or phrase to the details of a selection. The following strategies will help students distinguish main ideas from details:

1. *Telegrams*—This activity asks students to reduce the information in a selection to essentials so that it may be sent in telegram form. Explain how much it costs to send a telegram and give the students a budget to stick to. Let them see, too, how details add needed clarity and sometimes essential data.

Information	Budget	Telegram
Cousin Denise and Aunt Fay expect to take the ten o'clock shuttle out of Dulles Airport and will arrive in Philadelphia at 10:52. Please pick them up at the airport.	@ 20¢ a word $2.20	Denise and Fay taking ten o'clock flight. Meet them at 10:52.
	@ 20¢ a word $1.20	Meet Denise, Fay at airport 10:52.

2. *Categories*—Give students (a) lists of related words without their topic label, which they will supply. Move on to (b) related sentences that require a subheading and then to related paragraphs. When the latter text unit is used, we call this titling stories. Many teachers like to take newspaper articles or old basal stories and delete the title. An important adjunct to this activity is a discussion with students about the "why" of their choices. If possible, have them explain their reasoning, and if this proves difficult, explain your choice—model your thinking processes for them.

(a) ?＿＿＿＿＿?   (b) ?＿＿＿＿＿＿＿?

setter
poodle
terrier
shepherd

Some hypnosis is a condition of detachment. The everyday world fades and a new frame of reference becomes the focus of attention, and an altered state of consciousness or trance results. Under another form of hypnosis, the subjects seem asleep but can talk. In still other cases the subject seems wide awake and even responds more quickly than usual.

3. *Names of...* —The reverse of "Categories," this oral activity, a kind of chant, asks students to come up with the probable details of a main idea. The chant has four beats: First the players slap hands on thighs, next clap hands together, then snap right fingers and then left fingers. With the first round of finger snapping, students recite "Concentration," with the second round, "names of" and with the third round, one student chooses a category, for example, *dogs*. Now each player in turn names a member of the category, saying the name in time to the finger snapping (slap, clap, snap, snap). Now each player in turn names a member of the set (setters, terriers, etc.). When a player fails to name one, he drops out of the game. The last player left is the winner.

"Names of...." can also be played in a written game form we call STORM. (See the Activity Index.)

Building Outlines

Written outlines are particularly useful because they bridge the gap between all phases of study from information gathering to storage to retrieval. The outlining habit, too, is an excellent way to approach expository writing instruction.

Outlining should flow naturally from distinguishing main ideas and details. It takes many forms, most of which are quite similar. Of course, students and their teachers can use or create their favorites. We like using the initial letters of the main idea (MI) and detail (D) with subscripts to help remind students of the concept behind outlining:

$$MI_1$$
$$D_1$$
$$D_2$$
$$MI_2$$
$$D_1$$
$$D_2$$
$$D_3$$

At first, outlines should be created from brief selections that have clearly stated main ideas found either in subheadings or topic sentences, and evident supporting details:

> Gravity is a force that pulls everything toward the center of the earth. It is hard to lift a heavy package because gravity pulls it down. When you throw a ball up into the air, gravity brings it back down. It is easier to run downhill with the help of gravity than it is to run uphill with gravity working against you. In fact, if it wasn't for gravity, you'd float off into space. Gravity is the force that allows us to keep our feet firmly planted on the earth.

To begin the instructional sequence in outlining, you may wish to present a nearly completed outline to students, and then gradually withdraw the amount of information provided. If the selection above were used in a first lesson, the outline in (a) would be appropriate, the blank lines representing what students need to supply. Samples of what students would fill in if the selection were presented in subsequent lessons are found in (b) and (c).

(a)
MI_1 _____

D_1 It makes heavy things hard to lift.

D_2 When you throw something up, it will come down.

D_3 Going downhill is easier than coming up.

D_4 It keeps us from floating away from the earth.

(b)
MI_1 Gravity pulls things to the center of the earth.

D_1 It makes heavy things hard to lift.

D_2 _____

D_3 Going downhill is easier than coming up.

D_4 _____

(c)
MI_1 _____

D_1 _____

D_2 When you throw something up, it will come down.

D_3 _____

D_4 _____

When the main idea is inferred, as in the next selection, students may be required at first to choose among sentences, phrases, or titles (a), and eventually create them on their own (b).

Why not turn off a light if it's not in use? People can walk or use public transportation instead of driving everywhere. They can keep their house temperatures at a reasonable 67 degrees, and take a hot shower instead of a hot bath. Watching less television and reading more could save large amounts of fuel as well.

    (a) Choose the best topic sentence for this paragraph:
       (1) Americans need more physical exercise.
       (2) There are many steps to take to ease our fuel crisis.
       (3) Good conservation habits start in the home.
    (b) Write a good title for this paragraph.

What's in a Textbook?

The format of textbooks is relatively consistent across subject areas and grade levels—that is, there is usually a preface, table of contents, index, glossary, and a list of references. To get the most from a text, students should make use of these aids.

Probably the most useful technique for teaching such skills is the same one used to assess presence or absence of the skill—teacher-made questions about the content of a particular text which require using pertinent text features (see Diagnostic Procedures). Examples are:

(Table of Contents)	1. In what chapter can you find information about holidays?
(References)	2. Name two other books you might look at to compare information about the treatment of heart disease.
(Index)	3. What pages in this text deal with adoption?

How To Read a Textbook Chapter

Like the format of an entire text, individual text chapters have a structural similarity that allows use of a single approach for getting the most from them. There have been many techniques created to help students extract information from text chapters. Two of the acronyms of such approaches and their expanded titles are the ubiquitous SQ3R (*S*urvey, *Q*uestion, *R*ead, *R*ite / *R*ecite, *R*eview—Robinson, 1970) and PARS (set *P*urpose, *A*sk questions, *R*ead to answer, and *S*ummarize—Tonjes and Zintz, 1981). Our contribution to these systems is GRUNT (*G*uess what this chapter is about, *R*ead to check your guesses, *U*ncover the truth, *N*otetake, *T*est yourself).

Most important is not the differences between systems—their similarities are evident. What counts is that they give students something active to do when they approach texts, and bolster confidence about probable success with the material. Moreover, like outlining, parts of the system are written (write, summarize, notetake) and therefore can be stored for later retrieval.

In our experience, one difficult task for students is taking the content obtained from a survey of the chapter and turning it into questions or hypotheses to be confirmed by careful reading. To help students with that step, try one or two of these options with, for example, the subheading *The life cycle of a frog*.

Option 1. Just place a question mark at the end of the statement: The life cycle of a frog?

Option 2. Place the words "What is" at the beginning of the statement: What is the life cycle of a frog?

Option 3. Create a cloze statement: The life cycle of a frog _____

Graphically Speaking

Not only does the format of textbook chapters need special attention, but so too do the graphic or visual aids that are plentiful in expository writing. Usually students have had picture-reading experiences, but most often the illustrations in children's stories present the information representationally—that is, with the objects and persons children are familiar with rather than symbolically, as with bar graphs, maps, and cross-sections of plants. Instruction to gain facility with graphic aids is necessary for all readers; but, as usual, the remedial learner needs the most practice. Here are some suggestions:

1. Use the students' interests and immediate environment as data for class-made visual aids. For example, make graphs of students' shoe sizes, pets, ball team loyalties, and the like. Start with picture graphs, since those most closely resemble story illustrations, and then move ahead to bar and line graphs. Maps of the students' classroom, school block, or neighborhood should precede those of city, country, and continent.

2. To remove students one step from familiar contexts, have them make graphics that re-express information from familiar stories. Have them chart, for instance, how many siblings each of their favorite story characters has or diagram a floor plan of their favorite story family's home.

Finally, though, students must deal with totally decontextualized graphics; little personal or story experience can be brought to bear on textbook visuals. What follows are some suggestions to make that task easier.

3. Explain to students how diagrams usually represent a portion of a whole. The following diagram which depicts how a steam engine works is really a piece of the whole steam engine, and a cross-section at that. Moreover, scale considerations need to be noted.

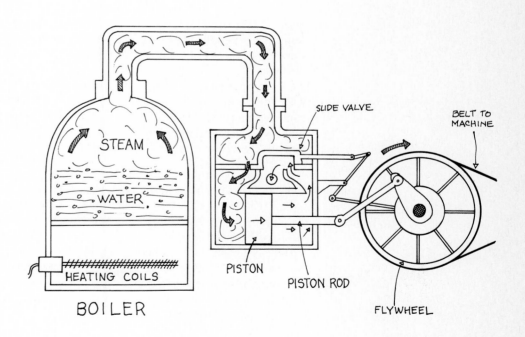

4. Tables, like the one below, are scanned differently from connected discourse. Row and column perusal need to be explained; otherwise, the untrained student may read the top and subsequent lines of chart titles straight across.

KIND OF MODEL	SOURCE OF POWER	SPEED OF TRAVEL FAST MEDIUM SLOW			DISTANCE OF TRAVEL (IN FEET)
CAR	COILED SPRING	X			35
BOAT	RUBBER BAND			X	10

5. Reading quantitative measures such as circle graphs is best shown by use of the "pie technique." Get a pie or other three-dimensional circular object and divide it up. Then move to a cut-out circle and finally a circle drawn on paper. Or take blocks and stack them in varied-size columns, one block representing each counted item. Then on a large piece of chart paper, trace the columns from the blocks. Finally, draw the bar graph directly on a smaller sheet of paper, reducing the column sizes proportionately.

6. Maps are, perhaps, the most difficult of all visual displays to comprehend since we never see the whole (city, country, continent) that the picture represents. For most of us, in fact, our inner perception of the United States probably looks very much like that puzzle map we worked on as children—pink, blue, and light green!

Nevertheless, finding locations, measuring distances, and interpreting legends are essential map-reading tasks. Each map or atlas uses its own set of symbols or abbreviations that depend on what is portrayed on the map. However, lines for roads, dots and stars for cities, blue symbolizing water, compass points, and a scale of miles seem to be universal.

Comparing map types is a technique that allows students to compare a text map with those found in other sources, particularly atlases. Atlases provide opportunities to compare map types of the same region—topological, population, animal, human, plant, weather, and production maps are examples. Have students identify places by matching a written description to several maps of the same area:

a. Find a city in the Southeastern United States in an area covered by standing water 10 to 50 percent of the time. You can travel there by car, south on Route 26. Many earthquakes have occurred there. The average family income in this city in 1959 was $4569. Current population is about 79,500.

b. Compare wildlife and human population maps of Australia to see which animals live closest to big cities and which live in areas of sparse human habitation.

c. Compare a modern map of Israel with one of the same area during the reign of King David. Are cities in the same locations and have place names changed? Note similarities and differences.

Atlases that provide answers to these and other like assignments are:

National Atlas of the United States of America. Washington, D.C.: United States Department of the Interior Geological Survey, 1970.

National Geographic Atlas of the World. Washington, D.C.: National Geographic Society, 1981.

Nayman, Jacqueline, Atlas of Wildlife. New York: John Day Co., 1972.

Rand McNally Road Atlas. Chicago: Rand McNally, 1983.

Reader's Digest Atlas of Australia. Sydney, Australia: Reader's Digest Services, 1977.

Terrier, Samuel, *The Golden Bible Atlas.* New York: Golden Press, 1964.

Looking It Up

In order to expand on information available in a text, it is necessary that students use reference books, particularly encyclopedias and dictionaries, along with other non-fiction sources. To make such books attractive for use, try introducing "fun" references first. *The Guiness Book of World Records, The Book of Lists,* and *The Baseball Almanac* are three well-known sources and the list below presents some reference books of this kind especially prepared for young readers:

Disney's Wonderful World of Knowlege. The Danbury Press, 1973.

Elwood, Ann, et al., *Illustrated Almanac for Kids.* New York: Macmillan, 1981.

McLoone-Basta, Margo, and Alice Siegel, *The Kids' Book of Lists.* New York: Holt, Rinehart & Winston, 1980.

Zimmerman, Jerry. *Book of Records.* New York: Platt & Munk, 1977.

Also motivating and important to master are nonschool references such as the phone book, cookbooks, and *TV Guide.* When students have enjoyed working with these references, more traditional school and library sources can be introduced.

Our Friend, Noah Webster

Special skills are necessary to make maximum use of a dictionary. Alphabetization usually comes to mind for one must first locate a word before reading its definitions. The remedial teacher should, however, be cautious about a plethora of activities for developing alphabetization. Remember that we are not training file clerks. Being able to alphabetize to the second letter is probably sufficient for remedial readers using abridged dictionaries. A little time spent scanning up and down columns of words isn't lost if, in the process, a student can uncover a word or two he or she didn't but always wanted to know.

However, when time is short, guide words can be helpful. Have students decide whether a particular word, let's say "heathen," can be found on a page with certain guide words, let's say "heater" and heather." Then reverse the process and have students make up probable guide words for the page on which one would find the entry for "basket." Explain the whys of right and wrong answers. Require functional rehearsals: (1) look up real entries and note the guide words, and (2) find actual guide-word pairs and note entries between them. This is recommended over the practice of alphabetizing lists of words to the third or fourth letter.

The more important skill in using dictionaries is being able to distinguish among available definitions for any entry. Students can:

1. Provide illustrations for varied definitions of one word:

    (a) run (in stocking)   (b) run (for president)

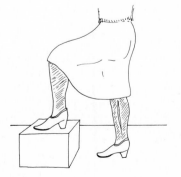
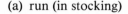

(c) run (an elevator)   (d) run (move fast)

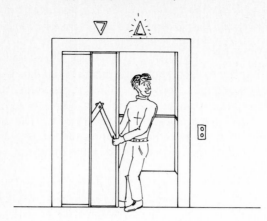

2. Urge students to use synonyms located in a dictionary or thesaurus for an overused word in a text or composition. To exaggerate the result of word overuse, try a selection like this:

Too Much Niceness To Be Nice

> One nice day, a nice man named Neil was waiting for his nice daughter Nancy in a nice park. Nancy had taken Neil's nice car and had gone to buy a nice dress. While waiting, Neil sat on a nice park bench to eat a nice lunch.

3. Play fictionary—Give students a sample dictionary entry with multiple definitions, one of which is false and has been created by you. See if they can find the fictional definition by (a) choosing what they think is the made-up definition, and, (b) checking their hypothesis with a dictionary.

Example: stand a. be upright on one's feet. Don't *stand* if you're tired.
                b. to attach. *Stand* these papers with a clip or staple.
                c. be in a certain place. Columns *stand* on either side of the door.
                d. a group of growing trees. Choose your Christmas fir from that *stand* of trees.

4. Give students sentences containing several meanings of a target word. Have them match each one to the appropriate dictionary definition. They can refer to definitions by number if you wish to minimize the writing associated with this activity.

Sentences	Definitions
a. The horses *draw* the heavy wagon.	1. gather
b. *Draw* fifty dollars from your bank account.	2. take out
c. It is difficult to *draw* conclusions from the little that you told me.	3. sketch
d. That juggler can sure *draw* a crowd.	4. pull
e. That artist can sure *draw* a crowd.	5. infer

5. Let students discover the fun that dictionaries can be. When unabridged, dictionaries are multipurpose references. Foreign language sections, a list of given names with etymologic information, atlases, symbol dictionaries (♋ = astrological Cancer; ⁒ = a split in bowling) may hold fascination for youngsters along with those detailed engravings of esoteric machinery and rarely seen animals. Dictionaries *are* appropriate for recreational reading!

Encyclopedias

These reference books are often misused even by the best of students, and remedial learners especially can be quite tempted to copy whole selections to use in classroom reports. Naturally, it is important to urge youngsters to use their own words.

That this is difficult for most elementary grade children has been pointed out by Dohrman (1974), among others. Encyclopedias are written at a level that makes them extremely difficult to understand, especially for remedial readers. If they must be used, however, Yonan's (1982) suggestions for neophyte researchers make sense for remedial learners too:

1. Start with report topics like animals because encyclopedia articles about them tend to be short and easy.
2. Have students use the first person ("Hello, I'm a fiddler crab") since it makes verbatim copying difficult and makes for more interesting (and we might add, amusing) reports.
3. Maximize comprehension of articles by requiring an advance organizer in anticipation of the reading task, listing everything already known about the topic.
4. Encourage students to improve on encyclopedia language by asking them "How can you make this shorter, clearer, and more interesting?"
5. At first, allow students to report on most interesting rather than most important facts since they have an unerring instinct for the interesting and only a rudimentary sense of the important.

It is also important to point out to students that encyclopedia content, though factual, is written by one author who sees the topic subjectively through her eyes and the sources available to her and for that reason is not exhaustive. Other references must be used in conjunction with an encyclopedia. After students select a topic from an encyclopedia volume, have them go to the card catalog and find at least two sources on the same topic and compare information. What do the books relate that the encyclopedia does not and vice versa? You may wish to employ this chart:

	Encyclopedia	Other Source 1	Other Source 2
Same			
Different			

Storing Information

After information from expository text has been gathered, it may be necessary to store it for a written report, oral discussion, or test. The storage techniques below have been shown to increase memory for text. Because retention is a highly individual matter, it may take a while to find the best-fitting method for each student. It is recommended that you ask a student to describe, if possible, how he best remembers something, giving several of the alternatives in this section as stimuli. But remember that describing one's own thinking processes is an advanced skill (Brown, 1980) and, moreover, that students may respond with inaccurate self-reports.

Outlines Before or After?

Have students outline a selection (or give them your outline of the content) in advance and attempt to memorize it before reading. This technique has been shown to increase memory for details (Gutherie, 1978). If inferencing is the goal of instruction, giving an outline or requiring one of students after their reading is recommended.

Highlight the Highlights

Tell students in advance which are the important ideas in a selection they are about to read. Have them mark, in pencil if this is a school text, these important ideas as they read by underlining or via marginal notes. Afterwards, have them reread the marked sections as many times as they like until they feel they know the material. A brief quiz will show students if the number of rereadings was sufficient for memorization. Later, to gain more independence in this skill, students can decide what the important ideas are as they read, mark them, and in a discussion be helped to decide if these are, indeed, the most important ones, and then commit them to memory via rereadings.

Note Taking

The form of appropriate note-taking depends, in part, on the kind of material used. Students can mark in texts that they own or on xeroxed or dittoed material but must use notebooks for school-owned texts. It seems wise to teach underlining or highlighting and marginal note taking so that students have a number of options. Whichever system is used, check notes that students have made to be sure that important ideas are noted and ancillary information is omitted. Because students often highlight information that interests them in addition to or instead of that which represents central thoughts, you may wish to require two-color ink or two-column notes—one color (column) for main issues, and another for personal interests.

If students use an outline or SQ3R to help with information gathering, the outline or written answers taken down during that process will serve as notes. When the material is unsuited to outlining—it is too brief or is fiction—written summaries or precis serve well as notes.

Seeing Aids Remembering

Have students form a visual image of events either in their heads or on paper. When descriptions are available (but illustrations are not) of a character's facial expression or a Puritan's household effects, encourage students to form a mental image by closing their eyes and attempting to "see" the scene complete with action and dialogue. Even better, albeit more time-consuming, is a drawing of the scene by willing and able students.

Our Thanks to the Spider

Another kind of visual image is that which connects words in a diagramlike form called a semantic web. Webs can increase memory for content by providing a framework or schema in which to house details. It is a specific physical arrangement which if pictured can later facilitate retrieval.

A semantic web also activates another memory aid. It seems that connecting two or more ideas in a selection improves memory for them. If a selection topic were "summer food," for instance, relationships from the semantic map below could be drawn several ways.

One could mention that sometimes fresh fruit is used in the creation of cold drinks. Grape or apricot juice, orange soda, and even that slice of lemon in iced tea show that connection. Popsicles, shish-kabob, and corn have similar shapes. The former two foods are prepared on a stick, but only the first is eaten on a stick. Seemingly limitless inventions, whether the creation of causal relationships or simply contrasts and comparisons, make this activity enjoyable as well as memorable.

Slow Down

It is important for students to adjust reading speeds. This approach will be given more attention in the next chapter. Here it will suffice to say that studying is better done at a slower pace than is recreational or even first-time reading of stories or texts in school learning situations.

Relate, If Possible

Have students attempt to assimilate content into their personal life. Content area reading is usually perceived by students as much removed from their lives. If teachers can create prereading activities that prepare students by tapping into their feelings and experiences, the subsequent reading will be more memorable. An example provided by Macklin (1978) is apropos.

In preparing for a selection on the Industrial Revolution, students can be given a list of statements about change to which they react [i.e., "It takes time in order for change to be felt." "Change is generally hard to stop" (p. 214)]. This provides the opportunity to search for and conceptualize what they already know or feel; it activates schema that provide links between the personal and the informative, and makes the content come alive.

Spaced Learning

Putting time between attempts to learn from text seems to increase memory for it (Collins et al., 1981). This is probably because each study session takes place under slightly different personal and environmental conditions, thus creating multiple memories, one for each study attempt. When students later try to retrieve and one memory path is blocked, they can attempt another one.

"Sensible" Learning

This suggestion is similar to spaced learning. Students attempt to remember content by feeding it to memory through several senses or modes. Listening to the information to be learned, given by teacher, studymate, via tape or record represents aural access. Reading about the information or seeing it on video or film provides visual data. Writing notes and outlines or answering study guide questions utilizes a fine motor pathway to memory. Finally, reciting the information aloud to oneself or to a studymate involves yet another communication mode—speaking. This may be an effective channel since it closely resembles teaching, a process we've found to be the best way to learn anything!

Retrieval

The last step in the sequence that begins with information gathering is called retrieval. This refers to the ability to gain access to information stored in memory.

Most strategies for retrieval fall under the heading "associations"—that is, the target information is compared to or associated with other data, usually more memorable or at least more personal than the target information. The more personalized data is joined with the target information during storage and later the former data is recalled first and pulls with it the targeted data.

At times, retrieval strategies are unplanned—a student may remember a word because it was the longest one they learned in a particular lesson. However, planning retrieval strategies takes a bit more work.

If students anticipate the task of retrieval during their information gathering and storage sessions, they'll be halfway home—that is, planning for retrieval or setting up associations in advance is essential. Giving students examples of retrieval strategies is the teacher's job, but students must eventually find their own tricks, associations that work for them. Some strategies that have been useful for many students are:

Spelling "Tricks"

These are good examples of planned retrieval strategies. A song like "There Was a Farmer Had a Dog and Bingo Was His Name-O" helps children spell one of their first words—B-I-N-G-O. "Look" is spelled with two o's, a fact made memorable by turning those o's into eyes which look out at the reader.

Category Structures

To remember a list of words, store it with a category structure. This helps to narrow possible members of the list. For example, when a teacher asks a child experiencing word identification difficulty to remember that "It's that word we had yesterday," she is calling to mind a category of items called "All the words we learned yesterday." That may not seem like much of a clue until you compare it with the categories "All we learned yesterday" or "All the words we learned last week."

Numbers

To help narrow the field of what needs to be retrieved still further, knowing the number of items for recall is also helpful. To remember the names of the New England States, it might help to first identify their number, six.

Acronyms

Using the first letter of each detail to be recalled to form an acronym or other mneumonic can also be helpful. ROY G. BIV helps us to remember the names of the colors in a prism or rainbow. HOMES reminds us of the Great Lakes (Huron, Ontario, Michigan, Erie, and Superior). "Homemade" mneumonic devices aren't as "neat" as ROY G. BIV, but they are equally or even more useful. If, for instance, a student was trying to remember the names of the New England States, he'd store them with the number six and, perhaps, this phrase (accompanied by an illustration if desired)—M & M's RuN for CoVer. (The double M's are Massachusetts and Maine, the R and N represent Rhode Island and New Hampshire, the Co is Connecticut, and the Ver is Vermont.) Although this may seem farfetched to some, the fact that students (perhaps with teachers' help) create the device makes it memorable and fun. The energy involved in the act of creating acronyms is often enough to imprint the information.

ACTIVITIES INDEX

STORM
STUDY SKILLS CROSSWORD

REFERENCES

Brown, Ann, "Metacognition Development and Reading," in Spiro, Rand, et al. (eds.), *Theoretical Issues in Reading Comprehension*. Hillsdale, NJ: Lawrence Erlbaum Associates, 1980.

Collins, Allan, Dedre Gentner, and Andee Rubin, *Teaching Study Strategies*. Report #4794. Cambridge, MA: Bolt, Beranek and Newman, 1981.

Dohrman, Mary H. "The Suitability of Encyclopedias for Social Studies Reference Use in the Intermediate Grades," *Journal of Educational Research,* December 1974, pp. 149–152.

Gutherie, John T., "Remembering Content," *Journal of Reading,* October 1978, pp. 64–66.

Mackin, Michael, "Content Area Reading Is a Process for Finding Personal Meaning," *Journal of Reading,* December 1978, pp. 212–15.

Robinson, Francis, *Effective Study.* New York: Harper and Row, 1970.

Tonjes, Marian J., and Miles V. Zintz, *Teaching Reading / Thinking / Study Skills in Content Classrooms.* Dubuque, IA: William C. Brown, 1981.

Yonan, Barbara, "Encyclopedia Reports Don't Have To Be Dull." *The Reading Teacher,* November 1982, pp. 212–14.

Eleven

Inflexible Reading Rate

SKILL DESCRIPTION

How fast or slow one reads is an issue of two dimensions. First, there are students who read too slowly in all contexts—recreational and text reading among them. As Frank Smith (1979) points out, a slow or word-by-word rate does not allow meaningful chunks of discourse to be passed from short to long term memory, and as a consequence, comprehension suffers. Moreover, as school reading responsibilities increase, these slow readers have difficulty finishing in-school and homework assignments.

Slow reading of all material is often the result of immature word analysis, when the need to decode each word puts primary focus on pronunciation at the expense of fluency, comprehension or rate. Even when decoding is mastered, the slow rate habit picked up during that stage may remain.

The second situation is related to the first in that students may read all material at the same rate, but this time the pace may be consistently average or fast. Because purposes for reading vary with difficulty of material, and with students' familiarity with specific content, the assumption is that reading rates should vary in order to maximize comprehension and retention. Comprehension would be impeded, for example, if a student used a habitual rapid rate with unfamiliar, difficult material.

The following strategies are the ones used by readers with flexible reading rates:

1. Slow down when studying, or reading difficult or unfamiliar material.
2. Speed up when reading easy or familiar material and when skimming, scanning, or reading recreationally.

Successful reading rates are also characterized by fluency—the abilities which make written text sound like natural spoken language during oral reading and allow for the sufficiently rapid silent reading that facilitates comprehension.

POSSIBLE REASONS FOR SKILL DEFICIENCY

1. Beginning or remedial readers who are attempting to master decoding often stop at every word, even those they can read by sight. These students are at a particular stage of reading development (Chall, 1979) when their concentration on word analysis precludes reading either for meaning or fluency. If levels of reading development are viewed as necessary and inevitable, it makes sense to wait until a child achieves approximately fourth-grade reading ability before instruction in rate increase or flexibility is recommended.

2. Using reading machines (those mechanical tachistoscopes that regulate with a light and automatic pacer how much of a line of print can be seen at once) may be detrimental to the development of flexible and effective reading habits and is a poor substitute for effective instruction. There are two reasons for this. The first is that mechanical devices do not allow the eyes to regress, a necessary movement for efficient comprehension. The second is that they promote a uniform rapid rate for all reading material. Once eyes are accustomed to moving at that rate, it is difficult to slow them down for studying, for example.

3. As with study skills and comprehension instruction, little classroom time is usually devoted to instruction in flexible rate. Most students are convinced of the necessity of reading every word, lest they miss something important. This attitude is often unwittingly reinforced by teachers who, when listening to students read aloud, correct them for omitted words or phrases, whether essential to comprehension or not.

4. Often no distinction is made between oral and silent reading speeds. During an oral reading performance every word counts. For silent reading, however, skills like skimming, or even skipping (because you know the content, or because it's boring) make sense. Because children begin their school careers with oral reading, they tend to apply every-word reading to silent tasks as well. Evidence of this can be observed in children who lip read during silent reading. Moreover, some older readers pronounce words internally. This is called subvocalization, and results in an unnecessarily slow silent reading rate.

5. When students with reading problems are given grade level instead of ability level material, they may slow their rate in order to deal with the decoding problems which result from text that is too difficult. Avoiding frustration level material is always important with remedial readers but seems particularly essential when fluency is a goal.

6. Once students are taught to skim or scan materials, some of them overuse these techniques. For example, students may skim stories or chapters that need slow or in-depth processing. Sometimes students who are given comprehension questions before a story read only those sections of it which supply the answers. (This may be appropriate behavior when taking a test, but is limiting when applied to instruction. For more about this, see Appendix A.)

SELECTED DIAGNOSTIC PROCEDURES

To have differing oral and silent reading rates is desirable; silent reading should be faster than oral for it is not dependent upon overt or covert pronunciation (subvocalization), processes which slow reading considerably.

CASE STUDY*

One test which can be used to compare oral with silent reading rates is the Spache Diagnostic Reading Scales.† The chart below shows Dennett's oral and silent rates of speed and comprehension on comparable Spache passages. She is a reading disabled fifth grader.

Passage Number	Passage Readability	Task	Number of Words	Speed in Seconds	Rate of Comprehension
16r	1.6	oral	57	52	100%
16s	1.6	silent	41	17	70%
22r	2.2	oral	81	55	100%
22s	2.2	silent	81	10**/45	15%/85%
28r	2.8	oral	119	102	87%
28s	2.8	silent	112	92	100%

**Because of Dennett's extremely poor comprehension score and unrealistically rapid rate on the first reading of this selection, she was asked to reread it with more serious intent. Her second attempt is more consistent with the results on other passages.

Dennett's oral reading seems to be appropriately slower than her silent rate which, according to Spache (*Examiner's Manual,* Table 4, page 45) is a fast one. At times, however, this faster rate appeared to be at the expense of full understanding since oral comprehension rates dropped 15 percent to 30 percent when passages of equivalent difficulty were read silently (from 100 percent to 70 percent on 16r and 16s respectively, and from 100 percent to 85 percent on 22r and 22s). When Dennett was cautioned to read silently with more care, her rate slowed a bit (from 128 wpm on passage 22s to 72 wpm on passage 28s) and her comprehension improved.

It is interesting to note that Dennett's most successful score in silent reading comprehension (100 percent) occurred with the highest level passage she read for this assessment. In diagnosis, it often happens that an observed pattern, in this case better oral than silent reading comprehension, is reversed in later testing. The reasons for this may come from the following: (1) Has the student finally warmed up? (2) Is the content of the more difficult passage more familiar or more interesting to that student? (3) Is she learning from the test? Any one or even all of these explanations could account for Dennett's performance on the Spache. Further observation is needed to determine whether Dennett's silent rate is overly or inflexibly rapid.

Other Assessments

Gates-McKillop, *Reading Diagnostic Tests.* New York: Teachers College Press, 1962.
    Subtest: Phrase reading

Durrell Analysis of Reading Difficulty. New York: Harcourt Brace Jovanovich, 1980.
    Subtests: Oral and silent reading

Stanford Diagnostic Reading Test, Blue and Brown Levels, Karlsen, Bjorn et al. New York: Harcourt Brace Jovanovich, Inc., 1977.
    Subtests: Skimming, Scanning

TECHNIQUES FOR REMEDIATION

Read in Idea Units

Segment a portion of written discourse into idea units. These are words generally phrased together when read aloud, or held together by punctuation or by phrase or clause characteristics. Show students how word-by-word reading or inappropriate

*See Introduction for function of Case Study.
†Spache, George, *Diagnostic Reading Scales.* Used with permission of the publisher, CTB/McGraw-Hill, Monterey, CA. Copyright ©1981 by McGraw-Hill, Inc.

segmenting can be harmful to understanding (*the quick/brown fox/jumped/over the/lazy dog*). You can mark segments at first and then later allow students to divide text on their own. Segments can be lined up under one another like so:

Example: now is the time
for all good women
to come to the aid
of their gender.

or indicate units by spaces or slash lines in between:

Example: time/like the river/races some/
on downhill stretches/slowing
only/for the fight/with gravity.

Naturally, the second strategy is more like a real reading task, but the first is a good starter for unit reading. Gray (1978) recommends placing a dot at some central point of the meaning unit to aid students' focus *and* peripheral print intake. The size of unit to be viewed depends on reader skill.

Example: Once upon
o
a time
o
in a kingdom
o
by the sea
o
there lived
o
an awful truth
o

Self-Improvement

Instruction in rate lends itself nicely to a unit in reading self-improvement. Since reading rates are timed and can be charted, it is easy to see progress. Students seem to enjoy this sort of self- or group competition. It must be stressed to students, however, that rate increase with an accompanying comprehension decrease is undesirable. A gradual increase in rate is best, so when students are tempted to hit number one on the speed charts, caution them that minimal comprehension rates of 70 to 80 percent are required to chart the increase.

Certain remedial materials lend themselves well to charting rate improvement. In these, selections of uniform length and difficulty are followed by comprehension questions:

McCall, William, and Lelah Crabbs, *Standard Test Lessons in Reading*. NY: Teachers College Press, 1979.
Smith, Nila Banton, *Be a Better Reader,* Basic Skills Edition. Englewood Cliffs, NJ: Prentice-Hall, Inc., 1977.
Reader's Digest, *Reading Skill Builders*. Pleasantville, NY: Reader's Digest Services, Inc., 1977.

Fast or Slow?

Urge students to take it slow on difficult material but speed up when the reading is easy. To raise their consciousness, it may be necessary to show them that their current rate is too uniform. Time students in different reading situations that have varied purposes (i.e., studying, light reading). Together, calculate their words per minute ($\frac{\text{words in selection}}{\text{seconds}} \times 60$) for each reading situation. Words per minute should be lower for the more difficult passages or for studying purposes, but rate of comprehension for any selection or purpose should be at least 70 percent.

Cues

Knowing something about how writing is crafted is important for skimming and scanning, two essential fast reading techniques. Knowing where main ideas are found and how to find signal words are two strategies which allow students to know when one idea is starting and the next beginning. When readers feel they know enough about one idea, they can skip to the next. Smith (1963) has identified many signal words and categorizes them as "go-ahead" or "turn-around" words. The go-aheads such as *more, also, and, therefore, consequently, finally,* and *in conclusion* tell the reader that either there will be another idea coming up or that they are nearing the end. Turn-around words such as *but, not, however,* and *rather* tell the reader that a change of idea or point of view is impending and that they need to pay strict attention again.

Skimming

Often students fear skimming because they believe they are missing something important when they skip words. To prove to them that they can get a wealth of information from skimming, xerox a selection and then blacken every nth word. Raise questions afterwards that can be answered by what information is available in the nonblackened sections. Later, ask other questions that tap on information hidden by the blackened spaces and ask students to make guesses. In some instances, you may need to convince students to be satisfied with comprehension scores that are less than perfect but still acceptable (not less than 70 percent). Explain that skimming is inappropriate in a read-study-test situation since they are then aiming at "perfect" comprehension.

Scanning

Locating specific information within text is simplified and speeded for students who can scan. Show them how to move their index finger rapidly over lists or connected discourse in order to find the key word(s) of the information they need. (Key words are usually the noun alone or noun and verb of a question or idea. "How far did Susan run?" "Susan ran _____.")

The use of practical sources such as phone books and dictionaries and textbook features such as indexes and tables of contents are ideal for beginning scanning instruction because information is found in list form, and there is often a single keyword, usually a noun. In subsequent lessons, the art of transforming questions into partial statements (two to three key words) and looking for them in connected text can be taught.

Eye Span

To help word-by-word readers, it is often necessary to increase their eye span for phrases. The techniques listed under reading in idea units are helpful here, too. It is also recommended that students be shown that their eyes are actually taking in more than the word they believe they are currently processing. To demonstrate that, slam (gently) the book they are reading and have the student finish aloud the line they were on. Students are often amazed to find that their eyes are quicker than either their inner or outer voices.

Sssh

There are a number of strategies for reducing subvocalization during silent reading, thus ensuring a more rapid rate. The push for speed in a self-improvement program, and an emphasis on reading in phrases are two strategies that have been discussed. Another two are similar to each other in that they force the student to abandon movements of the lips or throat because these organs are otherwise engaged. "Bite the bullet" has been recommended by Judson (1972). Here the student gently bites a finger or knuckle or clamps down on a pencil or popsicle stick, thus making lip and tongue movements difficult. To have students discontinue internal pronunciation, have them mumble numbers in order, or say repeatedly a sound like "Z-Z-Z-Z" or even recite a mantra or favorite song lyric or poem. Meanwhile, eyes are moving over the words, attempting to process them via the eye-brain connection, instead of the accustomed eye-voice-brain chain of oral or subvocal reading. At first, students may experience some detachment from the words when they can't hear them internally. Comprehension may suffer initially, but it will soon pick up again.

ACTIVITIES INDEX

GET THE SIGNAL
READING RATE RECORD

REFERENCES

Chall, Jeanne, "The Great Debate: Ten Years Later with a Modest Proposal for Reading Stages," in Resnick, Lauren, and Weaver, Phyllis (eds.) *Theory and Practice of Early Reading.* Hillsdale, NJ: Lawrence Erlbaum, 1979.

Gray, Lee Lerner, *Better and Faster Reading.* NY: Cambridge Book Co., 1978.

Judson, Horace, *The Techniques of Reading.* NY: Harcourt, Brace, Jovanovich, 1972.

Smith, Nila Banton, *Faster Reading Made Easy.* NY: Popular Library, 1963.

Twelve

Disinterest in Reading

SKILL DESCRIPTION

The best instruction in the world is wasted on students who aren't "there." Some of these students, openly hostile, disrupt the classroom. Others may appear attentive but their glassy stares are an attempt to hide disinterest and daydreaming. For still others, basic disinterest in reading limits their ability to translate school learning into a reading habit, thereby limiting their reading achievement and denying the pleasure that reading can afford.

Recently certain educators (e.g., Rosenshine, 1978; Harris, 1979) have reminded us about the importance of academic engaged time, the hours spent attending to textbook and workbook assignments, teacher-directed lessons and sustained silent reading. This academic engaged time, or for our purposes—reading task time—is proportionate to the amount of reading achievement as measured by standardized tests. Here research confirms common sense, but it is important to remember that academic engaged time is not measured by how much of a school day is allotted to reading tasks by the teacher, but rather by how much of that allotted time students are engaged, or attentive. This chapter deals with ways to increase engagement so that good instruction can have its effect.

POSSIBLE REASONS FOR INTEREST DEFICIENCY

1. One group of disinterested readers may have at one time in their school careers been considered good to excellent readers who tackled the demands of elementary reading instruction with ease and may have been enthusiastic consumers of leisure books. At about the middle grades, these good readers often get caught short. At that point reading demands grow to include inferential, critical, and evaluative skills, and careful reading of the content of textbooks which is usually outside their experience. Not to be ignored, too, is the influence of peer culture accompanied by an "addiction"

to TV and to video games. "Hangin' out" consumes a lot of study time, and moreover, it may not be "hip" to like school and/or reading.

2. A second group for whom disinterest is critical are the functionally illiterate. These students have only rudimentary reading skills, and reading for them is always a great effort. Naturally they wish to avoid a failure experience. It is important that their teachers understand that their rejection of reading is a defensive reaction, sour grapes if you will. These students may want very much to read well, but believe it to be impossible. Peer culture operates with this group too in that reading becomes a thing of adulthood and the dominant culture, something to rebel against.

3. Reading disinterest may result from a student's school experience. Dull, routine reading instruction is not uncommon. Kids brought up on the razzle-dazzle of Sesame Street have greater expectations about amusement than generations in the past. Much to our chagrin as educators who believe intrinsic motivation best, entertainment works (Lesser, 1974). The argument that school should be different, challenging and even frustrating at times to offset media influence is valid and persuasive (Postman, 1979) but when dealing with disinterested readers concessions must be made. We have to grab them before we can teach them.

SELECTED DIAGNOSTIC PROCEDURES

It isn't usually necessary to do formal diagnosis to discover reading disinterest. Simple classroom observation will reveal any of these six "warning" signs:

1. Daydreaming during reading instruction.
2. Incomplete book assignments.
3. Disruptive behavior during group oral or silent reading.
4. Difficulty with book choice. Several may be started or skimmed, but none is completed.
5. Frequent statements like "Not that book again!" "I hate reading," "All these books are stupid," "Reading is for wimps" should be taken seriously.
6. Reading activities are never chosen during time allotted for independent, optional work.

An interview may be the best technique, however, for discovering specifically what it is about reading or reading instruction that is boring or repellent to students. Howards (1980) provides an in-depth analysis of the reading diagnostic interview. Ekwall (1976) gives some do's and don'ts for effective diagnostic interviewing. It isn't as easy as asking a few "What's your hobby?" type questions, he explains.

Three of the techniques that Ekwall recommends follow. The fourth suggestion is one which the authors have also found helpful.

1. Use open-ended questions—let the student do most of the talking.
2. Give the interviewee time to think. It may be disquieting at first to have long pauses after your open-ended questions but soon students will "feel sorry" for your mute helplessness, and begin to fill in conversational gaps.
3. Refrain from expressing negative judgments or attitudes. This will close down communication.
4. Don't ask questions about the student's family reading habits or other teachers' instructional foibles. Some students will tell tales while others may react defensively. In either situation, the interviewer is in an awkward position, especially in the beginnings of a relationship with a student.

CASE STUDY*

What follows are brief excerpts from an interview with a reluctant reader, and an interpretation of his responses. Although the oral interview is probably less threatening than a written interest inventory or attitude scale for reading disabled students, written assessments can be handy. This is especially true when evaluating the interests and attitudes of larger numbers of students, or those of able but disinterested readers. Sources for such assessments come after the interview protocol.

Interview with Jaime

Interviewer: Tell me something about yourself.

Jaime: Anything?

I: Anything!

J: (big pause) I like the *Boston Sunday Globe*...I like math...that's it!

I: You don't have to tell me about school. If someone was interviewing you for *The Globe,* what would you say about yourself? How would you describe yourself?

J: Normal. I'm 11. I like the movie "Silver Streak." I like *The Book of Three* and *The Black Cauldron.* I'd like to go to the University of Chicago.

I: Any special reason?

J: Yeah, my brother goes there.

I: Anything else?

J: I like English, sort of. I'd like to be an engineer or doctor. My father is an engineer. I'd like a Rolls-Royce. I don't like horses.

I: I'm interested in why you don't like horses.

J: I can't draw horses.

I: Oh, it's about drawing.

J: Yeah. I like monsters. I made one. What it is, it's kind of disgusting (he looks at interviewer for approval).

I: I don't mind disgusting things.

J: Well, what he does is, he's sort of a see-through monster. You can see all his guts and stuff and all his blood and all his veins. And see he has this sword and the only thing he can live on is kidneys, human kidneys...

The reader will be spared the remains. Jaime followed his description of Boltar with a drawing. This took ten minutes and Jaime seemed hesitant to take up the interviewer's time, but because she was unhurried, Jaime became engrossed in his drawing. Afterward, he was livelier and relaxed. He told the interviewer about the plots and characters of the two Lloyd Alexander books he mentioned at the beginning of the interview. He also told of his dissatisfaction with other fantasy books, which he never finished, and of a comic strip about Boltar he envisioned.

Certain important ideas about Jaime, a reluctant, underachieving sixth grader are revealed in the interview protocol. First, he, or perhaps a parent, is scholastically ambitious. He expects or is expected to do well in and enjoy school. The fact that he does poorly and dislikes school is probably a major disappointment.

Second, Jaime needs an outlet for expressing what he believes to be the negative side of himself—his anger and aggression. Luckily, there are three books remaining in Lloyd Alexander's series about good and evil at war that Jaime has not read yet. After that, perhaps *The Hobbit.*

Other Assessments

1. Brown, Don, *Reading Diagnosis & Remediation.* Englewood Cliffs, NJ: Prentice-Hall, Inc., 1982. Semantic differential scale and sentence completion forms.

*See Introduction for function of Case Study.

2. Lapp, Diane, and James Flood, *Teaching Reading to Every Child*. New York: Macmillan, 1979. Reading attitudes and interest inventories.

3. *Estes Attitude Scales*. Charlottesville, VA: Virginia Research Associates, Ltd., 1976.

4. Warncke, Edna Wagstaff, and Dorothy A. Shipman, *Group Assessment in Reading*. Englewood Cliffs, NJ: Prentice-Hall, Inc., 1984. Chapter 5.

TECHNIQUES FOR REMEDIATION

The following additions and modifications of reading instruction for uninterested readers are divided into (1) those appropriate for the first group of readers discussed above, the average-high achieving middle- and upper-grade students who are unmotivated, (2) the functionally illiterate, and (3) techniques suited to both groups.

Middle-High Achievement—Low Interest

"Shock Therapy"

In general, average and high achieving students have been lulled into confidence about their abilities in reading as well as other subjects by the time they reach the middle grades. Just telling them and their parents that "things are different in junior high school" may have marginal effect. Showing them how things are different is better.

To start, find a passage or story written at the children's instructional reading level. It should be complex in meaning. Raise higher level (inference, critical, evaluative) questions about this material which you believe students will find difficult. Show how to "dig" for answers. Often for the high achieving–low interest child, this challenge sparks interest. An able teacher is then challenged to provide reading that will keep him interested.

Old Techniques in Sheep's Clothing

For college-bound students, study skills are a must. But although many of them have had such instruction before, the skills are yet unmastered. In order to get their attention, it is often necessary to rework the standard techniques for teaching these.

1. An example is what one extraordinary English teacher* calls "Harvard Outlining." Using the terms *sets* and *subsets* for main ideas and details, he puts in a new twist with status attached by linking Harvard's name to the pedestrian skill of outlining.

2. Use of reading pacers is another tool to restimulate interest. These machines are not recommended to increase reading rate, since it has not been sufficiently documented that machine-based increases translate to real reading. But the machines can awaken interest in skimming, and getting central thoughts, particularly of nonfiction material. Use of computers may also.

3. A final idea is the re-dressing of the standard book report. Textbooks on children's literature (Huck, 1976; Sutherland et al., 1981) and journal articles (Mason & Mize, 1975; Crisuolo, 1979) were helpful sources for us when adding to our personal bag of book report alternatives. Several of the best ideas are:

   a. *Use drama*—For example, interview one character from the story, dramatize a favorite portion of a book, arrange a story theater (one reader, others pantomime).

   b. *Re-read*—Exciting sections, or the whole book to younger children or, if polished enough, to the student's peers.

   c. *Book recommendations*—Rate books, use checklists, so that peers get a peek at what's good. (See Activities Index for Rate-A-Read.)

*Many thanks to Alan Goff.

d. *Have student-teacher conferences*—Have student retell favorite parts. Keep teacher questions to a minimum.

e. *Use another reporting or re-experiencing process besides words*—A picture, gather props from story, make a recipe mentioned in story.

Low Achievement, Low Interest

Tender, Loving Care

Students who have repeatedly failed in school need a certain degree of special handling. It is necessary to acknowledge their failure to learn without laying blame, and also important to convince students that you can and very much want to help. Tell it like it is, but immediately hatch a plot for change.

Other evidence of tender, loving care:

1. *Take it easy with corrections*—You or other students should do some correcting but only after discussing the difference between meaning essential and meaning nonessential errors (see Chapter Thirteen).

2. *Use "physical force"*—The force of the caring touch, that is. Students often respond to a hand on their shoulder, accompanied by a word of praise while they're working. Your physical closeness, too, may be sufficient. Get away from the desk and circulate.

High Interest, Low Vocabulary Materials

These especially prepared books, workbooks, kits, and tapes are not for everyone. But for those who accept these materials, they are worthwhile. First, they can provide the independent-level readability that is essential to improved achievement (Harris, 1979). Second, they allow for successful completion since most selections are short and at a low conceptual level. Too, these materials are frequently self-teaching so that individual instruction can occur. Some recommended programs are:

1. *Action* (upper grades) and *Sprint* (middle grades). New York: Scholastic Book Services.

2. *Rally!* (upper grades). New York: Harcourt, Brace, Jovanovich, 1979.

3. *Bridge: A Cross-Cultural Reading Program* (upper-grade black English speakers). Boston: Houghton-Mifflin, 1977.

4. *Reading for Winners* (upper grades). Austin, TX: Steck-Vaughan, 1980.

5. *Vistas* (middle grades). Boston: Houghton-Mifflin, 1979.

Use of High Interest, High Vocabulary Material

Sometimes employing frustration level reading material makes sense, especially when older students are insulted by easy texts. Particularly recommended are trade magazines such as *Hot Rod, Wrestling, Backpacker, High Fidelity,* and *Mademoiselle,* which contain articles and advertisements with adult vocabulary and motivating content. Usefulness of the articles in these magazines is maximized by teacher-directed lessons, with vocabulary and concept development and directed silent or oral reading. Just skimming these magazines may be fun too, and should be allowed on occasion.

Use of Low-Interest, Low-Vocabulary Material

Sometimes students can be convinced that material written at their reading level but below their age level should be read. This is especially needed for vulnerable children for whom mistakes are traumatic and for non-reading adolescents. Roswell and Natchez (1977) suggest that, "In these cases, the teacher explains that the simple books will be discarded as soon as possible" (p. 67).

Other times some upper-grade students can be convinced to perfect the oral reading of a low-level book or story in order to read it to younger children, students in their school or siblings. Cheek and Cheek (1981) describe how fifteen-year-old nonreading boys prepared a dramatization of *The Three Bears* for a kindergarten girl, complete with wigs and costumes. Such fun was had by all that these boys began to take requests for stories.

Why Read?

Reading materials come in three forms:

1. Those contrived to teach children to read. Examples are basal readers, workbooks, and kits.
2. Literature.
3. Functional materials, which exist to inform people and help them make their way in the environment. Examples are advertising copy, maps, menus, tickets, signs, catalogs, instructions, and newspapers.

The use of these latter materials with reluctant readers is advised to show them that reading is useful, purposeful, will increase their competence in their surroundings, and success with these materials may motivate them to go beyond functional reading.

Use of Kits, Games, and Self-Checking Material

Because skill levels are so low with this group, it is imperative to provide for skill practice. This is best accomplished through self-checked and paced work. Kits provide this. Students often feel bored or defensive when presented with teacher-directed lessons on topics they know they should have mastered long ago. Individual work that is self-regulating allows for self-respect. Some well-prepared reading kits in several skill areas are available from:

1. Curriculum Associates
   5 Esquire Road
   N. Billerica, MA 08862
2. Science Research Associates
   259 E. Erie Street
   Chicago, IL 60611
3. Bowmar Noble Pub. Inc.
   4563 Colorado Blvd.
   Los Angeles, CA 90039
4. Barnell Loft, Ltd.
   958 Church Street
   Baldwin, NY 11510

You can also create a "lap pack," so-called because of its size. This teacher-made kit on a single skill combined with a child's interest contains materials individually suited and motivating. This may be the most potent form of remedial material available. Lap packs are worksheets and games, reading selections and puzzles, among other activities, gathered together in a folder to be worked on at a pace and in an order contracted by student and teacher. Materials can come from comic strips, magazines, and the like.

Use of Brief, Frequently Changing Activities

Slow learners, like some preschoolers, have short attention spans. When the traditional academic period is forty minutes, schedule two to three reading activities for that time. Try to alternate active with passive, teacher-directed with independent, silent with oral reading and skills with pleasure-reading components to maintain attention.

Oral Reading

1. *By students*—Although oral reading has come under fire by many reading specialists because it leads to inappropriate silent reading habits and because it is over-used and frequently boring, in certain settings it can be used motivationally. Sometimes students beg to be allowed to read aloud. This may be because it lessens the load they are expected to carry with silent reading. (With five children in a group, for example, only one-fifth of a story is read by any one child.) Or perhaps oral reading maximizes comprehension for some auditory learners.

To improve conditions for oral reading, students who are listening should close or look up from their books so that slow silent reading rates, those which imitate oral reading in a word-by-word manner, won't be reinforced. Also, help with unpronounced words should be supplied quickly by the teachers. Finally, corrections should be made only when meaning is affected by miscues.

2. *By teachers*—Primary teachers are most likely to read to their students. As a motivational tool, reading aloud by the intermediate and secondary teacher as well has clear benefits. If the teacher is careful to (1) choose something to interest kids (see "sure-fire" choices, below) (2) vary selections so that many types of literature are sampled, (3) stop reading before the students get bored, and (4) use his or her dramatic talents, this technique is guaranteed to spark students.

Ready, Set—Let's Read!

Teacher-directed instruction (readiness for new vocabulary, guided silent reading, questions, and other follow-ups), although necessary for developing skills, may not be the best way to engender interest. So, on occasion, let students read without instructional responsibility. This is usually called *uninterrupted sustained silent reading,* or USSR.

Use of "Sure-Fire" Books

Whether students read these silently, or teachers read them aloud, the books below have the seal of approval of educators, librarians, and most importantly, kids. Of course, the list could be longer and not each child will love every book, but if you try these you're bound to have some success. Incidentally, most books by the listed authors are popular.

Middle-Grade Choices

Alexander, Lloyd, *Book of Three.* New York: Holt, Rinehart & Winston, 1964.

Blume, Judy, *Superfudge.* New York: Dutton, 1980.

Cleary, Beverly, *Ramona the Pest.* New York: William Morrow, 1968.

Corbett, Scott, *The Lemonade Trick.* Boston: Little, Brown, 1960.

Hicks, Clifford, *Alvin's Secret Code.* New York: Holt, Rinehart & Winston, 1968.

Juster, Norton, *The Phantom Tollbooth.* New York: Random House, 1961.

Rodgers, Mary, *Freaky Friday.* New York: Harper & Row, 1972.

Sobel, Donald, *Encyclopedia Brown Carries On.* New York: Four Winds Press, 1980.

White, E. B., *Charlotte's Web.* New York: Harper & Row, 1952.

Upper-Grade Choices

Blume, Judy, *Then Again, Maybe I Won't.* Scarsdale, NY: Bradbury Press, 1971.

Bradbury, Ray, *The Martian Chronicles.* Garden City, NY: Doubleday, 1958.

Childress, Alice, *A Hero Ain't Nothin but a Sandwich*. New York: Coward, McCann and Geoghegan, 1973.

Cooper, Susan, *Over Sea, Under Stone*. New York: Harcourt, Brace & World, 1965.

Cormier, Robert, *The Chocolate War*. New York: Pantheon Books, 1974.

Hentoff, Nat, *Jazz Country*. New York: Harper & Row, 1965.

Hinton, S. E., *The Outsiders*. New York: Viking Press, 1967.

Zindel, Paul, *The Pigman*. New York: Harper & Row, 1968.

Media Tie-Ins

The link between TV, movies, and the publishing world is well-established. Students respond to the advertising that accompanies new releases. Therefore, they may be interested in "novelized" scripts or the actual scripts themselves. (A good source for popular television scripts is Capital Communications, Inc., 4100 City Line Avenue, Philadelphia, PA 19131.) Comparing the book and the movie is a good way for students to discover the strengths of the print media. They often find that their image of characters and settings is superior to or at least more personal and satisfying than those depicted in the visual media.

That's Me!

Sometimes, as luck will have it, students will find themselves and/or their life situation in a book. The "shock of recognition" that occurs when book meets boy (or girl) can change a student's relationship to literature. The meeting described above is hard to arrange. But some blind dates do work. It's a matter of knowing student and literature well enough to be a good matchmaker. One resource that helps a teacher make potentially potent choices is Sharon Dreyer's *The Bookfinder: A Guide to Children's Literature About the Needs and Problems of Youth Aged 2–15,* (Circle Ponds, MN: American Guidance Services, Inc. 1977).

ACTIVITIES INDEX

REFERENCES

Cheek, Martha, and Earl Cheek, *Diagnostic-Prescriptive Reading Instruction*. Dubuque, IA: Wm. C. Brown, 1980.

Criscuolo, Nicholas P., "Effective Approaches for Motivating Children to Read," *The Reading Teacher,* February 1979, pp. 543–46.

Ekwall, Eldon E. and James Shanker, *Diagnosis and Remediation of the Disabled Reader*. Boston: Allyn & Bacon, 1983.

Harris, Albert J., "The Effective Teacher of Reading, Revisited," *The Reading Teacher,* November 1979, pp. 135–40.

Howards, Melvin, *Reading Diagnosis and Instruction: An Integrated Approach*. Reston, VA: Reston Publishing Co., 1980.

Huck, Charlotte, *Children's Literature in the Elementary School*. New York: Holt, Rinehart and Winston, 1976.

Lesser, Gerald, *Children's Television: Lessons from Sesame Street*. New York: Random House, 1974.

Mason, George, and John J. Mize, "Twenty-two Sets of Methods and Materials for Stimulating Teenage Reading," *Journal of Reading,* May 1978, pp. 735–41.

Postman, Neil, *Teaching as a Conserving Activity.* New York: Delacorte Press, 1979.

Rosenshine, Barak, "Academic Engaged Time, Content Covered, and Direct Instruction," *Journal of Education,* August 1978, pp. 38–66.

Roswell, Florence, and Gladys Natchez, *Reading Disability.* New York: Basic Books, 1977.

Sutherland, Zena, et al., *Children and Books.* Glenview, IL: Scott, Foresman and Co., 1981.

Thirteen

Speaking Nonstandard English

SKILL DESCRIPTION

As linguists have informed us, everyone speaks a dialect, a language variation which has special phonological, syntactical and semantic qualities. Dialects form(ed) because of closely knit regional and social groupings. Because certain regions or social classes have greater prestige, so too do certain dialects.

Such is the case with standard English, the dialect of the majority of Americans. Use of nonstandard English, the dialect of many black Americans, for example, can stigmatize speakers. Since standard English is the dialect of the mainstream, and of the institutions of the majority, reading teachers have believed that the ability to speak standard English is necessary for reading success.

In recent years that assumption has been questioned. First, because speech is an important part of personal identity, changing or adapting it to meet institutional demands is often traumatic and/or impossible. Moreover, researchers have shown that speaking nonstandard English doesn't usually interfere with comprehension of written standard English (Goodman & Buck, 1973; Melmed, 1973; Lass, 1980). It may, though, (1) disrupt student-teacher communication, (2) give a distorted view of a nonstandard speaker's oral reading ability, (3) occasionally interfere with comprehension, and/or (4) limit student horizons.

POSSIBLE REASONS FOR SKILL DEFICIENCY

Although speaking nonstandard English need not affect learning to read, under certain conditions it can cause problems.

1. When the teacher doesn't accept the child's language and demonstrates this through frequent corrections, the student may believe that the teacher is rejecting him, or his family and friends. Perhaps, too, the child surmises that the teacher is more interested in form than function. If his language is indeed serving him well in non-school situations, he may see the teacher and all of her messages as irrelevant. School will lose value to that student.

2. When the teacher judges the student's reading ability through oral reading alone, she may get an unwarranted picture of depressed reading ability (Hunt, 1976) particularly when the student's miscues are dialect related. Either those miscues should be discounted and/or a nonoral assessment technique used.

3. When a student wants to acquire a second dialect, standard English, and instruction is unavailable, s/he can become discouraged. Reading teachers often feel that second dialect instruction is not their job. However, since such teaching is neglected in classrooms and individual by nature, the corrective reading setting seems appropriate.

4. When a student must understand a portion of text that has been translated by him into nonstandard English and thereby made ambiguous (i.e., "He wait[ed] for Bobby."—When did the event occur?), comprehension difficulties may result.

SELECTED DIAGNOSTIC PROCEDURES

Two kinds of informal diagnoses are helpful to measure (1) nonstandard dialect usage and (2) dialect interference. Assessing (1) is helpful when you want to know how much nonstandard English is part of an individual's speech and which features* of the dialect he uses. This information is important when teaching standard English and evaluating oral reading.

The assessment of (2) is essential when diagnosing oral and silent reading comprehension.

Assessing Usage

To identify a student as either a standard or nonstandard speaker is difficult because of:

1. *Code-switching.* People can change their language to fit varied social purposes. A school-shy child, for example, may speak nonstandard English, but the teacher may hear only monosyllabic responses that are dialectless. Other students may be able to speak standard English but refuse to do so because of peer-group pressure.

2. *Dialect varieties.* There are varieties of nonstandard English which range from very divergent from to very similar to standard English. Some children speak "a lot" of black English while others use few features* infrequently. Because of the above factors, it is important to gather data about dialect usage informally, over time. If possible:

   a. Observe the speaker in several social contexts, formal to casual.

   b. Get a rough estimate of which nonstandard features the speaker uses and with what frequency.

*Nonstandard dialect feature list on page 122.

LIST OF BLACK ENGLISH FEATURES (Lass, 1976)

Category*	Feature	Explanation	Example(s) Written sE	Spoken bE
Phonological	1. Final consonant cluster simplification	Words ending in a consonant cluster have the final letter of the cluster absent.	desk	"des"
	2. *th* sounds	(a) Initial voiced *th* pronounced as /d/	that	"dat"
		(b) Medial and final voiceless *th* pronounced as /f/.	bathroom	"bafroom"
		(c) Medial and final voiced *th* pronounced as /v/.	mother	"muhver"
		(d) Final *th* in *with* pronounced /d/ or /t/.	with	"wid" "wit"
	3. Final consonant devoicing or absence.	(a) Voiced stops /b/, /d/, /g/ are pronounced like corresponding voiceless stops /p/, /t/, /k/, respectively.	fed pig	"fet" "pick"
		(b) Loss of final consonant sounds.	mad	"ma"
	4. Absence of medial consonants.	Medial consonants can be absent.	little help worry throw	"lil" "hep" "wo'y" "thow"
	5. Effect of nasal consonant.	(a) The /g/ in *ing* is absent.	running	"runnin"
		(b) Use of nasalized vowel instead of the nasal consonants.	balloon rum	"ballóō" "balloom" "ru" "run"
		(c) Short vowels "i" and "e" do not contrast.	pin and pen	"pin"
	6. *str-* cluster	*str-* clusters are pronounced /skr/.	street	"skreet"
	7. Long *i*	Long *i* is pronounced like the *a* in *father* ("ah").	time	"tahm"
	8. Article *an*	The article *a* is used whether the following word begins with a vowel or a consonant.	an umbrella	"a umbrella"
	9. Verb forms with *to*	When following a verb, *to* is pronounced "ta" or "a".	have to went to going to	"hafta" "went a" "gonna"
	10. Stress patterns	(a) Stress is placed on first syllable on some words which have second syllable stress in sE.	umbrella	"úm-brella"
		(b) First syllable can be absent when it is unstressed.	about	"bout"
	11. Final *t* followed by *'s.*	When final *t* is followed by the *'s* of a contraction the *t* is not pronounced.	it's what's	"is" "whas"
	12. *ask*	In the word *ask,* the final consonant cluster is reversed.	ask	"aks"
	13. Consonant *v.*	The consonant *v* is pronounced with a voiced bilabial fricative which is unknown in sE. It sounds somewhat like /b/ or /w/.	over	"ober" "ower"
	14. *don't*	This word can lose its initial sound (as well as its final sound, see Feature 1).	don't	"on"

*Semantic features, because of frequent changes, are omitted from list.

Category*	Feature	Explanation	Example(s) Written sE	Example(s) Spoken bE
Morphological	15. Loss of -ed suffix	The past tense marker -ed is absent.	*missed*	"miss"
	16. The present tense suffix	The present tense marker -s used for the third person singular is absent.	*He wants*	"He want"
	17. Plurals	The plural marker -s is absent.	*toys*	"toy"
	18. Possessives	The possessive marker 's is absent.	*boy's*	"boy"
Syntactical	19. Irregular Past Tense	Irregular past tense forms are replaced by present tense forms.	*said*	"say"
	20. The past participle	With irregular verbs, the past tense and the past participle may interchange.	*He has come.* *He has taken it.*	"He has came". "He taken it".
	21. The verb *to be*	(a) The verb forms *is* and *was* are used for all persons and numbers.	*They're running.*	"They's runnin' ".
		(b) The verb forms of *to be* are often missing.	*She is tired.* *They are busy.*	"She tired". "They busy."
	22. Invariant *be*	*Be* is used as a main verb, regardless of person and number.	*Sometimes he is busy.*	"Sometime he be busy.
	23. Auxiliary deletions	Auxiliary verb forms are absent.	*He is going to school.*	"He goin' a school".
			She'll have to go home.	"She have to go home".
	24. Negation	More than one negative marker is used.	*He doesn't know anything.*	"He 'on' know nothin' ".
	25. Relative clauses	(a) In relative clauses, relative pronouns are absent.	*That's the dog that bit me.*	"Tha's the dog bit me".
		(b) In relative clauses, *what* replaces relative pronoun.	*That's the dog that bit me.*	"Tha's the dog wha' bit me".
	26. Question inversion	(a) Indirect questions follow direct question rules.	*His mother asked why he was late.*	"His mother aks why was he late".
		(b) Direct questions follow indirect question rules.	*Why did he take it?*	"Why he did take it?"
	27. *There* constructions	Existential or expletive *there* is replaced by *it*.	*There was a convertible outside.*	"It was a convertible outside".
	28. Pronominal apposition	A noun and its pronoun are the subject of a sentence.	*His mother threw out the balloon.*	"His mother, she th'ew out the balloon".
	29. Use of *at* after *where*	Questions that begin with *where* end with *at*.	*Where is she?*	"Where she at?"
	30. Undifferenciated pronouns	Standard English nominative forms of personal pronouns are used to show possession.	*That's his book.*	"Tha's he book".
	31. Reflexives	Pronouns formed with the possessive form of the personal pronoun plus *self*.	*himself*	"hisself"
	32. Demonstratives	The use of *them* when standard English requires *those*.	*I want some of those candies.*	"I want some a them candies".

*Semantic features, because of frequent changes, are omitted from list.

To discover whether the dialect miscues made during oral reading effect comprehension, the following procedure is recommended.

After a selection is read with dialect miscues, make up questions which direct attention to the concepts possibly affected by those miscues. This suggestion contradicts conventional wisdom which asserts that better, higher level questions come with preplanning. True, but another purpose, assessing literal comprehension, is central here.

Incidentally, it is best to allow the student time to reread the selection silently before asking the questions. This should facilitate comprehension, since orally read material is not the best thing to use to assess comprehension. A student is often too concerned with pronunciation to pay attention to meaning.

CASE STUDY*

The sample passage from an Informal Reading Inventory (IRI) which follows illustrates that above technique. It was given to a third grade black English speaker reading at the second-grade level. Miscues are marked and answers to comprehension questions follow.

Sea Gulls†

A sea gull is a kind of bird.

Most sea gulls live near the water.

But some sea gulls are moving far away from the water.

They are making their nests in trees.

They are finding food on farms and in the fields.

Maybe we should call these birds land gulls instead of sea gulls.

**1. What kind of bird is important in this story? a sea gull

X2. Choose the sentence that gives the main idea:
  a. Sea gulls moved away from the water several years ago.
  b. Sea gulls will move away from the water in a year or two.
  c. Sea gulls are now moving away from the water.

X3. How many nests are made in trees?
  a. none
  b. one
  c. several

4. Name two places where gulls find food.
  nest *O*   field *O*

---

*See Introduction for function of Case Study.
†*Reading Diagnosis.* New York: Scholastic Books, 1975, p. 18. Used with permission.
**For a child whose miscue pattern is different, other questions should be asked.

124 *The Remedial Reading Handbook* Lass, Davis

The reader of this passage may have comprehension loss due to omission of morphemes *-ed* and *-s*. Further evidence for this hypothesis should be gathered during instruction. Questions about tense and number should frequently be directed at this reader. If a pattern of deficit is established, instruction in the pronunciation and meaning of the morphemes is indicated.

Other Assessments

These published tests may be helpful in gathering data about dialect usage:

Basic Inventory of Natural Language (BINL), Charles Herbert. San Bernadino, CA: Checkpoint Systems, 1979.

Teaching Black Children to Read, edited by Baratz & Shuy. Washington, DC: Center for Applied Linguistics, 1979, pp. 92–116.
Sentence Repetition Task

Language Facility Test, John T. Daily. Alexandria, VA: The Allington Corporation, 1968.

Michigan Oral Language Test, Ralph Robinett and Richard Benjamin. Ann Arbor, MI: Michigan Department of Education.

TECHNIQUES FOR REMEDIATION

Accept Dialect Renderings of Standard English Text During Oral Reading

This entails knowledge of dialect features. Study the list on pages 122–123. Your acceptance of a student's language helps to build self-esteem. It also sends this message to him: "Helping you *understand* what you read is the major purpose of our lessons."

Allow Child To See His Own Dialect in Print

This will build self-esteem through language pride. It also demonstrates the link between speech and print. Some reading materials have been written in black English. Here is a partial list:

Bridge: A Cross-Culture Reading Program, Simpkins, Simpkins & Holt. Boston: Houghton-Mifflin, 1977.
Trade books:
Clifton, Lucille, *My Brother Fine with Me.* New York: Holt, Rinehart & Winston, 1975.

Greenfield, Eloise, *Me and Nessie.* New York: Thomas Y. Crowell, 1975.

Lexau, John M., *Me Day.* New York: Dial Press, 1971.

Myers, Walter Dean, *Fast Sam, Cool Clyde and Stuff.* New York: Viking Press, 1975.

Steptoe, John, *Train Ride.* New York: Harper & Row, 1971.

Use the Language Experience Approach

You may wish to employ nonstandard dialect when children make their own reading material. You will probably want to copy the child's syntactic patterns and semantic choices. Phonological features, however, should not be incorporated into spellings (i.e., "fahn" for *fine;* "runnin" for *running*). The reasons? They make the story less readable (less legible—remember Uncle Remus?) and are frequently deemed racist by black educators (MacCann & Woodard, 1977).

Help Children To Acquire Standard English If They Wish

1. Although the reading period may not be the ideal time for instruction in a second dialect, for some children it's their only opportunity for individual attention. It is necessary, however, to take care that second dialect and reading instruction are not intermingled. That is, one portion of the remedial period should be devoted to reading instruction and another to second dialect acquisition. Otherwise, children may confuse the goals of one skill, speaking, with those of reading.

Second, it is important to note that standard English instruction will not take the place of the teaching of reading. It may be years before a second dialect is mastered and to delay reading instruction until then is ill-advised.

2. Remember that informal opportunities for standard English acquisition already exist, particularly if you have a linguistically mixed school and/or community. Television provides access to standard English for all, but live language models have greater impact. Most importantly, the teacher can be a model standard English speaker. An opportunity not-to-be-missed: Reading aloud to children daily. This will give them the chance to hear standard English at length instead of in conversational or instructional snatches.

3. Before formal instruction begins explain dialect differences to children. Emphasize functions of school (work) vs. home languages. Be sure students understand that they are not being asked to give up their primary dialect.

4. Use parallel, contrasting, structures as the primary instructional technique.

Examples:

a. Auditory discrimination

They are pin pals.   They are pen pals. | He miss the bus.
They are pen pals.   He missed the bus.

They are pin pals.   He miss the bus.
They are pen pals.   He missed the bus.

When it rain, he got a úm-brella.
When it rains, he has an um-brél-la.

b. Visual discrimination

I ain't got none.   He be my best friend.
I don't have any.   He is my best friend.

And his mother wonder why was he late.
And his mother wondered why he was late.

c. Call and response

1. Teacher gives a phrase in standard English. Students respond with dialect equivalent.
2. *Reverse roles:* Teacher gives the dialect phrase and the students, the standard English.
3. Eventually use student callers.

Teacher	**Student** (possible responses)
He hasn't any sisters or brothers.	He ain't got no sister or brother.
Fred loves all of his pets.	Fred love he pet.
Once upon a time there lived a girl named Cinderella.	One time it was a girl. She name Cinderella.

d. Black English/Standard English Dictionary

1. Allows students to share the wealth of their language with others.
2. Raises consciousness about dialect differences and language change.

*Sample entries

1. *scrub*—(n.) a person who is not good at anything
2. *smoking*—(adj.) describes something or someone super
3. *slick*—(adj.) clever, tricky
4. *bad, baddest*—(adj.) good, best
5. *cool-out*—(v.) to calm down (syn. to chill-out)

ACTIVITIES INDEX

MATCH-A-MEANING
WHO KNOWS WHERE OR WHEN?

*Because a dialect's semantic content changes with region and time it is important to place these entries: Boston, Spring 1981.

REFERENCES

Goodman, Kenneth and Catherine Buck, "Dialect Barriers to Reading Comprehension Revisited," *The Reading Teacher,* October 1973, pp. 6–12.

Hunt, Barbara, "Black Dialect and Third and Fourth Graders' Performance on the Gray Oral Reading Test." *Reading Research Quarterly,* No. 2, 1974–1975, pp. 193–211.

Lass, Bonnie, "The Relationship Between the Oral Language of Black English Speakers and Their Reading Achievements," Doctoral dissertation, University of Illinois, 1976 (unpublished).

Lass, Bonnie, "Improving Reading Skills: The Relationship Between the Oral Language of Black English Speakers and Their Reading Achievement," *Urban Education,* January, 1980, pp. 437–47.

MacCann, Donnarae and Gloria Woodard, *Cultural Conformity in Books for Children.* Metuchen, NJ: Scarecrow Press, 1977.

Melmed, Paul, "The Question of Reading Interference," in *Language Differences: Do They Interfere?,* (ed.) Laffey and Shuy. Newark, DE: International Reading Association, 1973, pp. 70–85.

Fourteen

Speaking English as a Second Language*

SKILL DESCRIPTION

Reading is a language-based activity. When English is not the first or primary language of students, certain difficulties can arise when they learn to read in English.

Although there are many other first languages currently represented in our schools (Italian, Vietnamese, Chinese, Russian, and Navaho are examples), Spanish will be the only one considered in this chapter, since (1) Hispanic students represent the vast majority of non-English speakers in schools in the United States, and (2) focus on a specific language allows for a pointed discussion and more practical chapter. However, it is expected that teachers of other language different students can apply the remedial suggestions in this chapter to their situations.

It should be noted that language differences exist among groups of Spanish speakers. Mexican-American, Puerto Rican, and Argentinian immigrants, for instance, use differing dialects of Spanish. Culturally, too, each of these groups is unique, a fact to consider when selecting interest-based reading materials.

Thonis (1970) has identified three groups of Spanish speakers who are learning to read English and for whom this chapter is applicable: (1) *preliterate:* Students who are literate in neither language because they have not yet been taught to read; (2) *literate in Spanish:* Students who are literate in their first language because of bilingual instruction in the States, Spanish instruction in another country, or reading instruction at home; and (3) *functional illiterates in both languages:* Students who have failed to learn to read in either language in one or a variety of settings. For them, limited oral proficiency in one or both languages is also characteristic.

Only the third group can be defined strictly as a remedial population. Yet individuals from the first two groups will also benefit from the specialized techniques outlined in this chapter.

*The authors wish to thank Betsey Anderson Reardon, bilingual teacher in the Lawrence, MA Public Schools for her direction in the writing of this chapter.

POSSIBLE REASONS FOR SKILL DEFICIENCY

1. Lack of English vocabulary is a most important factor in depressed reading comprehension for these students. (Suggestions found in Chapter Six should be helpful in most cases.) However, when this lack is profound, attempting reading instruction seems fruitless. Even if students can be taught to decode English, meaning will be absent. With such students, intensive oral language programs should precede or accompany reading programs.

2. Because of differences between Spanish and English, Spanish speakers may have difficulties when reading English. Phonics, morphemic acquisition, oral reading performance, and grammatical or conceptual problems may lead to poor comprehension.

What follows is a chart of some of the key phonetic and grammatical differences between Spanish and English. Knowledge of these potential points of interference can help teachers anticipate students' difficulties and plan appropriate instruction. It is important to note that not all listed features are characteristic of all Spanish dialects nor of the speech of individual learners.

Some Spanish Language Features Which May Cause Interference in Reading English*

Category	Feature	Explanation	Examples — Written English	Spoken ESL
Phonological	$/i/ = /e/$	Short *i* is pronounced as long *e*.	*sin* *ship*	"seen" "sheep"
	$/e/ = /i/$	Long *e* is pronounced as short *i*.	*sleep*	"slip"
	$/a/ = /e/$	Long *a* is pronounced as short *e*.	*late* *sale*	"let" "sell"
	$/v/ = /b/$	/v/ and /b/ are represented by only one sound in Spanish which is close to the sound /b/.	*very* *vote* *valentine*	"bury" "boat" "Ballentine"
	$/ch/ = /sh/$	The Spanish pronunciation of /ch/ sounds like /sh/ to English speakers.	*chip* *much* *teacher*	"ship" "mush" "tee-shir(t)"
	$/th/$	Initial voiced /th/ is pronounced as /d/ and final unvoiced /th/ is pronounced /s/.	*this* *bath*	"dis" "bas"
	$/j/ = /y/$ or $/ch/$ $/y/ = /j/$	J is pronounced as /y/ or /ch/, while initial y is pronounced in an approximation of /j/.	*job* *just* *yo-yo* *yes*	"yob" or "chob" "yust" or "chust" "jo-jo" "jes"
	Absence of final consonants	Because /p/, /t/, /k/, and /f/ do not appear in the final position in Spanish words, these sounds are often omitted from English ones. This is particularly true with multisyllabic words or words in phrases.	*hate* *economic* *student* *get off* *climb up*	"hay" "economy" "studen" "get o' " "climb u' "
	Final consonant cluster simplification	Spanish has no final consonant clusters so there is pronunciation difficulty with words in clusters.	*cats* *hopped* *moved*	"cat" or "cass" "hop" "move" or "mood"
	Initial *s* blends	Spanish has no initial consonant cluster beginning with /s/. There is a tendency for Spanish speakers to make a syllable out of an /s/ blend by adding /e/ to its beginning.	*sleep* *smile* *skin*	"esleep" "esmile" "eskin"

Category	Feature	Explanation	Examples Written English	Spoken ESL
Morphological	Superlatives	In English we inflect comparative adjectives (large, larger, largest). In Spanish, other comparative adjectives and articles are added to the first (grande, mās grande, el mās grande).	*larger* *largest*	"more large" or "more larger" "the more large"
	Possessive	There is no possessive case form in Spanish; "John's hat" is "El sombrero de Juan." This infrequently causes comprehension problems.	*John's hat* *the mother's cat*	"The hat of John" or "John hat" "the mother cat"
	Stress	Rules are different in Spanish—second, or third syllables, or marked vowels (ésta) are usually stressed while in English, first syllable of a root is emphasized.	*comment* *pilot* *language*	"commént" "pilót" "languáge"
Syntactic	Future tense	In Spanish, the most common future tense employs an inflected verb. In English, the modal "will" is the most common future marker. Consequently, "will" is frequently omitted and unless there is redundancy in the sentence (i.e., "tomorrow"), comprehension problems can result.	*She will laugh.*	"She laugh."
	Conditional tense	Conditional verbs are present in Spanish but uncommon in oral language of school aged children. Conditional markers are often omitted in verb phrases sometimes causing difficulty with the understanding of cause and effect relationships.	*She would speak.* *She may speak.*	"She speak."
	Possessive adjective	Spanish direct and indirect object pronouns come before the verb. English sentences with these features may be disordered by ESL students.	*He showed it to me.*	"He showed me it." "He show it me." "To me he show it."
	Pronouns	The Spanish word "su" means "his," "her" and "your" (formal case). So there may be some confusion among these words. Moreover, there is occasionally confusion between these adjectives and subject pronouns.	*Mary showed her mother the flower.*	"Mary showed his (or she) mother the flower."
	Negation	In Spanish a double negative is usual ("*No* tengo *nada*" = "he has nothing"). When reading English where only one negative marker is used, comprehension may be affected. After reading *He has nothing* and asked "Does he have anything?", the Spanish speaking child may reply, "Yes," since negative was not emphatic enough.	*He has nothing.*	"He no has nothing."

*Two sources served as references for this list: (Schneider, 1971; Stockwell, 1966).

SELECTED DIAGNOSTIC PROCEDURES

Two kinds of measures which are most helpful to the reading teacher of Spanish-speaking children are tests of (1) language dominance and (2) English proficiency (Murphy, 1980).

The first type of assessment is given by an English as a Second Language (ESL) teacher or by a bilingual person trained in the specific test procedure. Although reading teachers who don't speak Spanish cannot give these tests, they can be cautious consumers of results. (Many tests of language dominance are not established as valid or reliable.) Reading teachers need to know about language dominance in order to make informed judgments about whether a student has a reading disability or a language deficiency.

When the child has some English proficiency, the reading teacher will wish to know its level or degree and, moreover, which grammatical and phonological features of English still cause problems.

CASE STUDY*

One test of English proficiency, the English section of the BOLT (Bahia Oral Language Test),† is sampled below. What cannot be seen from the test protocol is that a child is shown picture charts and then asked the questions in the second column orally. Responses to the questions are the data used to classify a child in one of five levels of English. Also assessed is ability with twenty syntactic and morphologic concepts of English. The child whose test is shown below is a fourth-grade girl from a bilingual classroom who has English reading difficulties.

BOLT—English Test

CONCEPTS BEING TESTED	QUESTIONS OF LEVEL II
1. Plural formation: adding *s*	1. (Pointing to the "cars" in CHART 1) WHAT ARE THESE? *cars*
2. Simple sentence with subject and verb	2. (Using CHART 1) WHY ARE THE PEOPLE SITTING DOWN? *they tired*
3. Prepositional phrase	3. (Using CHART 1) TELL ME, WHERE IS THE SMALL CAR? *in the street*
4. Prepositional phrase	4. (Using CHART 2) WHERE IS THE FAMILY? *in the house*
5. *ing* form of the verb	5. (Using CHART 2) WHAT IS THE FATHER DOING? *reading*
	QUESTIONS OF LEVEL III
6. Plural: adding *es*	6. (Pointing to the "houses" in CHART 1) WHAT ARE THESE? *house*
7. Plural: *men*	7. (Pointing to the "men" in CHART 1) WHAT ARE THESE? *mans*
8. Possessive pronouns	8. (Using CHART 2) WHOSE SHOES ARE THESE? *father*
9. Use of past tense or future tense (implying the future)	9. (Using CHART 2) WHY DID THE FATHER TAKE OFF HIS SHOES? *for put the foots up here*
10. Possessive pronouns	10. (Using CHART 2) WHOSE TOY IS THIS? *the boy*
11. Use of past participle as adjective	11. (Using CHART 2) WHY IS THE BOY CRYING? *because the toy is broke*

*See Introduction for function of Case Study.
†Bahia Oral Language Test (BOLT), Berkeley, CA: (Bahia, Inc., 1977). Distributed by Bilingual Media Productions, Berkeley, CA. Used with permission.

CONCEPTS BEING TESTED	QUESTIONS OF LEVEL II
12. *ing* form of the verb	12. (Using CHART 2) WHAT IS THE OLDER SISTER DOING? *she is picking the cup up*
13. Use of future tense, or present tense (implying future)	13. (Using CHART 2) WHAT WILL THE FAMILY DO AFTER THE GIRL FINISHES SETTING THE TABLE? *they're going to eat* QUESTIONS OF LEVEL IV
14. Past tense	14. (Using the first picture of CHART 3) WHAT WAS THE DOG DOING TO THE CAT? *shaking the cat*
15. Past tense	15. (Using CHART 3) HOW DID THE CAT GET DOWN? *the fireman get off the cat*
16. "Would have" or "could have" plus participle	16. (Using CHART 3) WHAT WOULD HAVE HAPPENED IF THE FIREMAN HAD NOT COME? *he still stay in the tree*
17. "Could have" plus past participle	17. (Using CHART 3) HOW COULD THE BOY HAVE GOTTEN THE CAT DOWN BY HIMSELF? *when the dog went away the cat get down*
18. Past tense	18. (Using CHART 3) WHAT DID THE DOG DO AFTER THE FIREMAN BROUGHT THE CAT DOWN? *he went away*
19. "Would have" plus past participle	19. (Using CHART 3) WHAT WOULD HAVE BEEN YOUR REACTION IF THIS HAD BEEN YOUR CAT? *sad*
20. Formation of a question with a proper word order	20. (Using CHART 1) WHAT QUESTION IS THE LADY WITH THE RED DRESS ASKING THE POLICEMAN? *She said, "What's that?"*

LEVEL OF LANGUAGE CLASSIFICATION OF THE STUDENT:

LEVEL I   LEVEL I-S   (LEVEL II)   LEVEL III   LEVEL IV

The child assessed above is classified according to the BOLT as Level II—"Very Limited English Speaking." Although asking Level IV questions of this examinee is contrary to test procedures, the examiner, who is a bilingual teacher, did so to discover more about which English features are problematic for this girl.

Although generalizations should be drawn cautiously from so few items, it appears that this child has difficulties with (1) plural formation of both inflected and irregular nouns, (2) possessive pronouns, and (3) verb forms: past participles, the irregular past, and conditional tenses.

While observations made during instruction could confirm or dispute these tentative findings, it seems reasonable to suggest that reading comprehension difficulties in English could arise from such English language deficiencies. Oral language and reading comprehension instruction focusing on these concepts should be helpful.

Other Assessments (Oakland, 1977)

1. *Basic Inventory of Natural Language (BINL),* Charles Herbert. San Bernadino, CA: Checkpoint Systems, 1974.

2. *Bilingual Syntax Measure,* Marina K. Burt et al. New York: Harcourt, Brace, Jovanovich, Inc., 1975.

3. *Mat-Sea-Cal.* Joseph Matluck and Betty Mace-Matluck. Arlington, VA: Center for Applied Linguistics, 1974.

   An oral test of listening comprehension, sentence repetition, and structured responses.

4. *Test for Auditory Comprehension of Language English/Spanish.* Elizabeth Carrow. Austin, TX: Urban Research Group, 1973.

   It should also be noted that at least two reading achievement tests are available in Spanish to assess students literate in their native language and to provide contrast with reading ability in English.

5. *California Test of Basic Skills.* Monterey, CA: CTB/McGraw-Hill.

6. *Metropolitan Achievement Test.* New York: Harcourt, Brace, Jovanovich.

TECHNIQUES FOR REMEDIATION

Because oral language development is so important for Spanish-first students, many of the techniques which follow, focus on oral input from students, and do not always involve written language.

Talk and Talk Some More

Both informal "warm-ups" for lessons and more formal dialogues which are lessons in themselves are appropriate with ESL students.

Pictures can stimulate conversation. You can clip magazine photographs, use comic strips, or commercially prepared visuals to motivate discussion or prompt stories. Especially good for the youngest students are the "Sequencing Cards" that are part of Developmental Language Materials. For older students, *Story Squares* (Knowles and Sasaki, 1980), sets of interrelated pictures forming a complex story which they uncover by questioning the teacher, is recommended. Each set will elicit use of key problematic structures in English. (See the Activities Index for Get Talking!, a variation on *Story Squares.*)

Language Experiences Approaches

Using children's or adult's orally dictated sentences or stories as the basis for their reading material is a mainstay of ESL instruction (Thonis, 1970).

Miller (1982) explains a variation of the Language Experience Approach which, created by Paulo Freire, is popular with many ESL and bilingual teachers. Here is an adaptation for reading teachers to follow.

After problem areas in speaking, reading, or writing have been diagnosed, a list of observed points of interference, or errors, forms the goal(s) for instruction. From this, words are generated around an evocative theme. If a group of middle-grade children are substituting $/b/$ for $/v/$, for example, they need speaking, writing and reading opportunities to contrast $/b/$ with $/v/$. Their theme for a language experience unit might be *The Best Vocation for Me.* Examples of key words for discussions, dictated stories, reading experiences and follow-up activities are:

veterinarian	butcher	Boy Scout Leader
volunteer	baker	Vice-President
ventriloquist	Brownie leader	babysitter
barber	boss	

In another case, you may wish to combine problem areas. If /b/ is substituted for /v/, /ĭ/ for /ē/, conditional markers omitted, and comparative adjectives confused, *Vampire Bats* could provide the theme, albeit a gory one. Key words are:

bitten	*sleep*	*bloody*
bite	*bleed*	*bloodier*
biting	*blood vessel*	*bloodiest*

Points of Difference

Provide direct instruction for points of linguistic interference. Perhaps the most important graphophonic difference between languages is the amount of sound-spelling regularity. In Spanish there are twenty-nine letters and twenty-four sounds while English uses forty-three sounds but has only twenty-six letters (Barnitz, 1982).

Spanish speaking students need an explanation of irregularities in the rules of phonics, and much practice applying the rules flexibly. Detail comprehension instruction may also be necessary with ESL students. Recommended are pre-story discussions concerning time (tense), ownership of objects and relationships among characters (possession), as well as negative attitudes and actions (John did/did not want to go/ John did/did not go). Post-story questions assessing understanding of these as well as other details are also helpful.

"I Got Rhythm"

Help students with pitch, stress, and juncture. These terms refer respectively to the highness and lowness of words within contexts, emphasis on syllables or words within sentences, and pauses within and at the ends of sentences. Taken together, pitch, stress, and juncture give a language its unique rhythm. Instruction in language rhythm is rare but valuable. In some instances, halting, awkward reading, and inadequate reading comprehension may be improved. Some ways to help with English-language rhythms follow.

Oral Reading

Literature written to be performed (plays and poems) as well as fiction with an abundance of dialogue is suitable. For collections of such material see:

Dawson, Mildred and Georgiana Newman, *Oral Readers Series.* Westchester, IL: Benefic Press, 1969.

Martin, Bill, Jr., *The Sounds of Language Series.* New York: Holt, Rinehart & Winston, 1972.

Teachers and/or other proficient oral readers in a class or especially prepared tapes provide models of expressive, appropriately rhythmic oral reading for ESL students.

Silent Reading

To help ESL students transfer the rhythms of oral to silent reading in order to increase comprehension, a series of marked passages is useful. This is done by underlining, stress marking, and elaborating on punctuation via use of color or exaggerated size. An example of marked passages can be found in the Activity Index, "Reading with Oomph."

Use of Music

Folk tunes with multiple verses are particularly effective since students can learn the rhythm, orally, with the first verse and apply it to a silent reading of the others. Collections of such songs are found in:

Glazer, Tom, *New Treasury of Folk Songs.* New York: Bantam Books, 1978.
Keller, Charles, *Glory, Glory, How Peculiar.* Englewood Cliffs, NJ: Prentice-Hall, Inc., 1976.
Langstaff, Nancy and John, *Jim Along, Josie.* New York: Harcourt, Brace, Jovanovich, 1970.

Another noteworthy material is *Jazz Chants,* a cassette, child's book, and teacher's guide published by Oxford University Press, in 1979.

Develop Vocabularies

Naturally, the biggest challenge faced by ESL students is vocabulary acquisition. All of the suggestions in Chapter Six are relevant. Other techniques especially aimed at the unique needs of ESL students follow.

Begin with Spanish Borrowings and Spanish-English Cognates

Because Spanish and English have common ancestry (Latin) and mingled histories, a study of borrowings and cognates is profitable as well as motivating. (Borrowings are identical in spelling and meaning while cognates are the same in meaning but may be slightly different in spelling.) However, lest students overapply the similarities between languages, "chica" is *girl* in Spanish but in English "chick" won't do!

Here are examples of Spanish borrowings. Note that all of the words are not common in all regions or cultures within the United States.

adios	*coyote*	*poncho*
adobe	*fiesta*	*rodeo*
barbeque	*guitar*	*siesta*
burro	*macho*	*tacos*
canyon	*patio*	

Now an even briefer list of cognates. Any Spanish-English dictionary will provide many more.

alfabeto = alphabet	*pantalones* = pants
crayola = crayon	*Sábado* = Saturday
julio = July	*sinfonia* = symphony

Demonstrate Word Meanings

When a student's English is limited, it is difficult to define unknown words for them because the meanings of the explanatory words or synonyms may also be unknown. For example, explaining the word *hammer* is a challenge when students don't know *nails, strike, tool, wood,* or *build.* A picture of a hammer, though of temporary use, is not sufficiently language-rich for large scale vocabulary acquisition.

Demonstrating or pantomiming the driving of a nail into the wall makes meaning acquisition easier, especially if you explain simultaneously and then have students follow your lead. This technique was coined "an operation" by Nelson and Winters (1980). It is "a procedure for doing something using a natural sequence of events" (p. 1). The language makes the action operable while the action reinforces the language. In the case of *hammer,* the operation would be:

1. Hold a nail near the bottom between your thumb and your first two fingers.
2. Place the nail on a piece of wood.
3. With your other hand, pick up a hammer near the end of its handle.
4. Strike the nailhead lightly a few times with the hammer.
5. Release the nail from your hand and finish driving it into the wood.

Expand Conceptual Networks

Second language learners are frequently culturally as well as linguistically different. Even when they have learned the English word *yard,* for example, their image of *yard* may be quite different from the one in a story. Knowing and/or eliciting the children's experience with a word and then contrasting it with the story experience helps to expand the children's schema by "building bridges between the new and the unknown" (Pearson and Johnson, p. 24). One way to do this is by contrasting semantic webs, diagrams which illustrate word relationships. This is done for the word *yard* as follows:

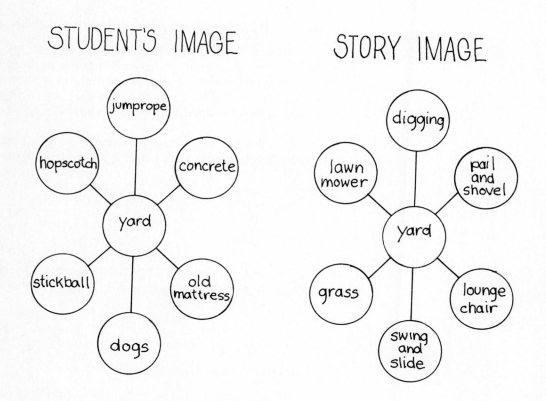

Provide Instruction for Figurative Language

Nonliteral meanings are among the most difficult for ESL students to acquire. With idioms and figures of speech, the parts do not add up to the whole and a dictionary is of no help. Often, it's hard to tell when you don't understand.

Reading teachers need to *anticipate* the problems ESL students will have with the figurative language in a given story and prepare them before reading begins. Direct skills instruction with idioms and figures of speech is also recommended. Students seem to love creating drawings of both the literal and figurative meanings of an expression. Some good ones are:

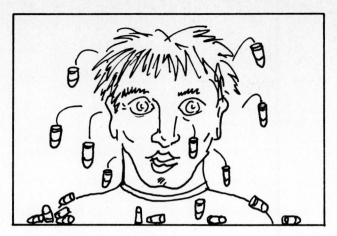

SWEATING BULLETS

BURNING THE CANDLE AT BOTH ENDS

Recommended books for teachers about the origins and explanations for figures of speech are:

Hog on Ice by Charles Funk. New York: Harper & Brothers Publishers, 1948.
Dictionary of Cliches by Eric Partridge. New York: MacMillan Publishers, 1950.

A superior book with ideas for instruction in idiomatic English is:

Idioms in Action: A Key to Fluency in English by George Reeves. Rowley, MA: Newbury House Publishers, 1980.

ACTIVITIES INDEX

REFERENCES

Barnitz, John, "Orthographies, Bilingualism and Learning to Read English as a Second Language," *The Reading Teacher,* Feburary 1982, pp. 560–67.

Knowles, Philip L. and Ruth Sasaki, *Story Squares: Fluency in English as a Second Language.* Cambridge, MA: Winthrop Pub., 1980.

Miller, Robert, "The Mexican Approach to Developing Bilingual Materials and Teaching Literacy to Bilingual Students," *The Reading Teacher,* April 1982, pp. 800–804.

Murphy, Barbara, "Second Language Reading and Testing in Bilingual Education," *TESOL Quarterly,* June 1980, pp. 189–97.

Nelson, Gayle and Thomas Winters, *ESL Operations: Techniques for Learning While Doing.* Rowley, MA: Newbury House Publishers, 1980.

Nilsen, Don, "Semantic Fields and Collocational Sets in Vocabulary Instruction" in *ON TESOL 74,* edited by Ruth Drymes and William E. Norris. Washington, DC: Teachers of English to Speakers of Other Languages, 1975.

Oakland, Thomas (ed.), *Psychological and Educational Assessment of Minority Children.* New York: Holt, Rinehart & Winston, 1978.

Pearson, P. David and Dale Johnson, *Teaching Reading Comprehension.* New York: Holt, Rinehart and Winston, 1978.

Schneider, Lois C., *Teaching English Sounds to Spanish Speakers.* Galien, MI: Allied Education Council, 1971.

Stockwell, Robert, et al., *The Grammatical Structures of English and Spanish.* Chicago: The University of Chicago Press, 1966.

Thonis, Eleanor Wall, *Teaching Reading to Non-English Speakers.* New York: Collier Macmillan International, 1970.

Appendix A

To Help Children Test Well

From the time children first enter school, we test them to find out what they know, how well they have learned, and what needs to be taught or retaught.

We use a variety of testing situations and instruments, some of which are standardized. Standard testing formats, however, may bear little or no resemblance to any instructions students have met in their daily classroom work. When, under these circumstances, students must try to figure out what they are being asked to do to demonstrate knowledge of a skill, they may fail to follow the directions correctly. This difficulty that the student experiences with the testing format is sometimes incorrectly interpreted as a problem with the reading skill task instead of with the procedure. Remedial students often have problems with testing format in addition to their skill deficiencies.

Testing is anxiety producing, particularly for children who have reading problems, no matter how much we try to sugarcoat the procedure with elaborate explanations and rationalizations. The factors of timed tests and IBM answer sheets automatically produce stiffened backs. The jury is still out on the role anxiety plays in achievement (Alexander, 1983). For some students, a little anxiety enhances performance, while for others it has detrimental results. In any case, *panic* is harmful.

We strongly recommend that teachers follow the suggestions below to attempt to allay anxiety and thereby increase the validity of test scores and diagnostic information they obtain.

FAMILIARITY BREEDS SUCCESS

Familiarize students with testing format so they may concentrate on the skill being tested. Find out what testing instruments are used by your school or school system. Be sure to use the testing format (not the test items) in your daily work with students. The example below is a format commonly used.

139

Example: Put your finger on the clown at the left.

R   R   R   R   S.   R

Look at the letters to the right of the clown. Circle all of the letters which are the same.

This procedure may be teacher-led or used with a tape and worksheet. The picture of the clown is used solely as a place marker. Its irrelevance to the task itself can be confusing.

TEST WHAT YOU TEACH

If you are using a beginning approach with students which focuses on one aspect of the reading process (phonics, word patterns, sight words) do all you can to obtain a testing instrument that also focuses on that aspect. Students who have spent six months learning short *a* patterns (*bad, bag, dam, can,* etc.) will not perform well at this point on a test which is better suited to those who have learned to read using a sight approach.

"HURRY UP, DON'T WASTE TIME"

For timed tests:

1. Teach students that when responding to paragraphs with comprehension questions it helps to read the questions first and then to read the *whole* paragraph underlining important points so that they can refer back quickly to specific information.

2. Have students answer the questions they know, skipping those they must mull over. (Be sure they have circled each number skipped. This will not only help students to mark the answer sheet correctly but will also facilitate their returning to difficult items later in the testing.) When the student has completed the first run through of the test, s/he may return to those items which will require more thought. Spending too much time on an early item can prevent students from showing what they know before time runs out.

TO LOSE ONE'S PLACE IS ONLY HUMAN

Losing your place on an IBM answer sheet when an item has been skipped or omitted is a problem most students encounter in their school careers.

Teach students to:

1. Circle or underline correct answers in the test booklet as well as on the answer sheet in case they need to go back and correct an answer sheet.

2. Circle the number of the omitted item on the answer sheet to highlight those questions unanswered.

Example: (6.)   a   b   c   d

3. With each item, make sure the question and the answer sheet numbers match before marking an answer.

We may also wish to make up worksheets for class exercises and use IBM answer sheets to give students practice.

HELP!

Encourage students to ask for help if they encounter a procedure problem. Demonstrate that help will be given promptly and gladly. Provide assistance to students before panic sets in.

WHEN TO GUESS

Test publishers often try to take into account the guessing factor by subtracting more for wrong answers than for omitted items. We as teachers want to encourage educated guesses. If the student has no idea as to what the answer is, s/he should go on to the next question and leave the unknown item blank. If however, s/he can narrow the choice to two answers, it is worth taking the chance and selecting one. Emphasize, however, that when only *one* answer is requested, only *one* may be marked.

Appendix B

Activities Index

NAME: *Don't Get Behind the Eight Ball*

SKILL: Reading Sight Words

MATERIALS: Game board, two packs of cards (12 in each pack)

PROCEDURE:

1. Have one pack of sight words which the student has learned easily (Easy pack). Each word card is written in blue. The other pack should have the sight words that have been difficult to learn (Demon pack). Each of these should be written in red.

2. The students each spin the die and move the number of spaces indicated by the die. If the space they move to has one star, they pick from the easy pack. Reading the word correctly, earns them one point. If the space has two stars, the student picks from the demon pack and receives two points for reading the word correctly. Play continues to the space marked END.

3. The student with the most points at the end wins.

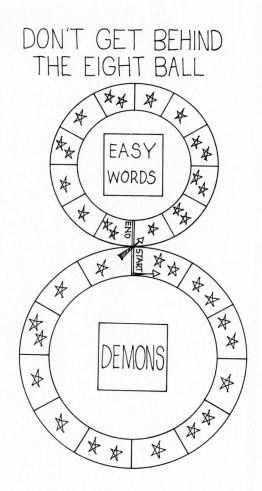

VARIATIONS:

You may use this board for any skill for which you can devise easy and hard items (words to practice vowels, synonyms and antonyms, etc.) You may also ignore the easy, demon designations and use two different skills for the packs—e.g., demon sight words and context sentences or words to practice vowels, etc.

DON'T GET BEHIND
THE EIGHT BALL

NAME: *Go Fly a Kite*

SKILL: Reading Sight Phrases

MATERIALS: Game board, ten different colored pens or crayons

PROCEDURE:

1. Use ten phrases (those below are from the Dolch list of sight phrases), one on each kite.

2. On each tail, print a word or phrase which completes the phrase on one of the kites.

3. Have the students use ten different colored crayons and draw lines from each kite to its appropriate tail.

4. If the teacher wishes to put this game on a worksheet, the student may use string and glue in place of crayons:

Example:

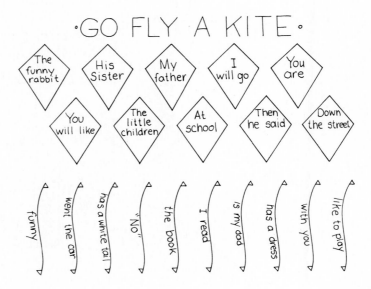

VARIATIONS: This game may be used with any skill for which you can devise pairs of words or sentences.
vowel symbol (*ă*)—vowel word (*cat*)
prefixes and/or suffixes—roots
synonyms—antonyms
words—definitions, synonymous phrases
cause—effect

Context or multiple meaning: The kites and tails may have pairs of sentences which can be completed by filling in the same word for each. The first kite might have the sentence: He hit the _____. The sentence on the appropriate tail might read: She danced at the _____. The word "ball" would fit both sentences.

1. She can _____ fast.
   The stocking has a _____ in it. (*run*)

2. Will you _____ that out to me?
   The pencil has a sharp _____. (*point*)

3. He lit the _____.
   Does this shirt _____ the pants? (*match*) etc.

Other possibilities in sentences: *star, crack, jar, trip, fair, play.*

GO FLY A KITE.

NAME:	*Be a Star*
SKILL:	Consonant digraphs, consonant blends, blending
MATERIALS:	Game board, die, board markers, paper and pencil
PROCEDURE:	The major purpose of this game is to build real and nonsense words. To do this the students roll the die to see (1) how many spaces to move; *and* (2) which phonogram to use.

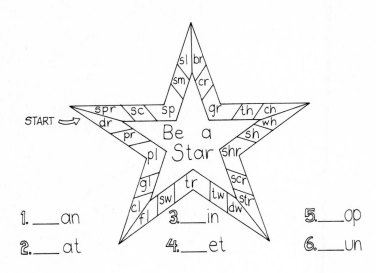

1. Fill in the star spaces and phonograms on the game board as shown above.
2. A six on the die would have the student move six spaces to the beginning consonant cluster "fl." S/he would also use the phonogram "un" to build the nonsense word *flun*. The word is written and then pronounced.
3. At the end, the students read all of their words indicating which are real words.
4. The game may result in different winners. One can be the student who finishes first. A second can be the student with the greatest number of real words.

VARIATIONS:	This game may be played with all elements which allow word or sentence building.

a. Use single consonants on the star spaces.

b. Use vowels and/or vowel digraphs on the star spaces. Instead of phonograms use six small words missing the vowel: *b__d, m__t, r__d, h__l, b__t, l__m*

c. Use root words like the following on the star spaces:
>   *lock, help, love, appear, fit,*
>   *read, care, place, work, arm*
>   *color, tie, mind, joy, close,*
>   *join, taste, prove, fear, play,*
>   *pack, like, do, cover, comfort*
> Use six prefixes and suffixes instead of phonograms:
>   *dis-, un-, -ful, re-, -less, -able*

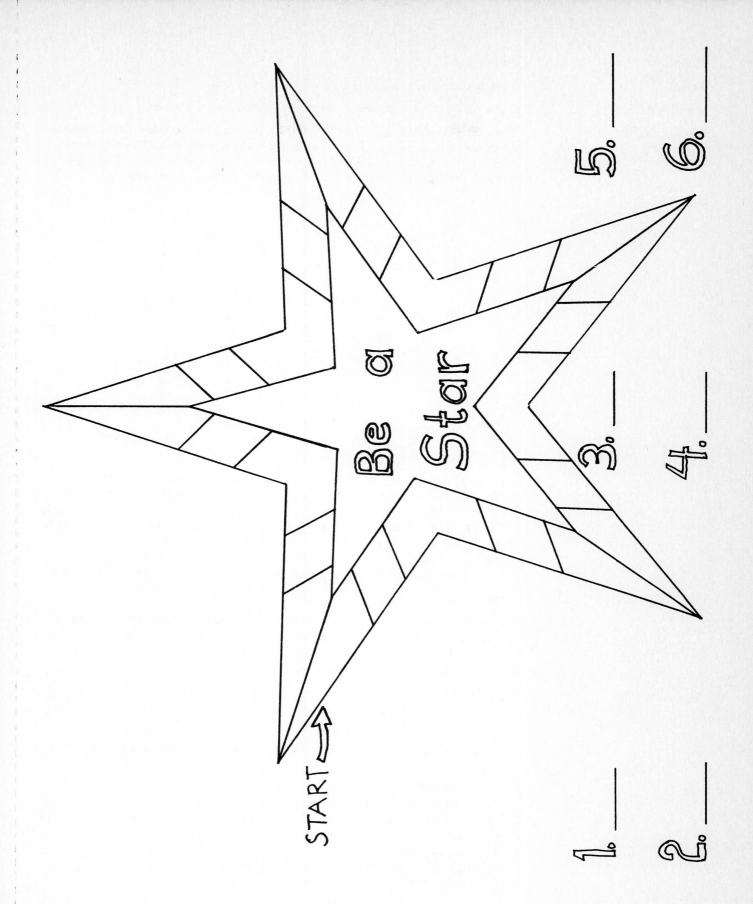

NAME: *Fishy Words*

SKILL: Consonants, Vowels, Blending

MATERIALS: Game board, two spinners (a. 1–6; b. 1–3), markers, paper and pencil

PROCEDURE: Three letter words are written on the squares of the fish as shown below. The students use the spinner with numbers 1 to 6 to see how many spaces to move. The second spinner (1 to 3) is then used to see which of the three letters to change (first, second, or third). By changing this letter to one of their choosing, students invent a new word.

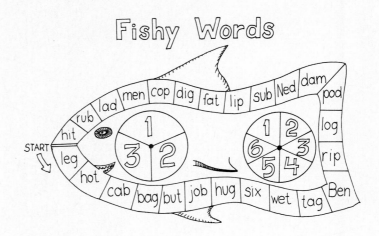

For example, if a six is spun, the student is on the space that says "job." If the second spinner indicates that the third letter is to be changed, the student can make "jot" or "jog." If the first letter is changed, the new word might be "rob," "gob," "lob," etc. If the second letter is changed, the result would be "jab" or "jib." Nonsense words may be used.

At each turn the students write the word from the game board on a sheet of paper and then write the new word next to it (job, jot). Winners must be able to read their whole list.

VARIATIONS:

Comparatives

1. *First spinner.* The words on the game board might include: *big, little, smart, tall, sad, happy, fast, bright, slim, nice, fine, funny, cute, fat, thin, good, careful, bad, naughty, sweet, kind, mean, silly, small, sleepy.*

2. *Second spinner.* Rather than numbers, the second spinner has the following sentences:

   a. She is a _____ girl.

   b. Jack is _____ than Tom.

   c. They are the _____ children in the class.

3. Students complete the sentences, using the correct form of the adjectives met on the board.

Multiple Meanings

1. The spinners used are the ones indicated above (a. 1–6; b. 1–3). The number on the second spinner indicates whether one, two, or three meanings must be provided for the word on the game board at each turn.

2. Appropriate words for the game board include: *well, run, light, hand, fire, hit, clear, iron, pen, save, spot, pick, star, note, hail, ball, point, bed, bill, jam, fine, sight, still, bear, hang.*

Fishy Words

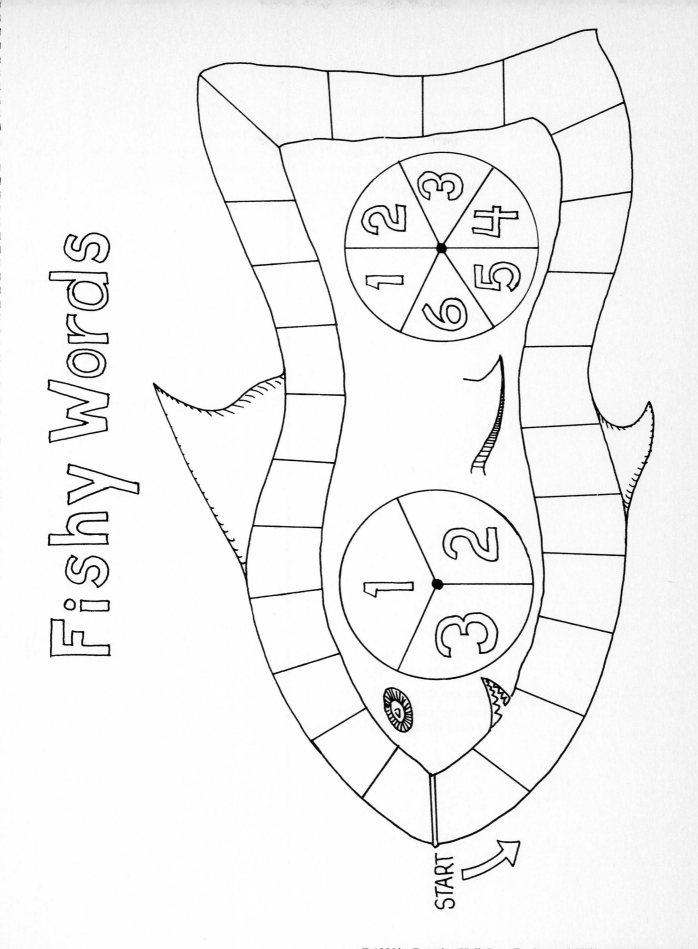

START

151

NAME: *Can You Strike 100?*

SKILL: Syllabication

MATERIALS: Game board, pen or pencil

PROCEDURE:

1. Fill in the game board with syllables as shown below.
2. Student pronounces the three syllables on each bowling pin, unscrambles them, and then writes the whole word on the line provided.
3. Each correct word is worth ten points.

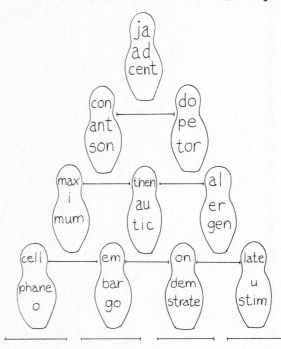

CAN YOU STRIKE 100?

Extra three syllable words: *invention, reproduce, unbutton, position, recognize, crocodile, episode, saxophone, satisfy, comical.*

VARIATIONS:

Long and short vowel words

On each pin write a vowel symbol (for example, *a*). Then write two words. Student copies the word which matches the symbol, writing it on the line provided.

ă-scratch, pain	ĕ-then, three	ĭ-kilt, kind
ŏ-clock, cloak	ŭ-cub, cube	ā-strap, stray
ē-treat, threat	ī-site, gift	ō-blonde, boast
ū-fuse, fuss		

CAN YOU STRIKE 100 ?

NAME:	*Rerouted*
SKILL:	Structural Analysis
MATERIALS:	Game board, pencil
PROCEDURE:	

1. Student finds and marks the open route through the maze, one in which only derived or inflected words are found (those with an affix). Each word a student encounters, s/he must read. If a word isn't affixed, the student must try another route.

2. The seven nonaffixed words are distractors—they look like derived words but they are only roots: *digest, remnant, presto, talent, jackal, unite, disco.* These words block maze paths and the student when encountering one must reroute.

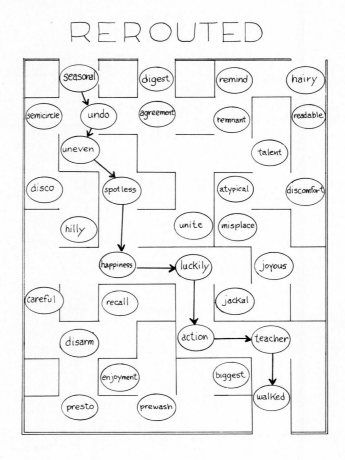

VARIATIONS:

    a. **Word Meanings:** Students find the route where all words are related in meaning.
    Related words: *say, talk, exclaim, shout, whisper, speak, remark, ask, nag, call, state, utter, tell, express, chatter, answer, beg, announce, voice, stutter, claim, suggest, relate, plead, reply*
    Distractors: *friend, seven, arrive, who, sense, chapter, want*

    b. **Phonics:** Twenty-five short or long vowel words may be used with seven distractors containing other vowel sounds.

REROUTED

155

NAME:	*Filling In*
SKILL:	Contextual Analysis
MATERIALS:	Game board, twelve game cards
PROCEDURE:	

1. On each of twelve cards write a skill sentence (see below).

2. Lay out the game cards with the skill sentences face down. On the side which faces up, number the cards from 1 to 12 so that the numbers are showing.

3. Have the students proceed along the board, space by space, clockwise, choosing which card to read, by figuring out the arithmetic problem in each space. For example, the starting space (10 + 1) equals 11. Therefore, the card 11 will be turned over and read.

4. If the student can get through the board with no mistakes, s/he is SUPER, 1 to 2 mistakes = GOOD, 3 to 5 mistakes = FAIR.

   There are different ways to write the skill sentences for the card. See sentence 1, below.

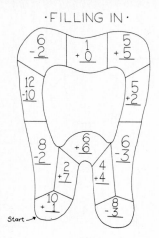

· FILLING IN ·

Skill Sentences for Cards:

1. The dog's _____ is Spot.*
2. He _____ the house white.
3. She wants _____ come, too.
4. She had a big _____ on her face.
5. _____ like to eat.
6. The _____ was beautiful.
7. What _____ did you come home?
8. He picked the lovely _____ .
9. Did you _____ that book yet?
10. He _____ the house today.
11. He felt _____ from eating that candy.
12. She _____ to school.

Example: A card might follow any of the following patterns:

    *The dog's _____ is Spot.
    The dog's n_____ is Spot.
    The dog's n_____e is Spot.
    The dog's n__m__ is Spot.
    The dog's __ __ __ __ is Spot.
    The dog's _____ is Spot. (*head   name   card   number*)

VARIATIONS:	

Almost every skill can be used with this board. Twelve cards are made with the words or sentences to be practiced. A combination of skills may also be used.

Examples: a. Consonant clusters: *pot   rave   sin*
                                 spot brave skin etc.

          b. Twelve sight word demons: *their who went,* etc.

          c. Twelve words underlined in sentences with two or three definitions given below. The student identifies the correct one.

·FILLING IN·

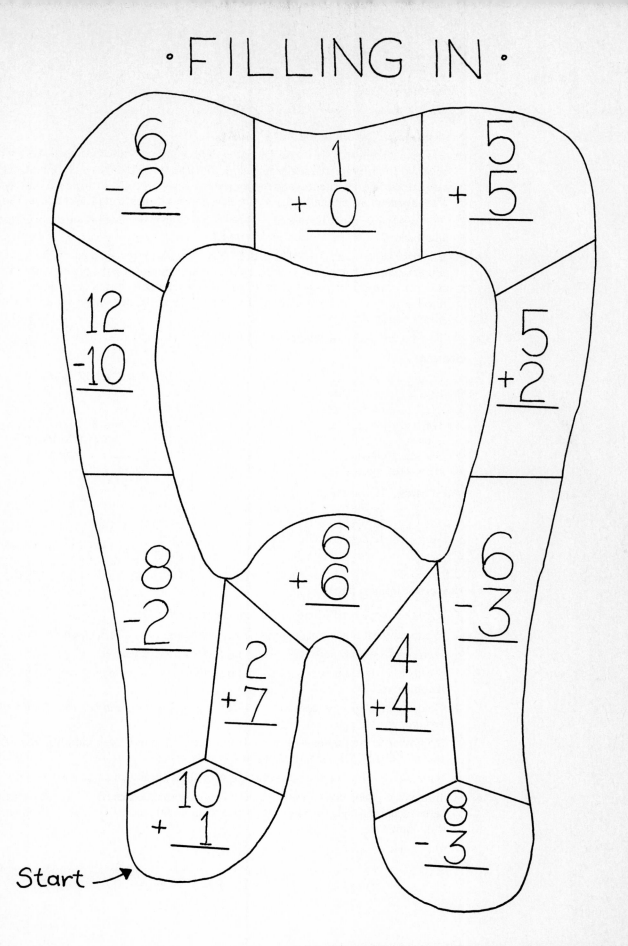

$\begin{array}{r} 6 \\ -2 \\ \hline \end{array}$

$\begin{array}{r} 1 \\ +0 \\ \hline \end{array}$

$\begin{array}{r} 5 \\ +5 \\ \hline \end{array}$

$\begin{array}{r} 12 \\ -10 \\ \hline \end{array}$

$\begin{array}{r} 5 \\ +2 \\ \hline \end{array}$

$\begin{array}{r} 8 \\ -2 \\ \hline \end{array}$

$\begin{array}{r} 6 \\ +6 \\ \hline \end{array}$

$\begin{array}{r} 6 \\ -3 \\ \hline \end{array}$

$\begin{array}{r} 2 \\ +7 \\ \hline \end{array}$

$\begin{array}{r} 4 \\ +4 \\ \hline \end{array}$

$\begin{array}{r} 10 \\ +1 \\ \hline \end{array}$

$\begin{array}{r} 8 \\ -3 \\ \hline \end{array}$

Start →

NAME:	*Concentrate*
SKILL:	Contextual analysis
MATERIALS:	Game board, eleven pairs of word (word and sentence) cards
PROCEDURE:	Students play "Concentration."

1. Eleven pairs of cards are made. On one card of each pair, write a sentence with a word missing. In the suggested sentences below, the missing word appears at the end, beginning, or middle of sentences and represents different parts of speech (noun, verb, etc.). For the matching eleven cards use the eleven words which complete the sentences.

2. The twenty-two cards are placed face down, one in each box on the board, covering the numbers.

3. The first player turns over two cards. If the two cards picked are a pair—that is, if the sentence can be completed sensibly by the word turned over—the player marks down the total number of points given in each box uncovered, keeps the pair, and takes another turn. If the cards do not form a pair, they are turned back over and the next player continues.

4. The winner can be the player with the most points or the most pairs.

Sentence cards

1. The ice cubes _____ in the sun.
2. That is _____car.
3. _____ did you go?
4. The book was _____two other books.
5. Her hair looked _____ .
6. He walked away _____ .
7. She needed to buy food at the _____ .
8. He was _____ the baby.
9. Put away your _____!
10. _____ came to the party.
11. She will _____ the letter.

Word cards
1. *melted*
2. *their*
3. *where*
4. *between*
5. *beautiful*
6. *slowly*
7. *market*
8. *carrying*
9. *clothes*
10. *they*
11. *write*

(See board on next page.)

VARIATIONS:	This game may be used wherever pairs of cards are suitable.

a. Word pairs with matching sounds—*cat, sad; made, rain; key, seal; comb, soap;* etc.

b. Homonyms—*hear, here; die, dye; their, there; brake, break;* etc.

c. Words with the same roots—*redo, doing; unhappy, happily; replay, playful; misread, readable;* etc.

d. Compound words or contractions—*base, ball; did not, didn't; I'll, I will; play, ground;* etc.

e. Synonyms or antonyms—*malign* (slander, praise); *lucid* (clear, cloudy). See words under TIC TACKY TOE (page 174).

f. Sight words—Eleven pairs of sight words or sight phrases must be created.

g. Inferences—Sentences using figurative language and sentences or phrases with the same meaning: "He was in the doghouse with his parents," "His parents were angry with him," etc.

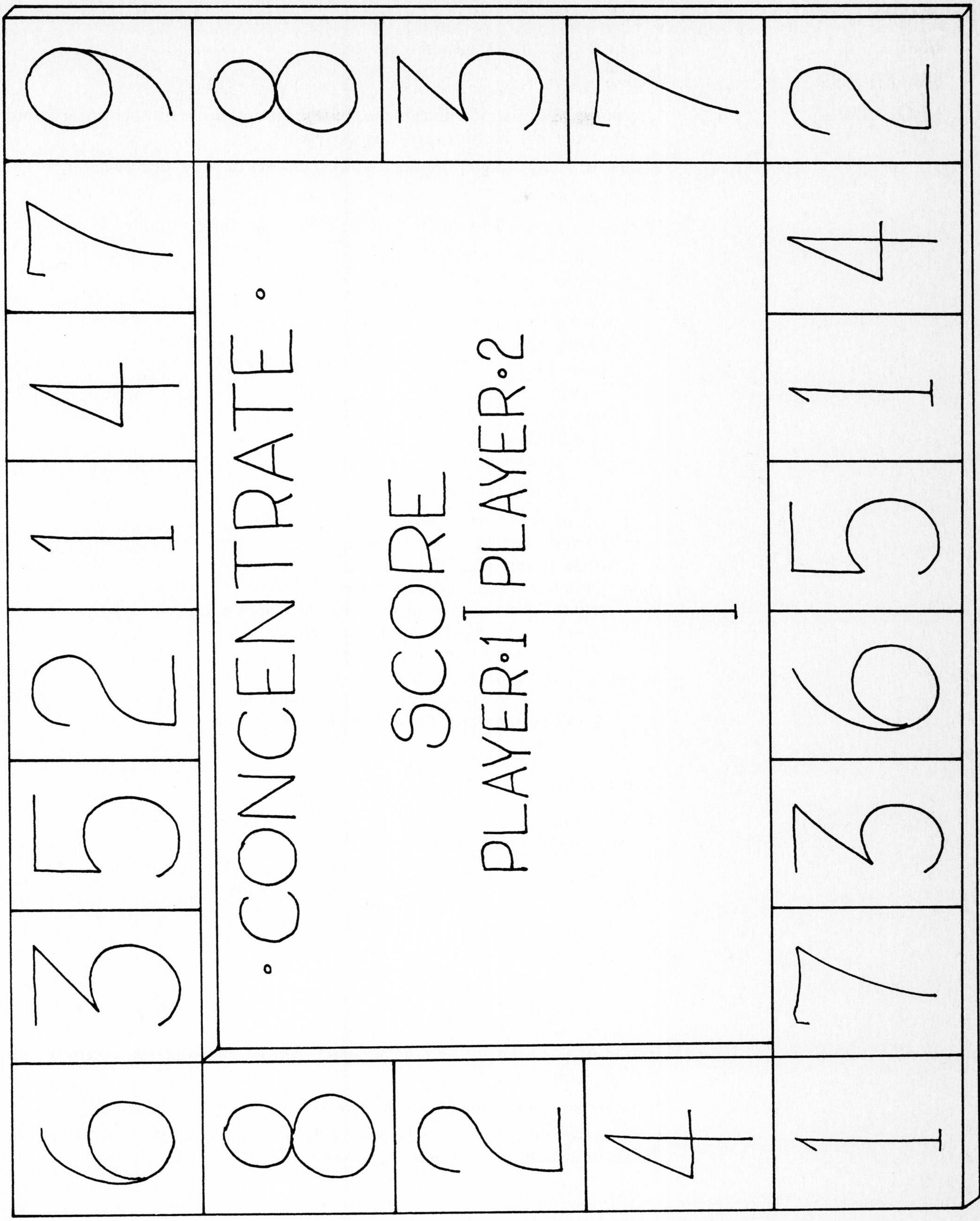
·CONCENTRATE·
SCORE
PLAYER·1
PLAYER·2

NAME:	*A Day in School*
SKILL:	Comprehension of Instructional Vocabulary
MATERIALS:	Picture board
PROCEDURE:	1. Student will either manipulate the student cut-out or use his/her finger in order to follow the oral directions given by the teacher.
	2. Teachers may choose from the following phrases or write their own.

Directions:

Place _____ (a name that the student chooses for the cut-out):

    to the left of the blackboard
    in front of the teacher's desk
    at the bottom of the room
    over his/her own desk
    beside the door
    below the flag
    next to the book shelf
    under the bulletin board
    to the right of Sally's desk
    above the window

Let _____ go to the blackboard and

    underline the word *brown*
    point to the first letter in the sentence
    circle the last word in the sentence
    put a box around the letter at the end of *fox*
    find the two words in the sentence which are the same
    cross out the animal words in the sentence
    tell which word comes after *jumped*
    put a line under the first letter in *dog*
    show how the words *fox* and *dog* are the same
    show how the words *fox* and *dog* are different

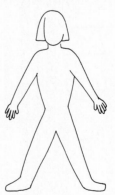

VARIATIONS:

Instead of using the prepared game board, cut out magazine advertisements with interesting settings and characters.

Have the student eventually give his/her own directions to the cut-out.

For help with the literal comprehension skill, following directions, have the student read directions instead of listening to them.

DAY IN SCHOOL

The quick brown fox jumps over the lazy dog.

NAME: *Story Shapes**

SKILL: Understanding Narratives

MATERIALS: Game board, marker

PROCEDURE:

1. Have student(s) place the events of a story into either diagram or shape on the game board.

2. The train shape is appropriate if skill to be practiced is beginning-middle-end.

3. The staircase is designed to contain the five-part narrative structure explained in Chapter Five (background, problem, attempts to solve it, climax, and resolution).

4. The completed shapes below demonstrate how the diagrams work.

STORY SHAPES

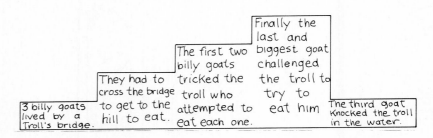

VARIATIONS:

a. Sometimes a central character can suggest a unique story shape. Two examples follow, but you'll need to create your own, given the particular stories your students read. Don't worry about lack of artistic gifts. Just trace a book illustration, as we did. Then write something about or from the story within the character shape.

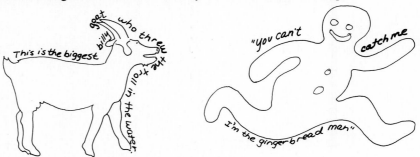

b. For inferential comprehension, write a sentence(s) in the middle of the train or on two or three steps of the staircase and have students fill in logical sentences to precede and follow.

*A tip of the hat to Dorothy Grant Hemmings, *Communication in Action: Teaching the Language Arts.* Boston: Houghton Mifflin, 1982.

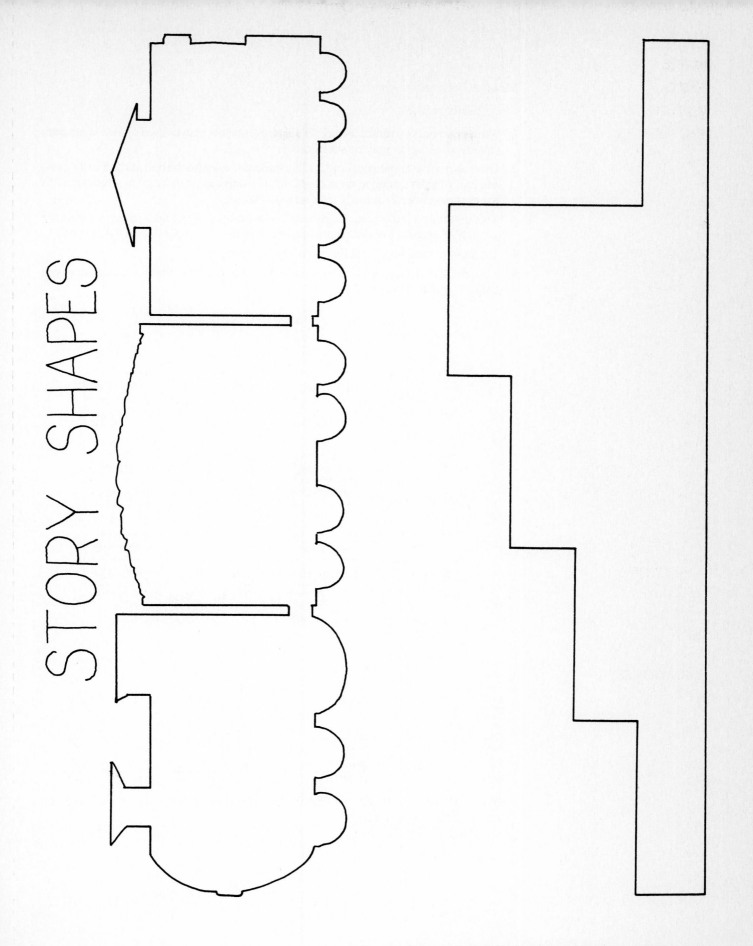

STORY SHAPES

NAME:	*Dominate*
SKILL:	Meaning Vocabulary—Synonyms
MATERIALS:	Game board, markers
PROCEDURE:	

1. Write two words on each domino. The examples below may be used or any vocabulary you are working on may be substituted.

2. There are twelve dominoes (1 to 12). The student starts with the bottom half of *1* (scent) and looks for its synonym on the top half of a domino, in this case at *9* (odor). S/he writes the number *9* on the blank line that follows *1*.

3. Now the student looks at the bottom half of *9* (expand). S/he finds its synonym on the top half of another domino and writes the number of that domino in the next blank.

4. The student continues until the top of *1* is reached.

5. It is helpful to put a check next to each domino that is used so that fewer dominoes will need to be searched each time.

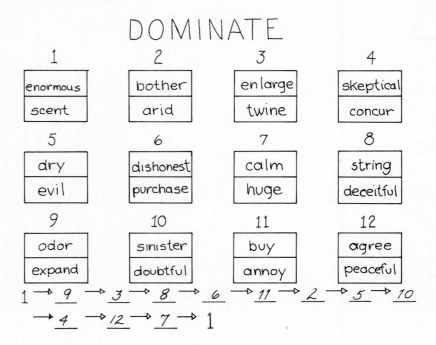

DOMINATE

1	2	3	4
enormous	bother	enlarge	skeptical
scent	arid	twine	concur

5	6	7	8
dry	dishonest	calm	string
evil	purchase	huge	deceitful

9	10	11	12
odor	sinister	buy	agree
expand	doubtful	annoy	peaceful

1 → 9 → 3 → 8 → 6 → 11 → 2 → 5 → 10
→ 4 → 12 → 7 → 1

VARIATIONS:

Vowels

1 raw	2 Fred	3 sweep	4 dime
chap	trip	turn	brake

5 sill	6 lack	7 mute	8 perk
toast	trust	shock	haul

9 stay	10 grow	11 club	12 flop
dent	cube	find	treat

1. Start with the bottom half of 1 (chap) and find a word with the same vowel sound on the top half of a domino.

2. Continue as described above.

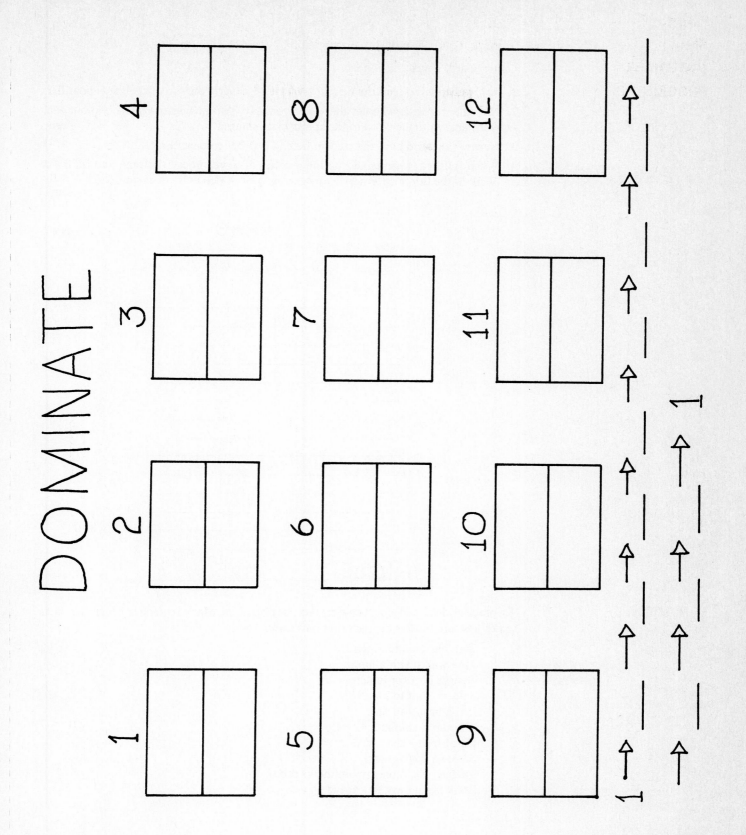

DOMINATE

NAME:	*The _____ Have It! (Yeas or Nays)**	
SKILL:	Multiple meanings and word connotations	
MATERIALS:	Game board, pencil, dictionary	
PROCEDURE:		

1. Ask student(s) to read the words you have written on the top of the game board.

2. Have them decide whether they feel positively (yea) or negatively (nay) about each word and write the word in the appropriate column.

3. Next to the word have the student defend his/her column choice.

4. When finished students add up the number of words in each column and fill in the blank in the title with Yea or Nay depending on which column has more entries.

The _____ Have it !

1. Power 2. Dough 3. Slight 4. odor 5. Plain

6. Squeal 7. Expand 8. Shallow 9. Ruffle 10. Relish

Yeas	Nays
Total:	Total:

VARIATION:

To practice distinguishing between fact and opinion: Mark sentences which are facts under Yea and those which are opinions under Nays.

Tom has an odd accent.
Jane walks with a limp.
George is in for lunch.
Sally is "out to lunch."
It is a beautiful day.
The sun is shining.
Carol seems distracted.
Richard appears lost.
Michael has three appointments today.
Betsy has a busy day ahead.

*Thanks to Beck, Isabel and McKeown, Margaret, "Learning Words Well: A Program To Enhance Vocabulary and Comprehension," *The Reading Teacher,* March 1983, pp. 622–25.

The _____ Have it !

1. _____ 2. _____ 3. _____ 4. _____ 5. _____

6. _____ 7. _____ 8. _____ 9. _____ 10. _____

Yeas	Nays
Total:	Total:

NAME: *Unlock the Meaning*

SKILL: Matching Synonymous Expressions

MATERIALS: Game board, a set of twelve cut-out keys

PROCEDURE:

1. Teacher will use key template below and twelve cut-out key shapes.

2. Twelve sentences which contain synonymous expressions (six matches) are printed one each on the keys, which are then placed face down over the key outlines on the board.

3. Student(s) turn over two keys at a time.

4. If a match is made, the keys are kept and a point is won. If a student can also identify key phrases *within the sentences which match or are roughly equivalent,* s/he may gain an additional point for each.

5. For example, in the sentences:
   a. Sue and Brian help out at the bakery after school.
   b. They work as baker's assistants from four to six on weekdays.
   There are four potential phrase matches:
   a. Sue and Brian / they
   b. help out / work
   c. from four to six on weekdays / after school
   d. at the bakery / baker's assistants
   If a student found all four, his/her total point count for that turn would be five, one for the sentence match and four for phrase matches.

6. If no match is found, the keys are turned face down again for the next student's turn.

Sentences for keys:

I hope you can come to my party.
Lenore, will you join us at my house Saturday night?
That outfit is too small on you.
Look how tight that dress is, Annie.
The soccer game ended with a loss for our team.
We didn't win the kicking contest.
Let's spread the picnic out here.
We can put the food on that table.
A magical creature came out of the woods.
An enchanting elf appeared through an opening in the thicket.
Are you feeling blue?
Why so glum, chum?

Key template

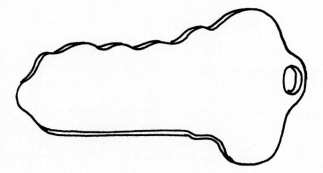

VARIATIONS: Synonyms (*moist / damp*), antonyms (*moist / dry*), or figurative-literal (*I could eat a horse / I'm very hungry*) matches could be printed on the keys.

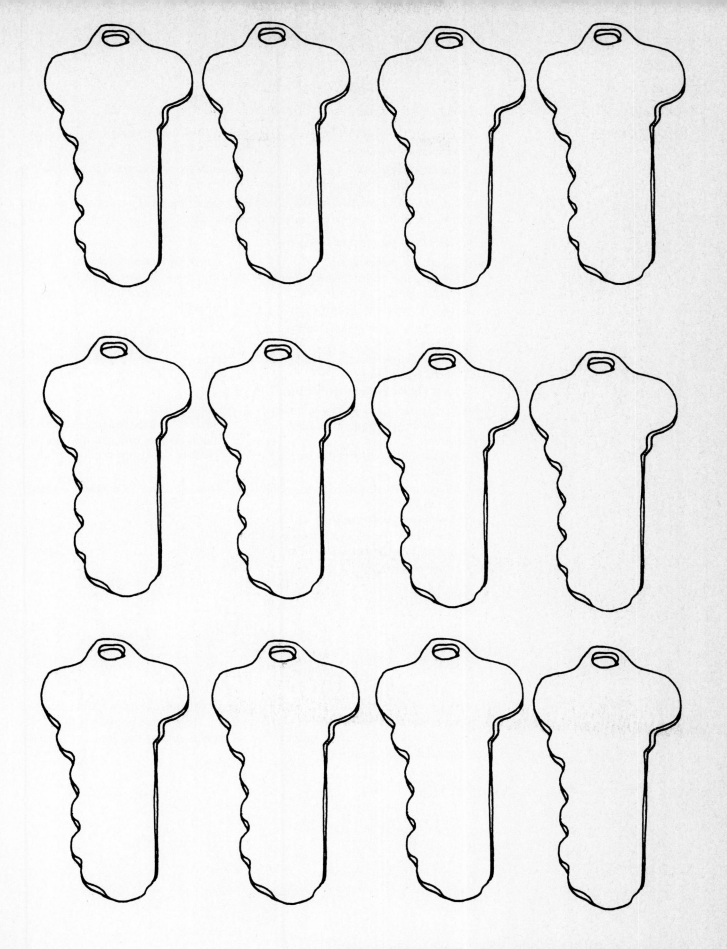

NAME: *Little Things Mean a Lot*

SKILL: Attending to details—detail comprehension

MATERIALS: Game board, colored markers

PROCEDURE:
1. Teachers add details to the game board drawings to grossly or subtly distinguish one drawing from the others.
2. a. *Teacher-directed activity*—Teacher asks student(s) to find or point to the drawing which matches a given oral or written description.
   b. *Independent activity*—Written directions (circle, underline, cross out, etc.) are given to a student who responds on the gameboard.

Sample directions for independent activity

Couch   Circle the messy couch.
        Draw a line under the neat couch.
        Cross out the old couch.
        (See illustrations below)

Other distinguishing details:
with many pillows, no pillows, two pillows, green, plaid, dotted, striped.

Girl   Put an X under the girl with the handbag.
       Draw a circle around the girl with the shoulder bag.
       Star the girl with the paper bag.

Other details:
mad, glad, sad
skirt and blouse, pajamas, slacks and sweater

House   Circle the house with no chimney.
        Underline the house with two chimneys.
        Color in the house with a single chimney.

Other details:
flowers, shrubs, vegetable garden, blinds on windows, curtains on window, shades on window

Shelf   Label the shelf with only books on it, "bookshelf."
        Put a star above the shelf with several tall books on it. Cross out the shelf with books and other things on it.

Other details: Put anything you like on the shelves.

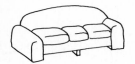  

VARIATIONS: This activity can be done by a small group of students who can take turns adding details to the pictures, creating the directions, and responding. To provide practice with instructional vocabulary, teachers can simplify the differences among pictures, and give the "cross out," etc., directions orally.

LITTLE THINGS MEAN ALOT

NAME: *Jumping to Conclusions*

PURPOSE: Making Inferences

MATERIALS: Game board, sentence cards

PROCEDURE:
1. The student begins at box 1 and picks a sentence card (see below). At least two inferences can be made for each sentence.*
2. If the student can make at least one inference, s/he moves to the next box and picks a new card. Multiple inferences, however, should be encouraged.
3. Play continues until box 8 is completed.

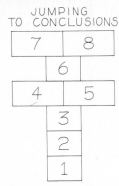

Sentences for cards:
1. Cindy was all dressed up, wearing a red skirt and sweater, and red bows on the new shoes her mom had just bought her.
2. Jed watched the screen, sitting glued to his seat for the whole two hours.
3. Zachary jumped on the brakes of his car and stopped just in time.
4. First Chip got out a map of the city and then he and Bonnie pulled over to the side of the road to plan their day.
5. Dan had to go to school that day so he carried a box of Kleenex with him.
6. Emily happily sat in her seat and looked down to the center ring where the lions were doing tricks.
7. David asked for seconds of eggs and juice before he gathered his books and left.
8. The snow looked clean and white but Michael knew it meant a lot of trouble for him.
9. Beth put on her boots and raincoat and carried her umbrella in her briefcase as she left for work.
10. Lee nervously packed his suitcase with his clothes for the next seven days as he prepared for the flight which would take him to see his father and stepmother.
11. The ten-inning game ended as Ann ran around the bases and crossed home plate.
12. Geoff called to say he'd be home in an hour and that the family should eat now and not wait for him.
13. Jon ran to pet the dog who quickly climbed into his lap.
14. Jenna was glad she'd worn boots because the path to the barn was muddy.
15. Wait until I change into a suit and then I'll race you to the raft.
16. When he got up during the night to go to the bathroom, Gordon tripped over a toy he'd left out.

   *If the first card reads "I was so hungry, I gobbled down my food, the carrots included," inferences could be:
   S/he had not eaten all day.
   S/he finished eating quickly.
   S/he did not have a stomach flu.
   S/he does not usually eat carrots.

VARIATION: Pick a card with a figurative expression and explain what is really meant.
Examples: It was raining cats and dogs. Has the cat got your tongue? There's no use crying over spilled milk. He was seeing red. John was in the doghouse. Et cetera.

JUMPING TO CONCLUSIONS

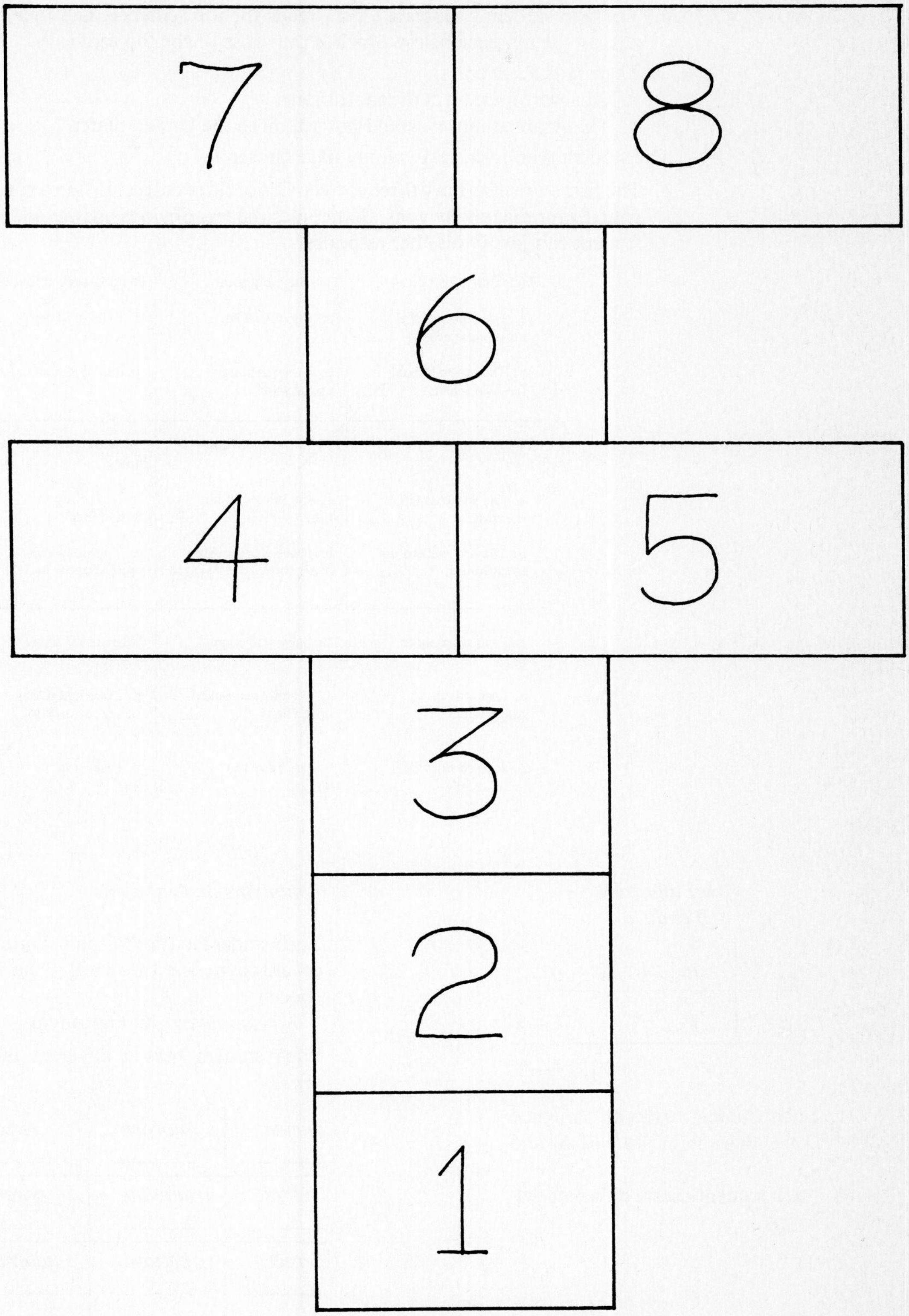

NAME:	Tic Tacky Toe
PURPOSE:	Inference: Cause and Effect
MATERIALS:	Game board, two pens (two different color inks)
PROCEDURE:	

1. Students play regular Tic Tac Toe using C (cause) and E (effect) instead of X and O. The teacher fills in the board with the sentences shown below.

2. The first student chooses a block, reads the top sentence, and then puts his/her C next to the sentence below which is the cause of the top sentence.

   There was a gas crisis.
   a. Cars were lined up at the gas stations.
   b. The Arab countries would not sell oil to the United States.   C

   The student who is using E would have chosen *a*.

3. The first student to have three correct C's or three correct E's in a row vertically, horizontally, or diagonally wins. Sometimes the less obvious answer will be correct if the student can justify his/her response.

He painted his house.	Tom ate a big meal.	The dog barked loudly.
a. The paint on the house was peeling. ___	a. Tom felt filled. ___	a. Sally held her dog tightly. ___
b. The house looked fresh and clean. E	b. Tom was hungry. ___ up the walk.	b. The mailman came
The bell rang.	Her toe was hurting.	The leaves were falling.
a. The students left the class. ___	a. She looked at her foot. E	a. It was late September. ___
b. The boy walked up to the house. ___	b. There was a pebble in her shoe. ___	b. The sidewalks were slippery in the rain.
Jane was learning to read.	The baby was crying.	Peter missed a day of school.
a. Jane was in first grade. ___	a. The mother picked up the baby. ___	a. Peter had a lot of schoolwork to do. E
b. Jane could read to her family. ___	b. The baby was hungry. ___	b. Peter was sick. ___

VARIATIONS:

Vowel digraphs, Blending

	r __l	m __l	b__t
X = ea O = ai	l__d	f __r	l__n
	h__l	m__n	r__d

1. Each student uses an assigned vowel digraph in place of X and O

2. Each student uses a different color ink.

Synonyms or Antonyms

1. Each student in turn fills in a synonym or antonym for the word s/he has chosen.
   X = synonym   O = antonym

2. Each student uses a different color ink.

ancient	morose	terse
___	___	___
lethal	amiable	potent
___	___	___
erect	blatant	adamant
___	___	___

Tic Tacky Toe

X =
O =

NAME: *Propaganda Points*

PURPOSE: Critical Reading

MATERIALS: Game board, sentence cards

PROCEDURE:

1. A student picks a propaganda sentence card (see below).
2. The student identifies the techniques used in the propaganda written on the card and adds the number of points indicated on the board.
   Example: Everyone knows that *Candyloo* is good for you. (4 [Bandwagon] + 7 [Glittering Generalities] = 11). Any reasonable answer can be accepted.
3. The next student picks a card and they compare point results. The player with the higher score gets a point and play continues until the cards are used. The one with the most points wins.
4. A single student may wish to go through all of the cards and see which card uses the most techniques and/or earns the most points.

Sentences for Cards:

1. The bounce of a real winner—buy the basketball the hometown team loves.
2. If Smellproof deodorant is good enough for heads of state in tense negotiations, then you know it's right for you.
3. All over the country people are saying, "It's Bonzo for me!"
4. Our all new liquid cleanser is 50 percent more effective.
5. The active ingredient in Glowy helps your dishes look terrific.
6. We may be small town folks but honesty is our trademark. When we say Hare is the best car available, we are telling the truth.
7. Whereas the cost of gas has increased 400 percent in the last twenty years, Blossom orange juice is up less than one-half of that.
8. For a sexy new look, use Curl-lash mascara.
9. Tired of looking ordinary? Players' clothes will make people sit up and take notice.
10. John Doe, the fast Olympic runner in 1980, runs for his Eatums each morning. A better breakfast cereal can't be found.

PROPAGANDA POINTS

VARIATION: The teacher may wish to have a student(s) search magazines for actual ads and see which product(s) collects the most points.

PROPAGANDA POINTS

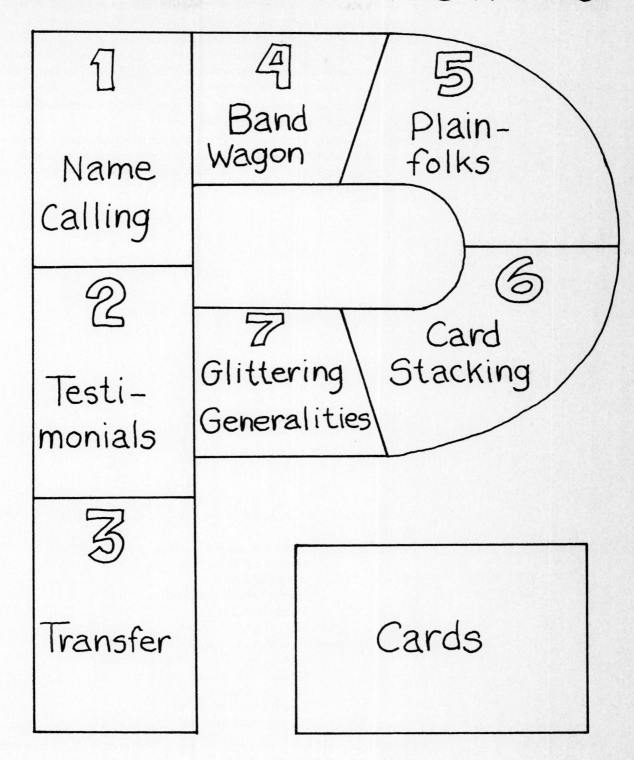

1 Name Calling

2 Testi-monials

3 Transfer

4 Band Wagon

5 Plain-folks

6 Card Stacking

7 Glittering Generalities

Cards

NAME: *Is That a Fact?*

SKILL: Distinguishing fact from opinion

MATERIALS: Game board, sentence cards, board markers

PROCEDURE:

1. Two cards each containing a fact or opinion sentence are placed on each space. The sentence side is facing up. The word *fact* or the word *opinion* is written on the reverse side.

2. The two students begin at start and move one space at a turn. The student reads the sentence card and identifies the sentence as fact or opinion. The reverse side of the card reveals the answer (fact or opinion).

3. If the student is correct, s/he receives a point. Students alternate turns. The student with the most points at the end wins.

4. Optional—After deciding whether the sentence is factual or not, the student changes it into an opinion if it was a factual sentence or vice versa and wins a second point. That racing car has been clocked at 100 miles an hour, may become: I'll bet that racing car can go 100 miles an hour.

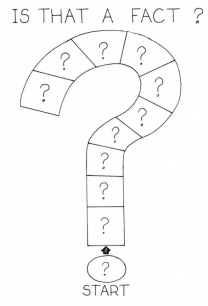

IS THAT A FACT ?

START

Sentences for Cards: See variation for *The _____ Have It! (Yeas or Nays)* for ten sentences.

Others: Facts: Susan is wearing a red dress.
I have a cut finger.
It is a Fall day.
John is President of the class.
Margie read a book.
Tim got an A in history.

Opinions: Mary looks very good.
John Doe is certain to win the election.
It's hard to believe the year is half over.
He's gotten so big.
That is a thick book.
The car needs washing.

VARIATIONS: Cards for any skill may be used with this board. Written answers, if applicable, are placed on the reverse of each card.

IS THAT A FACT ?

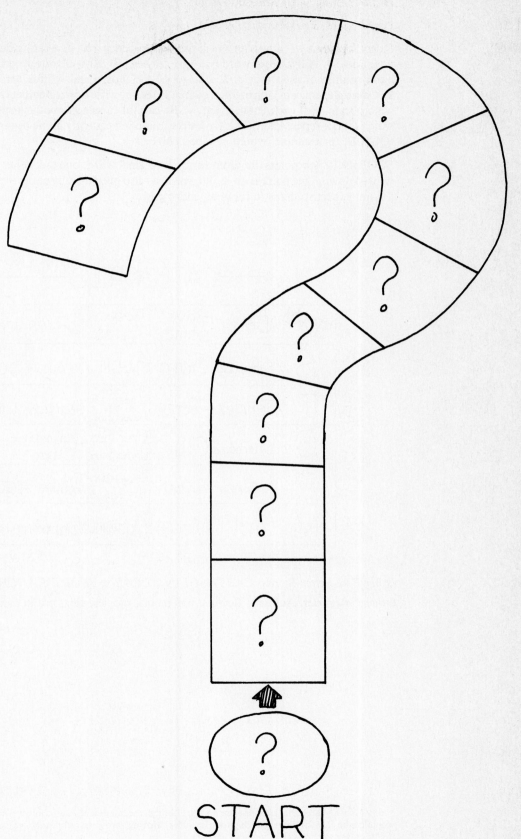

START

NAME: *Storm*

SKILL: Distinguishing Main Idea and Details

MATERIALS: Game board, markers

PROCEDURE: Storm is a game of categories which provides practice with generating details for a given main idea. 1. A five-letter word (we have chosen STORM) is written vertically in the left hand column of a 6×6 grid. 2. Categories are chosen and written across the top row. 3. Game players, working on their own or in teams, write down members of the categories which begin with each letter at left. 4. Be careful to select broad categories and words which do not repeat letters or have letters found infrequently at the beginning of a word. (QUILL, for example, would be a bad choice.)

SCORING: Two points are given for each original word, one that other players haven't written down. One point is given if a word has also been used by another player. *Caution:* Do not expect students to fill in an entire grid.

←———CATEGORIES———→

FIVE LETTER WORD ↑

STORM	Dogs	Boys' names	Book Titles	Cities	Veggies
S	Schnauzer	Sam	Sybil	Secaucus	Salad
T	Terrier	Terry	To Think That I saw it on Mulberry St.	Teaneck	turnip
O	Otterhound	Ollie	Over Sea Under Stone	Oklahoma City	Okra
R	Retriever	Roger	Return of the Native	Reno	radish
M	mutt	Melvin	Madeline	Minneapolis	mushroom

VARIATIONS: *Other Five-Letter Words:* EARTH, GLINT, LEARN, SPORT, RANCH, MELTS.

Other Categories: Animals, flowers, ball teams, movies, cars, brand names, clothing.*

*Not all categories need to elicit nouns, although the number of noun choices is usually greater than would be the case for other speech parts. Try these: Moving verbs (*run, skip, inch, go*), adjectives for food (*light, creamy, crisp, sweet, peppery, tender*).

STORM					

FIVE-LETTER WORD ←

Study Skills Crossword

Study Skills Terminology

Xeroxed copy of puzzle, pencil

1. Xerox the following page.
2. Have student(s) complete the puzzle in order to review what they have learned about study skills or to assess their understanding.
3. Allow student(s) to compare their completed puzzle with the answer key below.

ANSWERS:

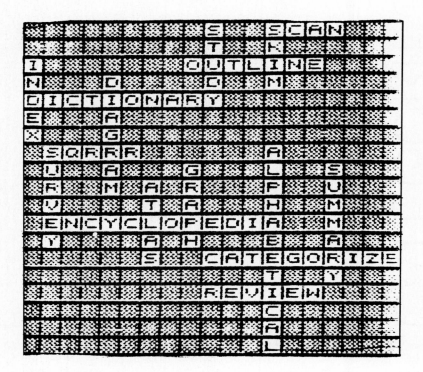

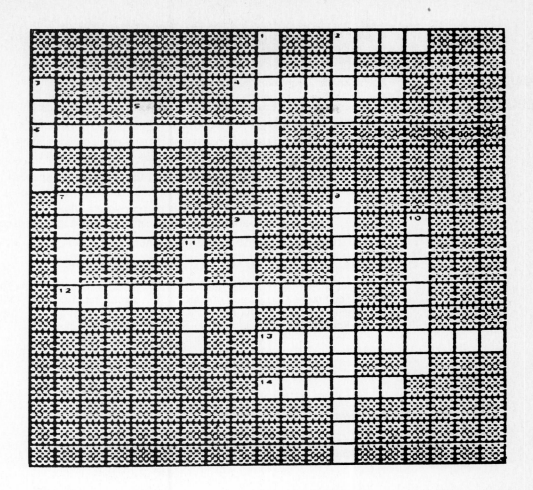

Across Clues

2. To read quickly to find a detail
4. Notes which show only the main ideas of a book or chapter
6. A book of the meanings and pronunciations of words
7. A system for the careful reading of a textbook chapter
12. A set of books with articles on many topics
13. To group like details together in order to remember them
14. Go over something again to refresh one's memory

Down Clues

1. Read carefully to try to learn something
2. To read quickly for the main ideas
3. An alphabetical list of the contents of a book
7. To get an overview of a textbook chapter
8. The order in which words can be found in a dictionary
9. A diagram which shows the relationship between two or more things by using dots, bars or lines
10. A brief statement of the main ideas of a book or chapter
11. A collection of maps

NAME: *Get the Signal**

SKILL: Understanding How Signal Words Affect Reading Speed

MATERIALS: Game board, twenty-six cards, a marker for each player

PROCEDURE:

1. The words and phrases listed below are printed on blank cards. The pile of cards is turned face down in the center of the board.

2. Students choose cards in turn. They read the word or phrase and advance their markers according to the following:

   If a "go-ahead 2" card is picked, move ahead two spaces.
   If a "go-ahead 1" card is picked, move ahead one space.
   When a "go-ahead 0" card is picked, do not move.
   When a "turn-about" card is selected, move back one space.

3. The student who finishes first is the winner.

GO-AHEAD 2	**GO-AHEAD 1**	**GO-AHEAD 0**	**TURN-ABOUT**
These words indicate that more of the same will follow. Reading can proceed fairly quickly.	These words suggest that an important idea will follow. Slow reading down a bit to insure understanding.	These words signal that one major idea or a whole story or article is about to end.	Such words prepare the reader for an abrupt change. They turn the written thought in another direction.
and	*thus*	*as a result*	*but*
more	*so*	*finally*	*yet*
moreover	*consequently*	*in conclusion*	*nevertheless*
more than that	*accordingly*	*at last*	*although*
furthermore			*however*
also			*still*
likewise			*otherwise*
in addition			*in spite of*

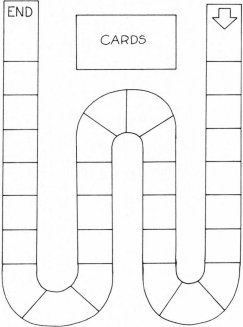

*The signal words used here were identified and classified by Nila Banton Smith in *Faster Reading Made Easy* (N.Y.: Popular Library, 1963).

GET THE SIGNAL

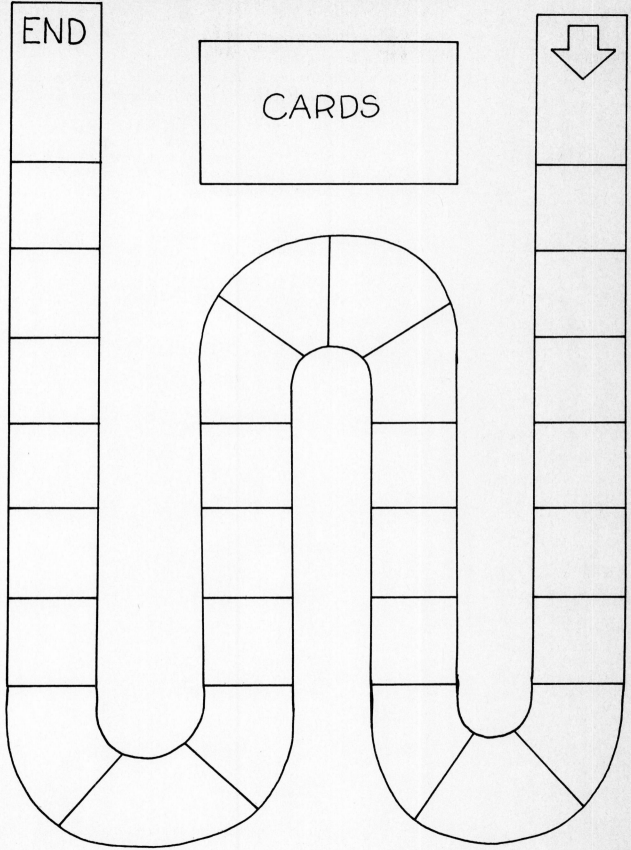

NAME: *Reading Rate Record*

SKILL: Flexible Reading Rate

MATERIALS: Copies of the chart, file folder, pen/pencil

PROCEDURE:
1. Teacher makes copies of the chart.
2. Students or students and teacher fill out a copy at rate improvement session.
3. Completed copies should be kept in a folder so that students can monitor their own progress.

READING RATE RECORD

NAME: _____ DATE: _____

I. BEFORE READING

Title of Material _____ Author _____

Number of Words _____

Your purpose for reading[1] _____

_____

Your interest in the topic[2] _____

Your previous knowledge about the topic[3] _____

Kind of material[4] _____

Pace at which you will read[5] _____

II. DURING READING

Time yourself—

Start: Hour _____ Minutes _____ Seconds _____

Finish: Hour _____ Minutes _____ Seconds _____

III. AFTER READING

1. Answer comprehension questions.

2. Computer comprehension score (% of questions answered correctly) _____ .

3. Compute words per minute $\left(\dfrac{\text{number of words}}{\text{number of seconds} \times 60} = \text{wpm} \right)$ _____ .

[1]*Purpose for reading:* to get ready for test, recreation, to get specific information, to get an overview, to enjoy the language, other

[2]*Interest in topic:* very high, high, average, low, very low

[3]*Previous knowledge:* very knowledgeable, somewhat knowledgeable, very little knowledge, no knowledge

[4]*Kind of material:* textbook, article, story, poem, other

Pace: study, average, rapid, skim, scan

NAME:	*Rate-A-Read*
SKILL:	Stimulating and Assessing Reading Interests
MATERIALS:	Rating sheet
PROCEDURE:	After finishing a story or book, a student completes the adjacent rating sheet. Both numbers one to five and smiling/frowning faces are offered so that students have a choice of response style. Writing space is provided after each response set, in case students want to explain or elaborate.
VARIATION:	When students read nonfiction such as text chapters or articles, the statements below may be substituted for those on the adjacent rating sheet.

1. This book (article, chapter) was so interesting, I could hardly put it down.
2. The author knows a lot about her subject.
3. I know something about this subject, but I found out even more.
4. This was the first time I'd read about this subject, and now I'd like to read more about it.
5. The author explained things well.
6. The author had facts to back up his opinions.
7. I liked the writing style.
8. I'd read another book by this author.
9. I'd read another book on this subject.
10. I'd recommend this book to a friend.

Rate-a-Read Rating Sheet

After reading each sentence on the left, circle a number or face which shows your opinion about your book or story. One (or the big smile) means you agree quite a bit. Five (or the big frown) means you disagree quite a bit. The other three numbers and faces are less strong opinions. If you wish, you may explain your rating in the "Why do you think so?" column.

Why do you think so?

1. This book (or story) was so exciting I could hardly put it down.

2. I learned something about myself from this book.

3. I was able to imagine places described in this book.

4. The author used language clearly.

5. The author used language beautifully.

6. The characters were interesting people. I'd like to know more about them.

7. I know some things about life I never knew before.

8. I like the author's sense of humor.

9. I'd like to read another book by this writer.

10. I'd recommend this book to a friend.

NAME:	*Snack-Man*
PURPOSE:	Motivation
MATERIALS:	Game board on adjacent page.
PROCEDURE:	

1. The "snacks" are left blank in the game board so teachers can print in the words which match one student's interests. The words below are useful for students who enjoy video games. Other high interest lists are found below in the Variations section.

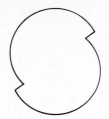

Video Game Vocabulary

asteroids	corridor
invaders	exit
monster	bonus
energizer	pattern
strategy	joystick
tunnel	

2. One student, using the Snack-Man cut-out as a game piece attempts to "eat" all the snacks (identify the words) located along a path s/he takes through the maze. Teacher or other student may check answers. The object is to get from start to finish following a single path. When a word is unknown, the player begins again, trying another path. Once a path has been mastered, a student can compete against himself to increase speed of word identifications.

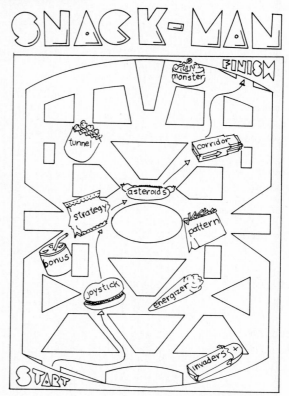

VARIATIONS:

Car Vocabulary

clutch	registration
radiator	transmission
battery	fender bender
accelerator	rear view
down shift	mirror
windshield	defroster

Sports Vocabulary

touchdown	inning
face-off	relay
tackle	marathon
strike out	slam dunk
foul ball	volley

SNACK-MAN

FINISH

START

NAME:	*Match-a-Meaning*
SKILL:	Matching standard and nonstandard English words, phrases, and sentences.
MATERIALS:	The game board on the adjacent page. Word, phrase and sentence lists are below.
PROCEDURE:	

1. Xerox enough copies of board for players.

2. Print in nonstandard words, phrases, and sentences in appropriate boxes. Be sure each student's card has these in a different order. Otherwise all will win simultaneously.

3. Play like BINGO. Caller reads standard words, phrases and sentences. Player(s) must cover with a marker the box which contains the equivalent nonstandard expression. Five across, down or on the diagonal wins.

Words:

a. *Nonstandard*—aks, bof, ain't, mas', hisself, wait, police, got, bloods, short

b. *Standard*—ask, both, isn't, mask, himself, waited, police, have, blacks, car

Phrases:

a. *Nonstandard*—be busy, the house what Jack built, runnin' a Joe, he shirt, Carla say, the hawk, hit you upside you head, messin wid, main man, run it by me

b. *Standard*—is busy, the house that Jack built, running to Joe's, his shirt, Carla says, windy cold weather, hit you on the head, damaging, best friend, explain it

Sentences:

a. *Nonstandard*—It was a garbage can on the sidewalk. Where Henry at? Judy, she be the teacher. They laughin.

b. *Standard*—There was a garbage can on the sidewalk. Where's Henry? Judy is the teacher. They are laughing.

VARIATIONS:	*Synonyms:*

Words:

a. dine, fall, chubby, mind, trip, start, trunk, road, stone, smart

b. eat, autumn, fat, listen, voyage, begin, suitcase, highway, pebble, brainy

Phrases:

a. very thin, chocolate bar, clothing, writing tools, cereal box, uncle, cup and saucer, father, in a minute, to the grocery

b. skinny, candy, pants and shirt, pen and pencil, breakfast food container, mother's brother, dishes, male parent, very soon, to the store

Sentences:

a. The robin sang a joyful song. Water splashed on my good shoes. Mom sent me to the store for a loaf of bread. I'll take the train to town.

b. The robin sang a merry tune. My good shoes were splashed with water. Mother sent me for bread. I will take the subway downtown.

	WORD				
PHRASE					
SENTENCE			MATCH– A-MEANING		
PHRASE					
WORD					

NAME:	*Who Knows Where or When?*
SKILL:	This activity focuses attention on the meanings of morphemes which signal tense or possession.
MATERIALS:	The game board on the next page; the sentences and questions below.
PROCEDURE:	The teacher chooses appropriate sentences from those below and / or creates her own. The sentences may be written or presented orally. The example below shows how answers are placed on the game board.

Example: We danced at Jack's house.
a. Where was the dancing? *jackhouse* *Jack's* *my house*
b. When was the dancing? *yesterday* *today* *tomorrow*
 "Jack's" is placed on the board in the "where" house.
 "yesterday" is placed on the board in the "when" clock.

1. Joan will slip three boxes into Lee's shopping bag.
 a. Where is Joan slipping three boxes?
 in a shop into Lee into Lee's bag
 b. When is Joan putting boxes in a bag?
 now later before

2. I jog four times around Darron's block.
 a. Where do I jog?
 around my house near Darron's house at four times
 b. When am I jogging?
 last week next month each day

3. They were swimming in Kevin's pool when it began to thunder.
 a. Where did they swim?
 in a boy's pool in thunder at Kevin's
 b. When did they swim?
 in the past in the present in the future

4. Frank says "This is my sister Laverne's house. Let's visit."
 a. Where does Frank visit?
 at his sister's at my sister's at Laverne's office
 b. When is Frank visiting?
 this day two weeks ago in the fall

5. The telephone rang three times before it was answered at the Johnson's.
 a. Where is the phone call?
 at John's at the Johnson home at John's son's home
 b. When is the phone call?
 three times several days ago tomorrow

6. Last week Bob pushed Fran across Kelly's lawn in the baby carriage.
 a. Where did Bob push Fran?
 into a baby carriage across Kelly on Kelly's lawn
 b. When was Bob pushing Fran?
 some time ago this afternoon on Saturday

7. She will take a trip to her grandmother's farm.
 a. Where is she going on her trip?
 to grandmother's to mother's farm to a grand farm
 b. When is the trip?
 this July some time in the future last Christmas

8. Five girls will present the play Thanksgiving Memory in Ms. Carol's class.
 a. Where is the play?
 in a classroom at Carol's in the carolroom
 b. When is the play?
 soon before on Halloween

VARIATIONS:	Literal comprehension: Teacher may compose sentences that contain both "when" and "where" information. Student writes "where" information in a house and "when" information into a clock. "Who" and "why" information from teacher-created sentences may be inserted into large drawings of a person and a question mark, respectively.

WHO KNOWS WHERE OR WHEN?

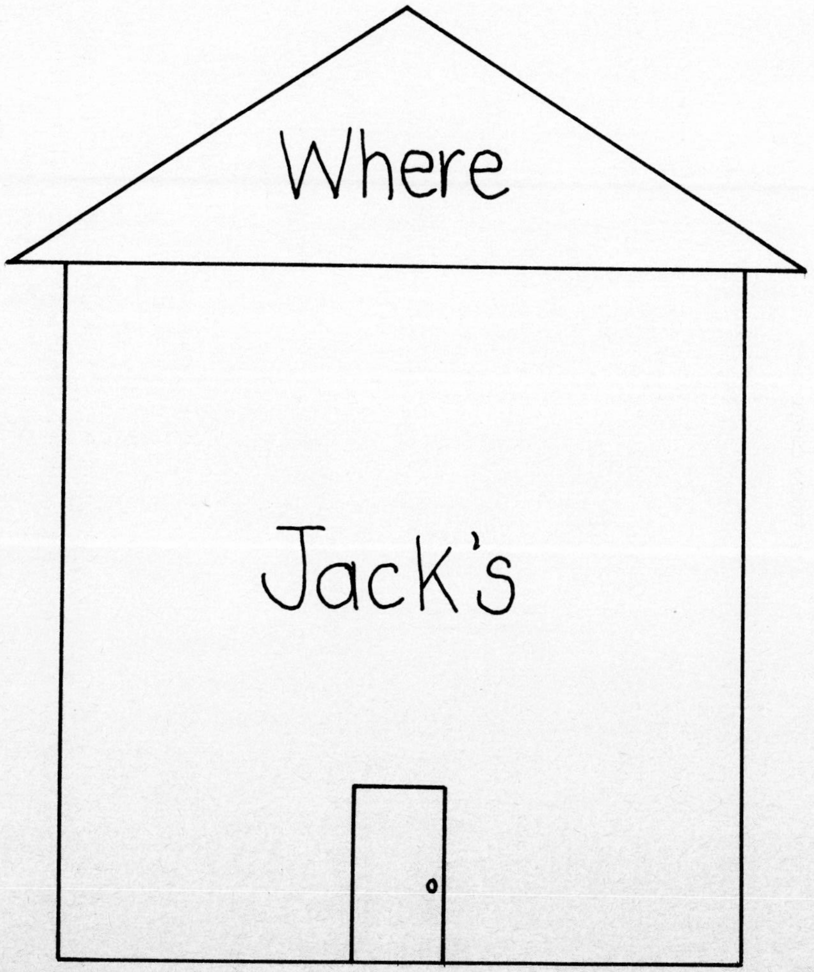

When

2
3
1
12
4
11
5
10
6
9
7
8

Yesterday

Where

Jack's

NAME:
SKILL:

MATERIALS:
PROCEDURE:

VARIATIONS:

Get Talking

The stimulation of oral language via practice with (1) the production of stories and (2) predicting outcomes.

The set of numbered illustrations on the adjacent page which tell a story.

a. Student(s) ask questions about each picture. There are answered by the teacher with only *yes* or *no,* according to the story the teacher has created to go with the pictures.
   Examples: Picture 1. Is that a stray dog? Yes
              Picture 2. Are those mean kids? Yes
              Picture 4. Are the children scared that the dog ran away? No

b. After the student(s) has exhausted the questions and knows all about the pictures, he puts together a story, using the pictures to help with the sequencing. A sample story for the adjacent page is presented below, to help the teacher answer student questions.

1. A boy and a girl are playing in a vacant lot with a dog. They are throwing a stick and their dog is jumping for it.

2. A group of bigger kids in another part of the vacant lot are putting together a kind of dog sled. They have one dog hitched, but the other harness is empty.

3. The first dog runs away and finds the harnessed dog in the lot. They're having fun playing together.

4. The first two kids are looking for their dog. One looks in a big box. Another calls "Here Chico" to the missing dog. They look worried.

5. The bigger kids start to hitch up the first dog to help pull the sled.

6. The younger children find Chico. They look happy and relieved. But the older kids stand in front of Chico. How this will end is unresolved.

Use a set of illustrations from:
   a discarded basal
   a wordless picture book
   a wordless comic strip

NAME:	*Reading with Oomph*
SKILL:	Practice with pitch, stress, and juncture
MATERIALS:	The marked narrative song below or teacher-marked printed matter. (Choose poems or song lyrics which, wherever possible, have dialogue and rhythm.)
PROCEDURE:	The song-story below is to be read aloud, using the following key to interpret the graphic markings.

1. Underlined <u>once</u>—say it softly.
2. Underlined <u>twice</u>—say it in a regular voice.
3. Underlined <u>three</u> times—say it loud.

Oh will you wear red

Oh my dear, oh my dear

Oh will you wear red, Jennie Jenkins

I won't wear red

I'll wear my jeans instead

I'll buy me a foll-de-roll-de

Till-de-toll-de seek a double

Roll Jennie Jenkins roll

Oh will you wear yellow

Oh my dear, oh my dear

Oh will you wear yellow, Jennie Jenkins

I won't wear yellow

'Cause I'm not a bowl of jello

I'll buy me a foll-de-roll-de

Till-de-toll-de seek a double

Roll Jennie Jenkins roll

VARIATIONS:

1. Put in stress marks (/) which mean "give this syllable emphasis". These may be put in instead of or in addition to the underlining.
2. You may also wish to put in punctuation marks which are printed and interpreted as follows:
   a. , (take a breath)
   b. . (take two breaths)
   c. ! (act excited or surprised)
   d. ? (act unsure or surprised)
   e. " " (act like someone is talking)
   These marks may be used instead of or in addition to underlining or stress marks.

Index